7.95

Continuing to Think
The British Asian Girl

Multilingual Matters

MULTILINGUAL MATTERS 81
Series Editor: Derrick Sharp

Continuing to Think: The British Asian Girl

An Exploratory Study of the Influence of Culture upon a Group of British Asian Girls with Specific Reference to the Teaching of English

Barrie Wade and Pamela Souter

MULTILINGUAL MATTERS LTD
Clevedon • Philadelphia • Adelaide

Library of Congress Cataloging in Publication Data

Wade, Barrie
Continuing to Think: The British Asian Girl/Barrie Wade and Pamela Souter.
(Multilingual Matters: 81)
Includes bibliographical references.
1. Minorities—Education—Great Britain. 2. Asians—Education—Great Britain.
3. Women—Education—Great Britain. 4. English Language—Study and Teaching
—Great Britain—Foreign Speakers. 5. Educational Surveys—Great Britain.
I. Souter, Pamela. II. Title. III. Series: Multilingual Matters (Series): 81.
LC3736.G6W33   1992
378.1'9829   dc20

British Library Cataloguing in Publication Data

A CIP catalogue record for this book is available from the British Library.

ISBN 1-85359-139-4 (hbk)
ISBN 1-85359-138-6 (pbk)

Multilingual Matters Ltd

UK: Bank House, 8a Hill Road, Clevedon, Avon BS21 7HH, England.
USA: 1900 Frost Road, Suite 101, Bristol, PA 19007, USA.
Australia: PO Box 6025, 83 Gilles Street, Adelaide, SA 5000, Australia.

Typeset by Editorial Enterprises, Torquay.
Printed and bound in Great Britain by the Longdunn Press, Bristol.

For Robert, Fiona and Mary

With chains of matrimony and modesty
You can shackle my feet
The fear will still haunt you
That crippled, unable to walk
I shall continue to think
Kishwar Naheed

One time we'll have a family of our own
and be able to stand up on our own
two feet and how do we do that if
we don't know nothing about the world?
Parveen (aged 15)

Contents

Acknowledgments

We are indebted, firstly, to the students and staff of those West Midlands schools which participated in our inquiry. The study derives its focus from the objectives of the BRITE Project, School of Education, University of Birmingham (Directors: Dr B. Wade and Mr E. Evans). It is the first of what is hoped will be a number of publications inquiring into and clarifying bilingual issues and offering practical support for secondary English teachers who work in bilingual contexts. This book has implications for all teachers, but we are glad to acknowledge the link with BRITE. We thank Mrs Napheas Akhter and Dr Lynn Davies who read our draft chapters and gave us positive encouragement and constructive criticism. We thank Mrs Jean Thompson for her immense care in preparing the manuscript and the publishers for the enthusiasm with which they received it.

1 Introductory

We have to thank the Pakistani writer, Kishwar Naheed, for our title and do so with the recognition that many hundreds of years ago in England Lovelace, writing to Althea from prison, said much the same about the impossibility of restricting thought by imprisonment:

> Stone walls do not a prison make
> Nor iron bars a cage.
> Minds innocent and quiet take
> That for an hermitage.

It is with more than merely literary satisfaction that we affirm, at the outset, the ability of thinking to make links between languages and cultures and to afford insights into both. Through language and literature, which are crucial elements of culture, we obtain perspectives on our human condition and gain insights into ourselves, our society and our common humanity. It is our view that the resources of British multicultural society and the wide range of world literature written in English should be made available to all pupils in schools whether or not they attend the 5% of schools in England

> that have a significant population of children for whom English is not their mother tongue. (DES, 1988b: 12.2)

It is the job (not exclusively, but mainly) of English teachers to deepen understanding of what language is and how it works within culture and society. In seeking to extend their pupils' insights into the structures of language and their control and satisfaction in using it, English teachers will want to use the experiences of pupils themselves as well as those of others in literature where language is often highly wrought and capable of making meaning most powerfully and intensely. In this respect, for us (and, we suspect, for Kishwar Naheed) *thinking* about experiences, about language and about culture also includes *feeling*.

Our own inquiries, reported later, are mainly ethnographic and focus on the experiences of pupils in the West Midlands as well as the ways in which these experiences are described. We have called this book an exploratory study. Partly we mean that what we have begun as a pathfinding inquiry could be continued (and we hope it will) in complementary, rigorous investigations by ourselves or others. Partly also we mean that the methods of investigation we used evolved from problems perceived by English teachers in secondary classrooms. The study is exploratory in that it tries to account for the causes of the problems, holds them up to scrutiny and tentatively makes recommendations for amelioration. We say this at the outset, not to escape responsibility for the approaches we have used: we take full responsibility and are well aware of shortcomings. Rather it gives us an early warning not to make extravagant claims from findings that are partial and restricted to one sample of youngsters in one geographical area. However, the views contained in this book are, we hope, both informative and insightful to teachers. We hope they will encourage reflection about current practice as well as about pupils in other classrooms.

First, then, we outline, in three general categories, the issues as we and other teachers have encountered them.

(1) Many Asian girls are intelligent, well-motivated pupils, achieving high standards in their schoolwork, who wish to continue their education and to seek satisfying careers. However, we have also encountered those wishing to undertake A-level studies, but who were prevented from doing so because a marriage had been arranged, or because parents were opposed to the co-educational nature of most sixth-form institutions. Pupils frequently expressed disappointment and anger because of being denied the opportunity available to some of their peers and, when interviews with parents failed to secure permission for their further education, clearly felt that they had been let down. More than one girl posed the question, 'Why doesn't anyone do anything about us?'.

(2) With some pupils, the enthusiasm for school work, demonstrated in the first years at secondary school, disappeared in their final school years. The transfer of interest from school to non-academic activities is not, of course, confined to Asian girls. This aspect of adolescence, however, is more likely to influence the work of the pupil who is aware that she will not undertake post-16 education and does not require qualifications for employment.

(3) A small number of pupils gave rise to concern because they failed to demonstrate competency in English and showed little interest in other school work. Once again, this phenomenon is not restricted to Asian girls and it is to be expected that some pupils, for one reason or another, will lack enthusiasm for education. Nevertheless, it was disturbing to find among the twelve third-year Asian girls, members of one class, poor reading ability, extremely immature writing, and a general reluctance to tackle even the most simple tasks without help. No matter how easy the assignment, they would initially say that they could not do it. Clearly they had low self esteem — possibly deepened by the fact that other people had

communicated their low expectations of what the girls could do. The girls' oral English was very poor and all had a tendency to speak English only when classroom activities required them to do so. This led to some resentment on the part of non-Asian children who sometimes accused the girls of 'talking about us in their own language'. An English teacher taking on this class for the first time might assume that the girls had been born in Pakistan without having had the opportunity of learning English in their early years, but, with the exception of one youngster, all had been born in England, had attended primary school (and, sometimes, nursery school) and had had the benefit of specialist (and possibly separate) ESL teaching throughout their schooldays. In secondary school they were taught in small withdrawal groups, or had been helped by language specialists in subject areas (again possibly separate from the mainstream). Although they had failed to make progress in most subjects, the majority of the group could not be regarded as being of low intelligence and, when interested in any activity, such as needlework or child care, the girls proved to be capable of producing work of a high standard.

The girls' perceived problems, as we have categorised them, encouraged us towards a closer examination in order to gain greater understanding through an analysis of their attitudes to education generally but, more particularly, to the teaching of English.

The way teachers characterised these problems indicated their perception and laudable willingness to provide equality of opportunity and to encourage enhancement of achievement. However, embedded in the views were two strands of stereotyped thinking apart from the tendency to think in 'problem' terms. Firstly, the assumption was being made that all causes of the problems identified lay outside the school. This would be convenient, but is hardly likely. One of the aims of this study is to illuminate the likely complexities of cause. Secondly, there was a tendency to talk, in the way we have reflected, about *Asian girls*, whereas the majority of pupils discussed had been born in Britain and all were British citizens. We recognise the importance of using exact and appropriate terms. Unfortunately, we found that some available statistics also use blanket categories such as 'Asian girls'. In fact, religious and linguistic groups may have different expectations and exhibit different behaviour from others. Muslim girls or Bengali speaking girls, for example, could be contrasted with other groups, but for this limited study that is not possible. Wherever we use the term 'Asian girls' it is with the knowledge that the generalisation covers specific differences.

In order to demonstrate the nature of the problems which cause underachievement, we devote Chapter 2 to a case study of the views of one girl,

Parveen, who tells her own story. Then, since Muslim girls form the majority of the sample we investigate, Chapter 3 focuses first upon educational and cultural integration of Muslim adolescents, then specifically upon Muslim girls in British schools. Reports and available statistics are used to investigate access to post-compulsory education and achievement by Asian girls compared with other groups. Chapter 4 relates the problems so far identified at both individual and society levels to the teaching of English in classrooms, firstly through a discussion of relevant recommendations for practice, then through a consideration of implications of a national curriculum for teachers in bilingual contexts. Chapter 5 presents the results of our inquiry into cultural context and English teaching. We offer evidence from unstructured discussion groups of girls' perceptions of their life opportunities, their understandings of sex roles and their attitudes to education. Chapter 6 presents the results of our more specific questionnaire survey of the girls' views on such aspects as leisure reading habits, television watching and reading in English lessons. Where relevant the findings are related to other more substantial surveys. Finally, Chapter 7 rounds off our study with conclusions and tentative recommendations.

2 Parveen's Story

In order to obtain initial perspectives on, and further insight into, the three problem areas we have identified in our introduction, we asked one 15-year-old, Parveen, to talk for as long as she liked without interruption on her feelings about herself. As will be seen, she ranged more widely than her initial brief and, though extempore monologue is naturally an unstructured and untidy kind of evidence, we present the transcript essentially unedited. After all it is her story.

At the outset Parveen speaks with some bitterness of the custom of arranged marriages when she says, contrary to the views put forward by a number of Muslim writers, that girls are sometimes forced into marriage:

> There's two types of arranged marriage — one where you're forced into it. The second is where the girl has agreed to it ... Most of us are in the former category, which is we are forced into it.

She switches then to the topic of education and her own situation and feelings:

> The situation I'm in is that I want to go on to further education and my parents think that's wrong, it's not very good for ... like — um — you get a bad impression by your relatives, your neighbours and these people say, 'Look at that — your girl's going to college, she's bad' and when you look at these people that say you're bad, their own daughter's at university or God-knows-what and I tried to talk — to tell my parents that isn't right, we should be allowed to go to college and they go, 'Your parents-in-law wouldn't like that' and I go and ask my dad, 'Why is this wrong? Why won't our parents-in-law like it? What's wrong with it? As long as we're not married we're your daughters, your property. You should know what's best for us, not our parents-in-law. You won't always be there. One time we'll have a family of our own and be able to stand up on our own two feet and how do we do that if we don't know nothing about the world, if we're locked up in our little houses 24 hours a day and all we ever see is our husband at night and then he goes off to work in the mornings or college or whatever.'

This description of her own situation prompts her to make generalisations about the role of Asian women in society:

The other point I'd like to make is that most Paki-Asian people believe that men are superior to women, like they should have the upper hand over women, they should decide what their wife does, what time she goes out. In other words, she has to, like, you know, sign a register, but you don't have to write it down, you've got to tell him. Like, if he doesn't agree, if he doesn't want you to go to a particular place, you can't go without his permission and, if you do, that could be a break-up of the marriage — in fact, that's happened in a few cases and I mean most girls in this day and age are split. Most of the girls I know in here, in England, at least, are split between two worlds. In school you're in a — or outside when you're in the street, they've got to adopt the white people's way of life. As soon as they walk into their house they're automatically just a person that's a number out of ten.

She develops her view of a woman's role strikingly and effectively as a stage performance until, almost with stage fright that the part is her own (and of the consequences of rejecting it) she switches once more to her own situation.

They're just considered a female fool whose parents decide what to do with them. Their life is, er, like, they plan it all out so that the girl has no part of it. She just has to — it's like a play — she's got to play that part and — er — you can't say what part you want to play, but in a play you have a right. You play that part and then forget about it. In the actual play of life, in this play it's your life an you've got to play the part. You can't even if you don't like it, you got to stick with it and that is wrong because that's ruining your life and I think most Pakistani-type Asian girls are too scared to speak out to express their views and — er like me.

It is Parveen's view that many Pakistani girls are denied the opportunity for further education because members of the Asian community regard education for women as inappropriate, with neighbours saying, 'Look at that — your girl's going to college, she's bad'. She complains that her own parents use the excuse, 'Your parents-in-law wouldn't like that' to prevent her going to college. She feels that most Pakistani people think men are superior to women, with women having few rights once they are married. There is no doubt about the strength of her feelings, but also no doubt about the intelligent and articulate way that she orders them, moving appropriately to make general points from personal anecdotes — to relate her experiences to a human issue.

Parveen complains that when she started secondary school, her father had led her to believe that if she worked hard and achieved good results, he would allow her to go to college, but that in her third year he began pressing her to leave school on the grounds that she had received sufficient education, even though she was only 13 years old.

First, when I started school — my secondary school that is — my dad he was on to me, like, I couldn't go to some kind of school and that, and he goes, 'My daughter's going to work hard and she is going to achieve everything there is and go on to further education'.

I thought, 'Great!' and I worked hard for the first two years of my life and in the third year, my dad suddenly goes, 'Haven't you done enough? Shouldn't you leave school? Shouldn't you pack up?'.

I goes, 'Dad, that's all … you had in mind', and he goes, 'Well, you've done everything you wanted to achieve. You've done your Biology. You've done this and you've done that, and you've done all subjects and they're useless'. I goes to him, 'How do you expect me to be able to go to college as you stated earlier on? How do you expect me to be a person of the world and how do you expect me to live my life?' And my dad he just thought I was being silly — I was being arrogant, that all the teachers had put this into me and I told him I wasn't a robot, I was able to think, like, you know, if I don't learn to — I was only 13 then. I goes, 'I'm only 13 and I'm not, I'm not, I can't cope with life yet. I need more experience. I mean I need to be able to communicate with people and that', and you know, my dad he thought that was wrong, that I was being arrogant. He didn't like it.

Not surprisingly the shock of this sudden shift of attitude made Parveen lose confidence and lose heart. Arguments at home, trouble and lack of commitment in school result:

So then I decided it was too late, I should have started bugging him earlier on and then, after that, I thought, 'He won't let me go to college and so why should I bother' so in the third year my work was a total flop. I didn't give it a second thought. I'd hand in all my homework a week late; I'd get detention. My dad wouldn't agree to that. He made up excuses, like I had to go to mosque. I mean, he got me out of mosque because he thought I was too old and that girls at the age of 13 start getting attention from boys — we can't help it. I mean, if I could create a world, if I, you know, we can't help it, you know, if boys, you know, girls, can get attention at that age and I told him, 'We can't help it. We didn't create the world. It's God's way. I mean, he made a perfect world, but it turned to take the wrong corner and we can't help it if we get lots of people's attentions, mainly men, and, er, I told him that, er, if you want you can't create an asexual race, like everyone was one, like, like some plants, like you don't have the opposite sex, that you can't, you know. The main setback to Pakistani girls is that, er, male sex … like, you know, they're more domineering in our lives and, er, I've just given up work after the third year. My work, I was a total failure at school and at one stage I even had to change my report because I had such a bad report that if I'd let my dad read that, my dad would think,

'Right'. He would have said, like, 'You're a total flop in school. What's the use of going?'. That would have given him even more reason.

We have so far direct exemplification of both problems 1 and 2 as we identified them in Chapter 1. Parveen clearly has ability, but has her hopes undermined as she sees it and gives up. Her resentment is expressed by the fact that she deliberately did little work, became 'a right old pain' to teachers, altered school reports and disobeyed her family by taking Physical Education as a subject. In the next stage of her story Parveen shows how alone she found herself even in a chosen subject. We wonder how many girls in similar conflict situations have to face them alone without the benefit of understanding or counselling either at home or school.

> So then I forgot all this for a year. Then we had our options and I've taken most of the options. Then there was an option about needlework, PE, Art and the creative subjects and, er, I thought about this particular option for a couple of days and I wasn't good at needlework, I wasn't good at Art. I wasn't good at anything apart from PE and I told him I'd like to do PE and that, er, and he goes, 'What's the use of a Pak- of an Asian girl doing PE' and, er, and that really got at me 'cause what's wrong with doing PE. Everybody now does PE, Physical Education. They move around, that's exercising, isn't it? In PE it's mainly movement of the body and you learn more about yourself and so, without telling my dad, I took the option and, er, when I'd chosen the subject, after a few lessons, er, I think it was three lessons, I got caught because I was the only Asian girl there and so I decided to leave the subject.
>
> So I went up to Mrs M. — and the year before that, in the third year — I'd been a right old pain to her. I'd accused her of being racialist and she wasn't. She was one of the nicest teachers there and, er, when I made that comment, that she was prejudiced against me because of the colour of my skin, right, she took it like a piece of cake and I've regretted that phrase ever since I'd said it, I, you know. And I went up to her and I goes, 'Miss, I'd like to do needlework', and I'd expected her to give me verbal abuse, like, you know, just to tell me to get out, but she didn't. She talked to me. We'd been talking for about half an hour, or maybe more, and she, she, er, then at the end, we did come to a conclusion ... She discussed it with my PE teacher and with the Head of Needlework, Mrs So-and-So and so, so, we left it alone for a couple of weeks and then, and then, I'd worked, I'd worked hard at PE without trying to, you know, I thought, I thought, if I didn't work hard at the subject I'd get out of it and somehow I'd managed to give my 100%.
>
> If you don't want something, like, if you're — I was good at PE but I felt lonely. I was the only Asian girl there and, at the end, the Head of PE Department, told me I was rude to the teacher and she'd discussed this with

my PE teacher and my PE teacher said I could, if I wanted to, get a good grade for it and so I had to stick with PE and I worked and I worked ... and after a bit they were really nice, like. They were very nice if I felt lonely, like.

I was good at trampolining, but I felt terrified. I thought they would all laugh at me and, er, my PE teachers they give me a lot of encouragement and at that point I learned what, what if I was the only Asian girl left in this country. I'd be scared stiff even to go out. I mean, it was definitely at that point that I discovered that communication with other people was good and how was I to get that ability to be able to communicate with people if I didn't know what anybody else is like. I mean, during my PE lessons, we had one lesson, practical and the other lesson we usually do theory and during the theory all the class would discuss pop music, what they saw on telly last night, and if I didn't know nothing about it, if I didn't know what the hell was pop, music, whatever, how would I be able to communicate with them, I'd be left out.

So, first of all, I kept quiet, then I'd start. I started to talk, then they'd take no notice of me. I'm a person, I mean, if I can't do what I want to do, I've got to make the most of what I have to do and, in a way, that's why I wanted to do PE and so I joined in and, you know, with my friends, I was joining the conversation and now I've got a quite good grade in PE and if I do good in theory, I might be for a Grade One and if my dad sees that ... he'd kind of be mad at me, 'cause, you know. I'll probably not get Grade One in all the other subjects and that's because my dad discouraged me against the subject and I'd worked hard at it, very hard, in fact. I worked the hardest for this subject and, you know, just to prove to my dad that I can cope with something he's against and, in the same way, I want to set out to prove he's against my ed-, my being educated and I'd like to prove that I can cope, you know, like even if he doesn't bless me, give me his blessings, I'd be able to cope without them and at one point he would. I know it, I can just feel it in my bones...

Parveen's account is honest and reflective, showing how she understands other viewpoints without sharing them and how keenly aware of her own situation she is. The narrative is full of self-knowledge but also balanced by self-criticism plus appreciation when she speaks of an occasion when she is treated with courtesy and sensitivity. Her maturity is apparent because, although her wishes and personality are not taken into account and this makes her patently unhappy, she makes something positive out of misery, beginning to articulate her wish to use her experience to help others.

At one point in the first years, he said he'd like me to make something of myself and now he disagrees. He's changed his mind, but I haven't. I agree

I haven't worked hard, but you know, just to prove my dad otherwise, just
to make the future bright for other Pakistani girls, I'd like to set out and
help anyone I can and from my own personal experience. I've tried discussing this with my dad and he goes, 'What's wrong with you? I mean,
how …' I goes, I told him, 'I want to help women who are in my situation'
and I've discussed this with the careers teacher as well and I goes back to
my dad.

He goes, 'What's wrong with you? I mean, you don't even have to do
the cooking, the washing, anything, you know. You get your breakfast and
your supper cooked for you and everything in front of you. What more do
you want? Why do you want to help women in your situation?'. What he
doesn't see is that I'm quite capable of cooking, you know, and so on, but
I want to be part of the world. I want to be recognised and I want to help
people with the same difficulties as me.

The utilitarian argument adduced by the English Working Group (DES, 1988b:
12.3) that command of English is necessary to avoid disadvantage to students
from ethnic minorities 'in their working life' (12.3) is shown to be irrelevant in
Parveen's case. She perceives her chances of working either before or after marriage as very slim.

I doubt it with the marriage my dad's got in mind. It's very difficult. I mean
the in-laws, I know them and, believe me, they're right old pains, you
know. Like they want the best for their daughter — they're going to send
her to college and why do they object to me going to college. Is it because
they can treat me like a rag doll or something? That's what most parents-
in-law want to be able to rule your life for you, just before, like your parents did, except they don't want the best. They want what's best for their
son or their daughter.

Her own lack of opportunity is highlighted by what she sees as a double standard in the family of her intended husband whose sister is encouraged towards
higher education. Her own role apparently is to be a wife and mother. For that
role, training rather than education is seen to be important by her family who,
she says, will insist she stays at home until her marriage.

What they've got in mind is to train me at home, meaning cooking, washing, washing the nappies, you know, all the household chores and I know
all that, that's common sense, that is, and what they've got is staying on the
dole for the first 12 months, right, and after that, sitting at home.

For Parveen the future appears bleak and it is no wonder that she has given
up in the later stages of her compulsory education. Without opportunity,
incentive or understanding she must submit or, with more difficulty and

danger, rebel. Her family may accept unemployment benefit, she says, but are well prepared to sacrifice her potential earning power to safeguard her reputation.

> Their status is more important than money, I mean, they'd rather, well, have to starve to death than let me go out to work and get, make a bad reputation. They think I'll be bad, like. You know, what I would like is independence. What they, their idea of independence is going out, going out with boys, you know, getting pregnant, and all sorts, and that's not it, that's what you call 'messing around' — that isn't independence. Independence is, like, when, like, you don't defy your parents, but you're able to sort out your own life and, you know, my idea of independence is being able to go to college and to decide my life the way I want to and not particularly mean that you have a boy friend every night, or this and that, which is what they think. Nice girls I know, it's not what they want. They want to be able to create a career for themselves, so at this day and age you need some kind of academic levels, you know, to get a good job.

Again Parveen's natural intellect and command of spoken English are admirable as she distinguishes between different notions of independence and shows her ability to 'decentre' by exploring other points of view. In summary, we have abundant evidence of her ability to understand her situation and give expression to her thoughts and feelings. We have, of course, only heard her viewpoint, but reality for the individual lies in the meanings made from the flux of experience of the world. Life for Parveen, with its frustrations and closed doors, is essentially as she sees it. Her account certainly helps us to understand some of the background to disappointment that able students experience when opportunities are denied them (Problem 1, Chapter 1).

Parveen's case is also typical of Problem 2, as we have defined it. She worked well in secondary school until she saw no purpose in continued commitment to her studies. It is hard to devote care and effort to schoolwork if that care and effort are not valued and are perceived as leading nowhere. In this respect Parveen shows that Problems 1 and 2 are possibly related, with disappointment and anger resulting in disaffection, withdrawal and apathy. Much depends on at what stage of education the process of realisation occurs.

Problem 3 does not apply in Parveen's case, for, as we have demonstrated, she is very competent in spoken English. However, her case does provide the insight that, if she withdrew effort from schoolwork because of her perception of her family's intentions, other girls might similarly rate competence in English as a low priority. Lacking incentive, motivation and commitment, naturally they would make less progress than their potential indicated. Further, if they too were aware of a role destined for them in the way Parveen describes it, that might account for potential being realised only in needlework or child-care subjects which visibly complement the perceived role.

At all events Parveen's case demonstrates, apart from damage to one individual's self-concept, two aspects of waste that our multicultural society can ill afford. Firstly, there is the waste of talent that is represented by the repression of potential in someone as articulate and intelligent as Parveen. We are not in a position to say confidently how great the loss is to both individuals and to society, since it is not possible to generalise from one particular case. This is a matter for further study, though the evidence we review in Chapter 3 indicates that the loss may well be substantial both to society as a whole and to certain communities in particular. The second aspect of waste that is highlighted lies in the restricted and inadequate concept of childrearing. In the modern world feeding, cleaning and washing are a minimal part of what we regard as an essentially creative process; furthermore, the time spent on these aspects is much reduced because of labour-saving devices. Physical health and well-being are an important part of a child's upbringing, but they are not the only part. Contributing to a child's full intellectual, emotional, social, linguistic, moral and spiritual development requires a fully developed intelligence on the part of parents who spend much time with, and so considerably influence, their children. These aspects cannot be promoted by the school system if they are undermined by attitudes in families such as Parveen's.

Throughout this chapter we have drawn attention to the limitations of a case study. Parveen, a Muslim, has contributed to our understanding of the problems we outlined, but there is no guarantee that other Muslim girls or their families think or feel exactly in ways described by her.

Parveen's unhappiness at being denied the career she wanted and her expressions of frustration are very real to her, but it does not follow that other girls will have the same difficulties and feelings. Before we turn to our explorations that were designed to derive further insights and to widen our field of inquiry, we will first locate our three problems in the context of cultural development and identity. Chapter 3 therefore discusses what we know about Muslim adolescents in Britain, then specifically focuses on the problems of Muslim girls using a wider framework than that of a case study. Then in Chapter 4 we will discuss the teaching of English in bilingual contexts.

3 Culture, Conflict and Identity

This chapter is in two parts. First we discuss the education of Muslim children in British schools against the background of development and change since the 1950s. We then proceed to the specific issue of Muslim girls, their access to education and evidence of their attainments within the system.

The Muslim Child in School

During the 1950s and 1960s, the need for an increased labour force in Britain led to Commonwealth citizens being invited to take up residence in this country. A large number of people from India and Pakistan responded, settling in large industrial towns, such as Birmingham, Bradford and Wolverhampton, constituting, with people of West Indian origin, about three-and-a-half per cent of the total population.

Despite the disadvantages of poor housing, frequently low wages, unfamiliar foods and customs and discrimination by some of the indigenous population, the Asian community, in a relatively short time, became an established part of British society, with Asians becoming increasingly involved in the commercial and professional life of the cities.

Integration into employment and civic life did not, however, lead to an abandoning of cultural identity. According to Dr M. Anwar (1981) 'integration means acceptance of their separate ethnic identity by the majority population and its institutions', while 'adapting to other aspects of the dominant culture' (p. 102). In some communities the mosque and the temple have become as familiar on the urban landscape as the church and chapel, just as businesses displaying names like Patel and Singh now seem no more unusual than those of Jones and Smith.

By the late 1970s, British society had become more overtly multiracial and multicultural, though unevenness of distribution of ethnic minorities meant that experience and attitudes differed widely. It is not, of course, a unique

13

phenomenon for groups of other races and nationalities to settle in Britain. Throughout the centuries immigrants and refugees have made their homes in Britain, their descendants becoming part of the established community. Many of these descendants no longer consider themselves as having a connection with their ancestors' place of origin except, perhaps, for an awareness that a surname has originated in another country. Others, the Jews for example, pre-serve not only their religious beliefs, but many aspects of their cultural her-itage too. The influx of Asian and West Indian immigrants was, however, a noticeable event, partly because of skin colour, partly because of concentration of numbers in particular areas.

Naturally the newcomers also had misgivings about the new society they were entering and some of these early worries continue. For Asian families and community leaders, the protection of their children's cultural identity causes some concern. Mustafa Yusuf McDermott & Muhammad Manazir Ahsan (1986) consider the major issues for Asian children in British schools as 'role conflicts, language, co-education, religious education in schools, sex education, dress and food' (p. 43). The difficulties experienced by the child who speaks only Urdu, Bengali, Gujarati or Panjabi at home, but Arabic when praying and English in school, may be easily imagined. Other problems, such as those 'aggravated by a hotch-potch of muddled notions created by different religions and cultural symbols like Father Christmas, Easter, Jesus and Muhammad ... God and Allah' are less obvious, but still create 'a confusion in communication and comprehension'. McDermott & Ahsan feel that a 'Muslim child faces a very distressing conflict situation with respect to the many and varied roles he is required to play ...' (p. 44).

A number of writers agree that many children belonging to an ethnic minority culture experience conflict between the culture of their families and that of the host community. R. Miles (1978), although rejecting this idea, sum-marises it in the following way:

> In essence, the argument is that these migrant groups are victims of 'culture clash' (there being conflict between their own, or their parents' culture and that of the receiving society) with the result that either their own culture is devalued or its basis or coherence is modified by 'western' influence ... (p. 1)

Miles' own view is that

> it might be more accurate to speak of the children of immigrants as being bicultural rather than between two cultures; the present 'second generation' live their lives in two cultural contexts, adopting by choice, within identifi-able constraints, the most appropriate norm or practice, depending on the circumstances they face. (p. 1)

J. Rex (1982) argues against the assumption that culture is the homogeneous attribute of an ethnic group or nation,

> The child of immigrant parents does not merely have to be socialised into some seamless British culture. He enters into a complex process of intergenerational and class conflict in which he will both share experiences with working class and middle class British youth and be divided from them. (p. 53)

However, an Asian writer, Bhikhu Parekh, more simplistically sees conflict as inevitable in the case of the 'black child raised on a mono-cultural diet in an English school' with the child experiencing

> profound self-alienation ... His present nothing but a battleground between his past and his future ... He feels suspended between two worlds ... . (Modgil, 1986: 26)

Whilst the assumption that British Asian children can be said to be subject to 'culture conflict' may be clearly a matter for debate, it cannot be denied that Asian families in Britain do consider that problems exist. The Union of Muslim Organisations has felt that a major worry for Muslim parents is that their children soon begin to adopt English standards and ideas.

> They start to question not only traditional customs, but religious ideas which seem strangely alien to life in a Western materialistic society ... Most Muslims acknowledge that Britain is a fair place to live ... but it is hard to judge how possible it is to live as a Muslim in British society as a whole. (UMO, 1975: 10)

Helwig (1979) documented a debate held in 1970 when Sikh parents and community leaders discussed the possibiity of setting up a Sikh school. One leader expressed the view that 'The British education system is narrow and only concentrates on teaching students to fit into a Christian world, not a universal world'. Parents complained of intelligence tests which discriminated against Sikh children and of girls being 'taught that their parents are wrong in not giving them freedom' (p. 96).

M. Amanullah Khan (1980), Secretary of the Muslim Education Consultative Committee, speaking about the provision for the 50,000 Muslims living in the Birmingham area, criticised the Local Authority's failure to provide separate facilities for Muslim youth.

> Attempts to provide some multicultural education have resulted in Muslim children being classified in the all-inclusive category of 'ethnic minority' children. At best the term 'Asian' is applied and at worst the description 'Pakis'. This leaves Muslim youth at a grave disadvantage,

since they cannot make full use of the various facilities for youth activities.

Khan outlines the conduct which is acceptable to 'Western, free, permissive society' which he sees as 'violations of the principles and limits laid down by God and a sure and certain way to hell'. Because this conduct is permitted in youth and community centres, Khan maintains, young Muslims are withdrawn from them and 'confined to their homes due to the lack of alternative facilities', with those who 'decide to break the monotony of staying at home' becoming involved with the 'worst elements' indulging in

> anti-social activities which not only create worse tensions at home but in many instances lead to court cases, detention and admission into care. (MECC, 1980: 10)

The view that Western society in general is 'liberal, permissive and materialistic' is also put forward by Ghulam Sarwar (1983). He sees Western standards as allowing a 'person to do whatever he likes regardless of any accountability and with few moral controls'. He suggests that Muslim children are taught to live according to Islamic beliefs and practices at home but

> At school and elsewhere outside the home, they come into close contact with features of the Western culture with its materialistic outlook, family breakdown, free-mixing of the sexes, alcoholism and loose moral standards.

This, he believes, leads to the Muslim child facing 'a conflict within himself' (p. 7).

These Sodom-and-Gomorrah views of the Western way of life would, we are sure, be contested by many non-Muslims whose religious beliefs and traditions uphold similar moral values to those of the Islamic faith. Nevertheless, where such views are sincerely held, it seems likely that the 'cultural conflict' denied by Rex, Miles and others, will exist in some measure for Muslim children living in a Western society and mixing with those whose way of life, rightly or wrongly, is believed by their family and religious leaders, to be immoral and ungodly. Parveen indeed found herself in such conflict. Although her account highlights her morality and maturity, her father's lack of confidence in her is nonetheless real, even though mistaken.

Attempts have been made to suggest remedies for the problems arising since the 1960s in multicultural education. A number of reports and surveys, such as the Schools Council's 'Immigrant Children in Infant Schools' (1970), the Bullock Report (DES, 1975) and The Swann Report (DES, 1985), emphasise the need for all children to be prepared for life in a multicultural society. Much

Very important

has since been done to improve matters, with many schools attempting to develop more suitable curricula and changing attitudes to dress, food and customs, but it would be incorrect to suppose that all difficulties have been resolved. Anwar's survey of Muslim parents and children revealed that over half of the young people interviewed faced problems connected with religion (food, dress, school curriculum, facilities for prayer) whilst many Muslim parents continued to express distress at the permissive attitudes of young people in British society which gave rise to concern about the moral socialisation of their children at school.

Muslim Girls in British Schools

If the British Asian male child may be said to suffer from a conflict of cultures, his female counterpart is likely to be faced with even greater problems.

For the past hundred years a stream of English educationists have pressed for girls to be allowed equality of opportunity with boys. Legislation has achieved a measure of equality in employment and other areas, but more remains to be done in education. Attempts are being made to ensure that the school curriculum is developed in a way that does not discourage girls from undertaking what have been regarded as traditionally male subjects. However, attitudes expressed towards female pupils may radically differ from those towards boys. In one school known to us the subject known as Personal Development consists mainly of child care studies with some hygiene and sex education, but with no component that suggests that a female has any role apart from those of wife and mother. Higher education, for whatever reasons, still favours male candidates in Britain with, according to Sanderson (1987), Britain 'having one of the lowest populations of women among university entrants of any major country' with only 35% (of entrants) being female (p. 133).

It is hardly surprising that teachers who wish to see sex equality in education (and elsewhere) should encourage female pupils to take part in those subjects previously considered to be for boys only, and to urge girls to seek entrance to universities and colleges. Society is never static, but is changing and is sometimes a whirlpool of conflicting currents. Schools to some extent reflect these tensions and developments. Well-intentioned encouragement of more active female participation could conflict with the ideas of Asian parents about what is considered to be a suitable education for their daughters in the light of their religious beliefs and customs. Opposition to the type of higher education available for women in the United Kingdom can be seen in the guidance given by leading Muslims.

In 1977, the First World Conference on Muslim Education, for example, criticised co-educational schools or those whose curricula were originally 'formulated to suit men's nature and their needs' as being 'without regard to the delicate nature of women' bringing the 'evil consequences of moral corruption, family disintegration ... the susceptibility of criminal and abnormal tendencies at variance with the Islamic outlook'. The Conference recommended a 'special female educational system' offering courses designed 'to suit the nature of women, fulfil society's needs for female service, realise the objectives of Islam, preserve the ideas of chastity, strengthen family ties and morals ...' (p. 8).

It is apparent that the teachings of Islam are not opposed to the education of women. ' "It is a duty for every Muslim, male and female, to seek knowledge" said the Prophet' to which McDermott and Ahsan add, 'there is nothing at all in Islamic teaching that could be interpreted to mean that Muslim girls or women have less right than Muslim boys or men to an education related to their intelligence, ability, natural inclination and aptitude; from play school to university, from O-levels to a doctorate degree'. They maintain that within the Muslim community in Britain, 'a high percentage of Muslim girls continue their studies beyond O-level and are certainly encouraged to study at A-level and prepare for University, College and professional/vocational courses' (p. 83).

They admit, however, that the freedom to pursue higher education does not extend to all Muslim girls in Britain. In the same volume, McDermott & Ahsan acknowledge that 'the mixing of the sexes in and out of the adolescent stage is contrary to the ethos of Islamic teachings' and that 'it is not infrequent to hear of cases of girls being sent back to their country of origin or kept at home in England because of the lack of facilities for single-sex education'. This denial of educational opportunities clearly places such girls in a less favourable position than their peers, restricting their career opportunities and limiting their activities to those areas of life where sometimes only very basic literacy and numeracy are regarded necessary. It also, as we argued in Chapter 2, limits the way in which they will be able to help their future children to prepare for and make the most use of education.

In our view McDermott's & Ahsan's view that the deficiency in single-sex schools may be overcome because of the 'multi-style system of schooling in this country and a growing shift towards free parental choice' (p. 47) may be over-optimistic. Birmingham, for example, listed twelve county girls schools in 1980, seven of which were oversubscribed. Since then a number of girls schools have closed or merged with other schools. The 1988 Instrument and Articles of Government for County Schools issued by the Birmingham City Council lists seven schools, only three of which are situated near to areas where large numbers of Asian families are living. A discussion document drawn up in 1980 stated that,

The Committee will clearly wish to give every consideration to the wishes and beliefs of parents in respect of single-sex education. It must also be borne in mind, however, that some urban authorities with multi-racial populations have no or very few single-sex schools (such as Sheffield with none or Bradford with one of each sex), and that there is more than one viewpoint within Islam on the subject. (Birmingham Education Committee, 1980: 20)

The Committee pointed out that they had considered the diminution of single-sex places caused by amalgamation and had taken the view that 'public demand, as expressed at public meetings, had been increasingly for co-education ...'. It cannot be said with certainty that those parents speaking at public meetings represent the views of all parents, some of whom are less articulate or are not aware of ways of making their views public. Some parents speak very little English and would be unable to make their wishes known without an interpreter.

Some change is likely in the case of Birmingham. At the time of writing the Authority is facing prosecution in the European Court because it offers fewer selective school places to girls than it does to boys.

In a survey carried out by the Union of Muslim Organisations, community relations officers were questioned about Islamic Education and Single-Sex Schools (1975). Out of twenty-one authorities who took part in this survey, only fourteen provided secondary education in single-sex schools, four of which were to become co-educational. Comments from the officers included the opinion that, 'There has been a silent protest on the part of Muslim parents with regard to the non-existence of single-sex schools' so that

what happens is that Muslim parents do not send for their daughters in Pakistan for various reasons. And those few who don't encourage their daughters to go to school it is because they are mixed and parents don't approve of them. (p. 29)

In view of the strong condemnation of co-educational schools expressed by the Conference on Muslim Education, it is not surprising that some Muslim parents, in the survey conducted by Anwar, expressed a preference for their children to attend single-sex schools and registered concern that the number of these is diminishing. It is likely that this issue will remain a live one and it may actually flicker alight as the Education Reform Bill fosters local management of schools. Parental choice is an accepted principle of recent legislation and clearly much will depend upon the articulacy of communities in expressing their views. Placement is not the only cause for concern, however. There are disturbing signs of inequality of achievement which seem to indicate differences in opportunity and support rather than ability.

Although the pursuit of knowledge by Asian women is claimed to be encouraged, the reality is that females from Indian sub-continent origins do not match their male counterparts in the attainment of academic and professional qualifications. The Central Statistical Office Survey (1988) of academic qualifications of a group of people aged 26 to 59 years, revealed that, although 15% of the Indian females achieved higher qualifications (compared, however, with 24% of Indian males), no Pakistani/Bangladeshi women interviewed held any higher qualifications (compared with 12% Pakistani/ Bangladeshi males).

At O-level, vocational or professional studies, trade apprenticeships or City and Guilds, 29% of the Indian females and only 14% of Pakistani/ Bangladeshi females had gained qualifications (compared with males: 34% Indian, 21% Pakistani/Bangladeshi). The total percentage of those without any qualifications was higher in the case of Indian and Pakistani/Bangladeshi women than in any of the other female ethnic groups studied (see Table 1). With the exception of the West Indian and Guyanese women, females of all ethnic groups possessed fewer qualifications than males in the same ethnic groups, but with the difference between the Pakistani Bangladeshi males and females being greater.

Notes on the survey suggest that women from the Pakistani/Bangladeshi group are likely to be more 'economically inactive' than females in other groups and this would influence the qualifications, particularly those which were gained in connection with employment. Early marriage, too, is likely to prevent many girls in this group from taking part in post-16 education.

An earlier survey was carried out by the Policy Studies Institute (Brown, 1984) but with a more restricted group of informants who were aged 16 to 24 years. This showed that 50% of the young Asian women interviewed (compared with 21% West Indian and 22% white) possessed no academic or vocational qualifications. Brown points out, however, that 70% of the Asian girls in the 16 to 19 age group had succeeded in achieving academic qualifications which suggests that a change may be taking place in the pattern of education for Asian girls.

An interesting aspect of the survey showed that, although only Asian males and females in the sample stated that they had completed their full-time education before reaching the age of 13 years, the percentage of those continuing education to the age of 17 years or over was higher for both men and women in the Asian group than it was for the white informants. (The differences between the women in the three groups were not as marked as between the men, with the white male group percentage being half that of the Asian males.)

TABLE 1 *Highest qualification level of the population by sex and ethnic group 1984–1986 (aged 25–59) (HMSO, 1988)*

Highest qualification held (percentages) (4)	White	West Indian	Indian	Pakistani/ Bangladeshi	Other (2)	All (3)
MALES						
Higher	17	—	24	12	33	17
Other	47	35	34	21	37	46
None (5)	36	58	42	67	30	37
FEMALES						
Higher	14	16	15	—	23	14
Other	36	30	29	14	34	35
None (5)	50	54	56	80	43	51
ALL						
Higher	15	12	20	9	28	15
Other	41	33	32	18	36	41
None (5)	43	56	49	73	36	44

(2) Includes African, Arab, Chinese and other non-white groups.

(3) Includes those who did not state their ethnic origin.

(4) Higher = first or higher degree, other degree level qualification, teaching or nursing qualification/HNC Scot. BEC grad. membership of professional institutions; other = trade apprenticeship C & G or 'O' professional or vocational qualification.

(5) Includes those who did not know or did not state qualification.

The Swann Report (1985) included a DES survey of school leavers in 1981/82. From this survey it was concluded that girls in the sample 'noticeably those from ethnic minorities, are more likely to stay on at school past the school leaving age than boys' with 'Asians and West Indian children much more likely to leave school to follow full-time education in 1981/82 than the "other" leavers' (p. 111).

TABLE 2 *Academic and vocational qualifications (percentages), informants aged 16–24 years (Brown, 1984)*

| | Men | | | Women | | |
	White	West Indian	Asian	White	West Indian	Asian
(1) Highest acad. qual.	4	*	5	1	—	1
(2) GCE A, HND/C or above (no degree)	8	6	14	10	5	8
(3) GCE O, ONCD, CSE	21	32	28	42	36	28
(4) CSE	34	24	18	22	36	14
(5) No acad. qual. but voc. or prof.	5	3	1	1	2	*
(6) Highest voc. qual.	5	3	3	19	22	7
(7) Apprenticeship	9	7	4	2	—	1
(8) C & G	8	8	3	5	5	—
(9) No voc. qual. but acad. qual.	50	48	56	53	52	43
(10) None of these qual.	27	35	35	22	21	50
Age on completing full-time education:						
under 13	—	—	2	—	—	15
17 & over	29	41	58	47	51	50
Base: All Adults (weighted)	483	476	718	470	495	684
(unweighted)	123	185	272	146	219	311

TABLE 3 *Age of school leavers from maintained secondary schools (DES, 1985: 112)*

	Asians		West Indians		All Other Leavers		Total School Leavers from 5 LEAs		All Maintained School Leavers in England	
	78–9 (%)	81–2 (%)	78–9 (%)	81–2 (%)	78–9 (%)	81–2 (%)	78–9 (%)	81–2 (%)	78–9 (%)	81–2 (%)
BOYS										
Age at 31 Aug.										
	51	54	79	68	74	70	7	368	77	73
16	21	24	16	23	12	14	13	16	8	10
17	19	14	4	6	12	14	12	14	13	15
18+	9	8	1	3	2	2	3	3	2	2
Total (Number)	262/	319	378/	315	2,487/	2,363	3,127/	2,997	353,580/	357,440
GIRLS										
Age at 31 Aug.										
	36	46	59	56	71	64	67	61	74	69
16	34	25	32	31	13	19	16	21	11	13
17	21	22	9	11	15	16	15	16	14	16
18+	9	7	1	3	2	2	2	2	1	2
Total (Number)	204/	252	340/	338	2,525/	2,355	3,069/	2,945	341,260/	349,240

The figures produced (see Table 3) suggest that Asian boys and girls have similar access to post-compulsory education, a contradiction of the situation sometimes described by Muslim girls. Statistics of this type, of course, show only the total numbers of an ethnic group, but do not offer finer analysis into

religious groupings or areas of family origin. Figures detailing the pattern of
education for children of Asian families generally cannot be said to be representative of particular sections of the British Asian community. The description
'Asian' may be applied to the child of a family originating in a poor rural community in Pakistan or Bangladesh whose outlook may be very different from
that of a middle-class family from a city in Kenya.

The Report, in listing the academic achievements of the sample, shows that
17% of Asians achieved GCE O-level or CSE Grade 1 passes, as compared with
6% of West Indian leavers and 19% of all other leavers in five LEAs, with A-
level passes of 5% West Indian leavers and 13% Asian leavers (national average
13%). The figures do not attempt to break down the category 'Asian' into
Chinese, Indian, Pakistani, etc.; nor do they show the percentage of passes
obtained by male and female candidates. The general suggestion that the
achievements of Asian children compare favourably with those of other ethnic
groups may mask specific inequalities.

Extracts from a study by G. K. Verma, which are also included in the
Report, show that some children interviewed felt that girls were not offered the
same opportunities for education as boys by their families. A Pakistani boy
spoke of Asian parents 'looking towards a good future for their sons', adding
that 'actually the girls do the housework'. A Pakistani girl mentioned her wish
to work with old people and of being prevented from taking part in work experience because 'work experience is mixed for girls and boys and my parents say
it's no good thing being with boys ...'. Although some young people felt that
their families were imposing restrictions upon them, respect for parents and the
realisation of the importance of family support was stressed throughout the
interviews (p. 104).

The anxiety of parents about their daughters mixing with boys, referred to
by the Pakistani girl, gives rise to the main problem encountered by Asian girls
wishing to obtain higher academic qualifications. We have known Muslim parents who, supporting their daughters' wish to undertake post-16 education, have
sought help in finding a single-sex college or sixth form. A small number of
girls are able to gain admission to sixth forms in single-sex schools and,
although some of these express a preference for college, accept that their parents
will not permit them to attend a co-educational institution. For others, education
ends at 16 years.

Even if the girls are able to overcome the obstacle of finding a place for A-
level studies, their problems are not over at 16+, as some parents will continue
to oppose their daughters' admission to co-educational establishments at 18+,
ruling out colleges of higher education and universities. We have known girls
who have worked hard, enjoyed school-life and looked forward to higher

education, only to be disappointed in the final year at secondary school and we mention two illustrative cases. Shamin, who gained good O-level results, was married between O-level examinations and entering sixth form college, having been promised that she would be allowed to continue her education after marriage if she married without creating difficulties about it. After the ceremony, she found that this was not the case. Within a year, she had given birth to her first child and had accepted that her only role was to be that of wife and mother, with little opportunity for any outside interests, apart from meeting with other married women.

Nasreen, who had throughout secondary school, spoken of the time when she would become a teacher, found when she entered her fifth year at secondary school, that her family's support for her ambitions vanished and that she was destined to become the wife of a cousin who lived in Pakistan. When she continued to adhere to her plans to achieve examination success and to seek a career, she was first sent to Pakistan for several months. Upon her return to this country, she found that her grandmother was to share her bedroom in order to prevent her from studying. Despite family opposition, she refused to abandon her studies, working in lunch-times and other breaks to complete homework assignments and eventually gained O-level passes, but at a lower grade than had originally been anticipated before her family's opposition became apparent.

In addition to lack of single-sex educational provision, parents of Muslim girls may find other aspects of the British educational system difficult to accept. They may feel 'great anxiety at the possibility of their daughters breaking Islamic laws pertaining to dress' which have lead to 'incidents in which Muslim parents have fought vehemently over the issue of school uniform' (McDermott & Ahsan, 1986: 47). Anwar's survey shows that, although attitudes to the wearing of Western clothes are varied amongst Asians generally, the majority of Muslim parents and children did not feel that the traditions of the Muslim community would permit them to be worn, some feeling that they were 'not decent'.

Other matters of concern for parents of Asian girls, even those in single-sex schools, are the arrangements for physical education and the subject of sex education. The Islamic Foundation states that girls should have 'proper covering' in female shower rooms, a requirement which could lead to conflict with some teachers. A Muslim Teachers' Conference held in 1979, argued against sex education in schools on the grounds that 'sex education and sex aids are for a society of people sick and disenchanted with their own promiscuity' (McDermott & Ahsan, 1986: 47). From this, it would seem that in schools where sex education is part of the curriculum, the Muslim girl is faced with the choice of undertaking teaching unacceptable to her religion or being withdrawn from classes, thereby becoming isolated from her peers. In practice, parents are not always as opposed to sex education classes as might be expected. For example, in one girls' school which arranged talks by a trained nurse on sexual development and contraception a maximum of two Asian girls in any one year failed to obtain parental consent to attend. This was true over a three-year period with an intake which included 80 or more British Asian girls — mainly Muslim.

In many instances, difficulties about these subjects and about dietary and devotional matters, are resolved by the sensitive and sympathetic attitudes of teaching staff, but this may not always be the case, not necessarily because of prejudice or intolerance, but sometimes because of lack of knowledge on the part of the teacher about the religious beliefs and traditions of pupils.

Despite the insistence of Asian writers and religious leaders that Asian girls enjoy equality of educational opportunity with boys, the evidence on attainment does not point in the same direction and accords with Parveen's view that she and possibly others are being deprived of a full education because of the influence of families and community. Whatever the truth of the matter many Muslim girls believe that they cannot aspire to any academic achievements beyond GCSE. Since such beliefs influence pupils' motivation to learn, we determined to seek the views of a larger sample of Asian girls about their anticipated qualifications, attitudes to schools, post-school plans and their perceptions of their roles in the community. The findings of these exploratory investigations will be discussed in a subsequent chapter. First, however, we proceed to our specific focus on the teaching of English language.

4 Teaching English in Bilingual Contexts

This chapter will place the problems that we have identified so far into the context of national consciousness, as explicated by major reports and selected research inquiries into the teaching of English since the mid-1970s. Having discussed those issues and recommendations relevant to teaching English in bilingual classrooms, we finally consider the implications of a national curriculum for teachers in bilingual contexts.

The Rampton Report makes an explicit statement of the issue and provides a convenient starting point:

> The aim of all schools should be to provide a 'good education' for all their pupils ... to encourage the individual development of every child to acquire knowledge and skills ... to provide every individual child with an equal opportunity of playing a full and active part in adult social and working life. To benefit from education in all these respects a child must possess the basic tools of learning: the ability to read and to use language. (DES, 1981: 19)

The importance which the Rampton Report places upon language learning had previously been emphasised in other official documents. The Plowden Report (DES, 1967) refers to language as 'central to the educational process' (p. 19), and the Bullock Report (DES, 1975) describes its 'unique role in developing human learning' with the 'higher processes of thinking ... achieved by the interaction of a child's language behaviour with his other mental and perceptual powers' (p. 49).

In an introductory letter to a recent Report into the Teaching of English Language (DES, 1988a), Sir John Kingman writes: 'It must be the primary objective of the educational system to enable and encourage every child to use the English language to the fullest effect in speaking, writing, listening and reading' (p. iii). The child, of Asian or other culture, who does not succeed in mastering English will forever be at a disadvantage while living in a predominantly English-speaking society, both in social life and in career advancement. Mastery of English is of even greater importance if it is the medium of instruction in schools.

For many British Asian children entering the education system, language therefore presents additional problems to those experienced by all children. John Rex (Modgil, 1986) sees these problems in three types:

> the problem of the non-English speaking child of approaching his school work with the linguistic capacity he or she actually commands ... the problems of maintaining his or her skill in the mother tongue ... the problem of acquiring sufficient English to be able to work with English as a medium of instruction.

Rex outlines three approaches in dealing with the last at the moment of entry into the school:

> children have been sent to special centres for English instruction; peripatetic teachers have served schools with non-English-speaking children; and, finally, and worst of all, the children have simply been left to cope with English as best they can.

These techniques, Rex maintains, are 'unsophisticated, callous and cruel' because they 'fail to cope with the basic problems facing all school children which is that at the outset they have not merely to learn but to learn to learn' (p. 209).

Rex advocates the adoption of the Swedish approach, that of learning initially in the medium of the mother tongue and introducing English later as a second language by stages. Such a policy has worked well as a short-term strategy. In European countries where it has been adopted, children who are taught in this way are members of families who are not likely to be permanently settled and will eventually return to their countries of origin. On the contrary, in Britain, the Asian communities cannot be regarded as being anything but permanent residents. Many of those permanent residents are also keen for their children to develop competence in English as speedily as possible. The system Rex advocates could become, in its early stages, a form of cultural division, separating children at an age when they should be working and playing together and gaining a greater understanding of each other's lifestyles and cultures. Institutional separation of ethnic groupings in Britain is to be considered with caution as it is likely to lead to racial disharmony.

Apart from political, educational and cultural considerations, there are economic constraints which affect the issue of mother tongue teaching for minority groups. With limited funds available, it would be difficult to implement any policy which requires the recruitment and training of a large number of teachers able to speak Asian languages. (With present recruitment problems it is not even known if sufficient candidates for such posts would be available.) The alternative would be to draw the children into specialist centres, in the way that was adopted in the 1960s and 1970s, then abandoned. The problem is that, as well as separating children from their indigenous contemporaries, special centres distance them scholastically from their communities and make contact between parents and school more difficult when it is desirable for parents to become involved in the learning and school activities of their children.

The Swann Report (DES, 1985) uncompromisingly classifies the teaching of English in separate language centres to children for whom English is not the mother tongue, as assimilationist, with 'the thinking behind these centres ... in retrospect ... an example of institutional racism' (p. 389). However, it is our view that segregation can just as easily occur within institutions as between them. Again the Swann Report cites the argument that

> second language learners should be in mainstream classes rather than the situation we have more commonly encountered where second language pupils are withdrawn to be taught away from the general run of mainstream activities. This more common situation not only institutionalizes second language pupils to failure but also compounds the difference between second language pupils and other members of the community ... it leads to both their curriculum and social learning being impoverished, and thus both language and intellectual development is held up. (p. 390)

This argument coincides with our own observations of pupils who have been segregated for the whole of their secondary schooling into special ESL classes and have become less able to work on their own initiative, as well as more isolated from other pupils in school, mixing only with members of their immediate group. These pupils are often regarded by their peers (both Asian and non-Asian) as of inferior intelligence, their practice of speaking an Asian language for all communication, except to the teacher, being taken as evidence of lack of ability.

The opinion expressed in the Swann Report that teaching English as a second language should be 'viewed as an extension of the range of language needs for which all teachers in schools should, provided they are given adequate training and appropriate support, be able to cater' is to be supported. The difficulty lies in the proviso. Many teachers have not yet been trained to cater for language needs and feel themselves that they have not been given the opportunity to make good this deficiency.

The degree of parental involvement in the child's early language learning, known to be an influential factor, gives rise to another problem for the British Asian child. We have argued elsewhere (Wade, 1978, 1990) that parents are most important resources in helping young children to master and enjoy reading, and the Bullock Report stresses the vital part which parents play in helping children to develop an interest in reading and a knowledge of the conventions of reading.

Some British Asian mothers, with whom their children will spend most pre-school time, may have limited English and be unable to engage their children in the type of talk which they will experience at school, nor will they feel able to help their children with pre-school reading in English. Figures quoted by Abdul Rehaman Khan (1986) in the *Pakistan Times* indicate a literacy rate of only 26.2% (in Pakistan). Amongst women, the rate is 13%. In rural areas the problems are even worse with a general literacy rate of 10% and 5% for women. It is likely that a number of mothers now living in Britain have not had the opportunity of becoming literate and cannot, therefore, be expected on their own to introduce their children to books in the early years. Much can be achieved in partnership with the school, however, and elsewhere (Wade, 1984) we have drawn attention to the role of older siblings and to the importance of telling and listening to stories in the home *in whatever language.*

If children are to receive maximum benefits from language teaching, it is necessary for links to be established between their schools and their parents, especially if the latter speak little English. Valuable work has been done by home–school liaison teachers in areas such as the West Riding and Birmingham, whereby help is given, not only to the child, but to parents who may feel isolated by the inability to communicate adequately with non-Asian members of the community.

In order to ensure that non-English-speaking children reach their full potential, teachers must possess the attitudes and skills necessary for this task. Too often, even specialist English teachers have not had the opportunity of learning such skills with some teacher training institutions, as the Rampton Report said, 'offering optional courses in such subjects as English as a Second Language' which are 'little more than token gestures' (DES, 1981: 61). There is much to do in the field of inservice education also. It remains to be seen whether these language initiatives, set up in the wake of the Kingman Report and using a cascade model of teaching beginning with 'expert trainers', can develop teacher competence to the levels necessary.

Effective use of reading is necessary for success in all subjects at secondary level. In English lessons, reading for many purposes additional to information gathering occupies a central role. Consequently the availability of books and other reading materials together with adolescents' reading habits are important considerations for English teachers. A number of studies have been carried out into the reading habits of school-children. In one of these, Frank Whitehead and others carried out an extensive survey of the reading habits of children aged 10 to 15 years (Whitehead *et al.*, 1977). They discovered a marked swing away from book reading as children grow older, with the percentage of girls interviewed who had not read a book in the month prior to the survey, rising from 9.4% at the age of 10+, to 32.4% at the age of 14+ (p. 272) and the books chosen by them being almost entirely confined to fiction. A large percentage of girls did, however, continue to read magazines and comics, again with a preference for those with a high fictional content. The researchers list a number of variables which are positively associated with the amount of book reading: size of family, number of books owned by the child; and so on, but no reference is made to the effects of ethnic origin upon the quantity and 'quality' of books read.

Wade & Cadman (1986) show that it is not uncommon for teenagers to reveal a reluctance to read and that it would be strange if this were not the case. Human beings do not all share the same tastes and interests. Nevertheless, as they point out, 'today's fourteen-year-old reluctant readers will be the parents of the next generation of reluctant readers unless we actively attempt to break through' and it is essential that the material presented to pupils be appropriate and capable of stimulating interest. The supply of books which appeal to ethnic minority groups is increasing, but obtaining books which will prove enjoyable reading for Asian girls feeding 'their imaginative development' and enabling them 'to see books as a necessary and natural part of daily life' presents a problem (Wade & Cadman, 1986: 27). If we accept the assertions of a number of Pakistani girls that their future lives will be restricted to their homes, it becomes even more desirable for them to be encouraged to find pleasure and meaning in literature.

The successful teaching of English to all pupils of Asian origin is vital, not only to enable them to achieve academic rewards and personal satisfaction, but to ensure that they are able 'to participate effectively in democracy'. As the Kingman Report (DES, 1988) argues, ' the discriminating use of language on the part of all its people' is necessary to the working of a democracy. Those unable to communicate effectively will be without the means of fully participating in the society of which they are members, unable to 'defend their rights and to fulfil their obligations' (p. 7).

This link between language and the political context brings us now to our discussion of a national curriculum, its rationale and its specific implications for bilingual children.

Towards a National Curriculum

Political pressures as well as utilitarian considerations have always placed constraints upon the cultural and educational arguments for teaching children in their mother tongue. Bilingualism in education by definition means that some kind of compromise is effected between education entirely in the mother tongue and education exclusively in the second language. The position is crucially affected by whatever language or languages are designated 'official' by particular countries. Britain is no exception. In England, for example, it is proposed to assess all young children's abilities in English whatever their mother tongue. In Wales, where there are two official languages, young children whose mother tongue is Welsh will be exempted from programmes and assessment in English. The problem is, of course, that many children achieving low scores in an official language have hitherto been regarded as possessing low general ability. The TGAT's report (DES, 1987) suggested that 'assessment in other skills and understanding, particularly at age 7, should wherever practicable and necessary, be conducted in the pupil's first language' (para. 53).

When, soon afterwards, the English Working Group received their terms of reference and guidance from the Secretaries of State they were enjoined to observe the 'cardinal point':

> that English should be the first language and medium of instruction for all pupils in England. (DES, 1988b: 12.1)

Clearly the term 'first language' is here being deliberately or mistakenly used in a different sense from *the first language learned* and the English Working Group thus inherited confusion and ambiguity centred on a 'cardinal point'. They attempted (DES, 1988b) a partial resolution by reference to the arguments mentioned at the beginning of this section. Firstly, the utilitarian:

> We believe that all children should be enabled to attain a full command of the English language, both spoken and written. Otherwise they will be disadvantaged, not only in their study of other subjects, but also in their working life. (12.3)

Then, making a cultural argument, they referred to a generalisation made by the Swann Committee (1985) that parents from all ethnic minority groups in England:

> want and indeed expect the education system to give their children above all a good command of English as rapidly as possible'. (DES, 1985: 7.3.13)

Significantly, the first argument assumes the status quo of no access to any other medium of instruction in perpetuity; the second ignores demands for, and developments in, instruction in languages other than the official language of the country. Further, as Parveen's story (Chapter 2) shows, the utilitarian argument does not account for attitudes in families where cultural differences actively discourage or even prevent youngsters from engaging in a 'working life'. To that extent the assumption is ethnocentric.

Positive attitudes towards bilingualism are, however, encouraged:

> Bilingual children should be considered an advantage in the classroom rather than a problem. (DES, 1988b: 12.9)

Such children may have advantages of experience which will help them (and others) both in the study of language — its structure, functions and usage — and in the discussion of literature as an element of world culture. Helpfully the linguistic and cultural aspects of English studies for bilinguals are now made positive. One could argue that the valuation is not positive enough. For example, mother tongue languages are seen as means rather than ends to be valued in their own rights: their importance is made specific to the better study of English:

> such children will make greater progress in English if they know that their knowledge of their mother tongue is valued. (DES, 1988b: 12.9)

Clearly the Working Group were seeking to find a subject-specific argument to change certain attitudes to a positive direction and were working under the constraint of its guidance that English should be the 'first language'. Further, they recommend that English language support for bilinguals should be offered in the mainstream classroom not in segregation groups and this is an important step towards recognising good practice and that bilinguals developing a second language are not (in any sense) less able.

This idea is returned to in the English Working Group's second report (DES, 1989) when integration and collaboration are recommended across the curriculum:

> Bilingual pupils at secondary school should be helped to extend their range of English so that they can undertake high level tasks alongside their peers.

and the crucial issue of attitudes is underlined:

> Expectations need to be appropriately set and as high for bilingual pupils as for all others. (10.11)

Cultural issues are referred to again, this time with useful advice for secondary teachers of English that they

> need to be alive to cultural differences which may particularly affect bilingual pupils' handling of literature. Many secondary pupils are likely to be

more aware than younger children of their cultural and religious frames of reference. (10.16)

This is an insight of great significance; unfortunately there is not space in the Report to underpin it with examples and pupils' viewpoints and perhaps the evidence was not then available. It is, however, the central stage of exploration that this book offers.

In one other respect the English Group has gained a perspective on what we have referred to as its ambiguous guidance from the Secretaries of State. Notice the inverted commas in their statement:

English is clearly the 'first language' of the education system. But it would be a great loss if pupils' knowledge of a range of other languages was to decline.

It is a mark of subtlety in writing English that even punctuation marks can mark out a concept to be critically distanced (i.e. not the views of the writer) as well as simply a statement for reference. Obscurity and inaccuracy can thus be met with critical distancing which calls the concept to question. Importantly the Working Group stress that bilingual language development need not be an *either/or* affair, but should be a *both/and* increasing of linguistic repertoires. Here 'a range of other languages' is viewed as an essential part of that repertoire and an important aspect of cultural identity.

We have shown in this critical discussion of official views an increasing willingness to take into account the needs of minority groups. Yet what is most apparent perhaps are the continuing complexity, ambiguity and even conflict which accompany such discussion. In this sense the national level is not dissimilar from the individual tensions and conflicts that we discussed in Chapter 2. It is to this more local level that we now return in Chapter 5.

5 The Girls Speak for Themselves

Our exploratory study has two centres of inquiry which correspond to what we have written so far on cultural context and on English teaching. There is, inevitably, some overlap between the two.

We set out to encourage British Asian girls to talk about their expectations of academic success in their secondary schools, their future ambitions and the possibilities of achieving them, the likelihood of undertaking higher education, opinions on school subjects and the changes they would make in their lives if it was possible to do so. We hoped to gather the information by allowing pupils to take part in discussions about a variety of subjects which interested them as part of their normal classroom activity in speaking and listening.

Our second area of investigation focused upon the subject of English and upon the leisure activities connected with, or having an influence upon, English learning. We wanted to obtain information about:

(1) the amount of reading done by pupils and their preferences in reading material (including periodicals);
(2) the reading habits of pupils' families;
(3) the amount of time spent in television/cinema viewing as compared with leisure reading;
(4) the extent to which non-English authors are read in schools;
(5) the use of school and public libraries and other sources from which pupils obtain books;
(6) pupils' attitudes to English lessons;
(7) the extent to which pupils had undertaken specialist English teaching;
(8) family differences which might influence reading habits.

Since we knew these were sensitive areas, we were prepared for difficulties and lack of co-operation which we, in fact, discovered in some of the schools initially approached. For this reason we made no attempt to obtain a random sample across Education Authorities and concentrated instead upon achieving contrasting schools which to some extent would be typical of the West Midlands as a whole.

We concentrated upon pupils in the 15 to 16 age group because, we argued, they would have had the benefit of most of their compulsory schooling and so have more informed views. They would also be at the stage when plans for their future lives might be exerting an influence upon their outlook. We decided upon an exploratory survey to be carried out by means of a group administered questionnaire plus discussion groups in which pupils could express opinions.

In deciding upon this methodology, we were aware of the shortcomings of the group questionnaire. One set of problems concerns a small sample; another set concerns intelligibility of the questionnaire itself. Cohen & Manion (1980), quoting Tuchman, see questionnaires as representing 'a problem to people of limited literacy' which we thought might be the case with some of the pupils whose views we would seek. They note that 'interviews allow for greater depth ... with extensive opportunities for asking, response keying and probing' (p. 291) with open-ended questions allowing 'opportunities for deeper investigation or clearing up misunderstandings. They encouraged co-operation and established rapport and made it easier for a true assessment of what the respondent really believes' (p. 297). Whitehead (1977) also feels that 'The nearer the chosen technique is to individual interviews conducted by a trained interviewer, the greater the control that can be exercised over the method of collection' and that 'the use of interviewers can produce a higher response rate' allowing for 'full and more complex questions' to be asked (p. 29).

We intended to allow pupils even more freedom in open discussion groups to balance any constraints imposed by the questionnaire. Also it was possible for one of us to be present during the completion of all questionnaires so that any misunderstanding could be ironed out. In this way we hoped to gain the advantage of avoiding any 'subjectivity and bias on the part of the interviewer' (Cohen & Manion, 1980: 292).

In preparing the questionnaire, a number of problems had to be taken into consideration. The questions had to be designed so that they would be understood by pupils of varying abilities, and ambiguity had to be avoided. It was necessary to ensure that questions were not too numerous, otherwise the respondent might become bored and fail to give proper consideration to the answers. For the same reason a minimum amount of writing was to be required from the girls. Wherever possible, questions were required to be answered by a tick or one word, but in other cases this would not suffice. Those questions requiring longer answers were kept to a minimum.

Certain difficulties in questionnaire design and intelligibility were removed after a small pilot study carried out with ten Pakistani girls of varying abilities, including some from a remedial group. (The full questionnaire is reproduced as the Appendix.)

The sample of fifty girls who assisted in our investigations was made up of twenty girls attending a single-sex school situated in a large council estate, to which girls travelled by bus; twenty-two girls from two co-educational Inner City schools, and eight girls attending suburban schools. We did not restrict the sample by reference to religion or origin but found, upon collating information, that all girls, with the exception of one Sikh and one Hindu, were Muslim. All came from Pakistan or Bangladesh, except one girl from East Africa, one born in Czechoslovakia, but whose family originally came from Pakistan, and one whose family originated in India. Our findings cannot be said, therefore, to be representative of all British Asian girls, restricted as it is mainly to Muslim girls with origins in Pakistan and Bangladesh.

Before offering the questionnaire to pupils we discussed it with all staff members concerned, giving them the opportunity of commenting upon the questions and method of research. Since one teacher objected to certain questions, it was necessary to exclude these from all questionnaire sheets as we wished each group to answer the same questions. The teacher concerned felt that questions such as 'Is your religion important to you?' and 'Do you think your parents are satisfied with your education?' were likely to cause offence. He was initially uneasy about other questions, for example: 'What do you like or dislike about English lessons?' and 'Is there anything about teenage magazines that you dislike?' on the grounds that they could not be answered without a great deal of thought and preparation, if at all, but agreed, after discussion with a colleague, to allow them to remain. Pupils were assured that their answers would be treated as confidential and that information would not be relayed to their teachers without their consent.

The discussions which were recorded were carried out in circumstances to fit in with teaching plans in individual schools. Some groups therefore consisted of Asian girls only, some were all-girl groups, but with pupils of different ethnic backgrounds; one group consisted of both boys and girls from a variety of ethnic groups. In some cases the pupils worked from a predetermined agenda; others talked freely about topics of their choosing. For example, one group was engaged in a discussion on prejudice as part of their GCSE oral work. In all groups, except the mixed sex group, no teacher was present. In one school the discussion was videotaped for the English teacher for use as part of GCSE coursework. Initially we thought this might inhibit some pupils from expressing themselves fully, but they were not deterred from giving their views and qualitatively this group's talk was similar to the others.

The strands that we tease out of discussions and the tentative generalisations we make are very different from measures of significance that may be obtained from a large empirical study and statistical analysis. For the reasons we have stated such statistical methods are inappropriate for our purposes. The value of our explorations lies in the fact that they give a voice to a minority which is usually lumped together with a much larger grouping, the majority views of which may not be applicable to it.

Our presentation of the mainly unstructured discussions must, of necessity, be selective. We identify typical topics of interest and illustrate the views offered by examples from transcripts. The remaining part of this chapter is organised in three topic sections:

(1)   perceptions of life opportunities
(2)   understanding of sex roles
(3)   attitudes to education

with the proviso again that, in the flux of conversation, there was overlap between these and that, in any case, there are connections between them.

Perceptions of Life Opportunities

We recall Parveen's bleak exposition of her restricted opportunities in Chapter 2. All the discussion groups concentrated on this issue, adding support, but also some variation, to Parveen's perceptions. For example, it is clear that it is not always fathers who set the limits of achievement and possibility.

Shabana appeared to be experiencing similar problems to those of Parveen, but in her case she felt that it was her mother who was preventing her from obtaining the education she wanted:

> My dad doesn't want to cause a family row, like. He wants to please me and, at the same time, he wants to please my mum, so if I went to college, you know, it'll break the family up and, um, you know, my mum wouldn't talk to my dad and she wouldn't talk to me and it'll be, um, me and my dad versus mum and that's it, I suppose. But she's stronger, our mum is, you know, she's a really strong willed woman.

Shabana sees her situation as impossible to change because of her mother's inflexibility:

> She's, she's been brought up from one of those really strict families, like, you know, where you can't even, you know, like, look outside your

window, but think you're doing something bad, you know, she's been really strict family and, um, I've tried talking to her, it's like talking to a brick wall. It's always the same conclusion. I mean, you always bump into it. There's no way out. You can't break through a brick wall. It's like that with her. I've tried talking about it.

Noreen offers a different viewpoint, showing her own mother's attitudes differ and further shifting us from accepting a stereotype of male-imposed restrictions:

My mum's strict, like, but she's not that strict. I mean, I'm allowed to go out with my friends on my own. I'm allowed to go to the parties, right, and I can stay out till 7 o'clock now and by 7 o'clock I have to be in and, um, I don't have to marry somebody, right, of their choice, right. I can choose my own husband and, er, I can go to college, right.

These choices and privileges point up differences between Noreen's and both Shabana's and Parveen's opportunities and reveal the diversity of attitudes within Muslim households. Noreen does complain about other restrictions placed upon her choice of career:

The only thing I've against them, right, they want me to study, right, or to be what they want me to be which I don't, I mean, I'm really interested in music and all that, into acting, for which they don't want me to be. They want me to go into something like teaching, or in medical, or something like that.

We must remember that adolescence frequently brings the need to test, resist or complain about adult authority. If major obstacles are not evident, then others less insuperable may promote conflict. In this respect Noreen is not different from teenagers in many cultures. She makes the connection herself:

It's not just Asian, or the, um, Asian people, there are problems, the white girls have the same problems.

and recognises diversity even within her own community:

I mean, it's not all the parents are the same. I don't think so.

Shabana interrupts to say that only a minority of girls are allowed freedom of this sort:

But what I'm trying to say is it's only the minority who are like you. Most of the girls I know aren't allowed to go out after school. I know I ain't and a few of my friends, quite a lot of them, aren't allowed to do that. It's only, you know, a few people, that I know who are in … situation here and it's

well, I think it's wrong. We should be allowed some amount of, like, we
need to get socialized, we need to, I'm not saying we should be out there
till 12 o'clock, going to nightclubs, disco's, whatever, we should be able at
least to go out once a day and, you know, see what the world around us is
like.

Shabana argues reponsibly for a limited freedom, intelligently perceiving the
need for socialisation and for seeing 'what the world around us is like'.
However, in her own case, she is virtually incarcerated:

I'm not even allowed to go to supermarkets and, you know, I'm not
allowed to go out and get an icecream on my own. I mean, never mind, my
own. I would like to go. I have to tell my brother to go and get it or whoever's about. If there's no-one about, I just, tough, I just have to do without
icecream, and, you know, a regular walk round the shops and do a little
shopping. It's just out of the question and, er, you know, I think that's
wrong. I mean, say if we was locked up for the next four years and out
there people could be walking round in plastic bags and you walk out with
something really weird on, that isn't right. You look really stupid, you
know, even though you think they look stupid.

Shabana believes that the situation is different in Pakistan, that the girls there are
allowed to go outside their homes, whereas in Britain parents are afraid that
daughters will 'adopt a white way of life'.

The suggestion that girls in Pakistan are allowed greater freedom than their
counterparts in England is not new, for we have encountered the view from
Muslim girls on previous occasions. Khawar Mumtaz & Farida Shaheen (1987),
however, do not share this view. They assert that

in Pakistan the attitude towards women as inferior beings is visible from
the birth of a girl, which is greeted with guilt or despair on the part of the
mother, shame or anger on the part of the father, and the general family ...
A woman's assets are calculated only in terms of her power of reproduc-
tion, and as an object of sexual satisfaction. In a country where the mere
suspicion of 'indecent conduct', let alone premarital sex, is enough cause
for 'crimes of honour', such assets can only come into play after marriage
... consequently, young girls are under constant surveillance and an appropriate marriage is arranged as early as possible. (p. 23)

Mumtaz & Shaheen maintain that young girls look forward to marriage
because they have 'no other dreams open to them and because all spinsters carry
a stigma'. They add that young girls are often 'told (erroneously) that they shall
have greater freedom after marriage' and that although this may be untrue and
the union may be unhappy, 'even the worst are endured for fear of society's

ostracization and a woman's own helplessness ...' (p. 24). They quote the saying that 'once she leaves her father's home for that of her husband ... she enters it in a bridal-suit, and will only emerge in her coffin' (p. 23).

In Britain, some families have retained a firm attitude, possibly an even more inflexible approach to their daughters' wishes in the face of what they perceive as lax Western morality. Others have shifted to accommodate girls' wishes substantially or in part. Thus the conflicts perceived by girls do not solely exist between the Muslim Asian minority and indigenous groups, but also within their own community. This hardly makes punitive restriction easier to bear for girls in families which take a hardline view when they see other friends allowed responsible freedoms. Shabana is convinced that pre-marital sex in her family leads to the family sending the girl 'off to Pakistan and kill them', whilst Noreen tells of a girl who had found herself in that position, but had been subjected to nothing more than 'a row' and marriage to the father of her child:

> She had a row, her parents they told her off, right, but I don't think they battered her up or anything like that.

Shabana counters with another story about a relative who fell in love with a young man of whom her parents did not approve:

> Her parents believe falling in love is a sin.

Shabana says,

> I've heard my mum say it, she's been, you know, a victim of physical violence, absolutely battered and, you know, that's not right.

Shabana complains that there was no organisation to help her relative, that in Pakistan even the police would be unsympathetic because the girl had gone out with young men. Shabana feels that she would like to be able to do some sort of work helping girls who were in difficulties with their families, a wish that had also been expressed, we remember, by Parveen.

We have noticed that life chances depend upon attitude differences between families. Another discussion group illustrate that attitudes within a family are also subject to change over time and according to circumstances. Provided girls tread carefully they can enjoy privileges, though Shabana reminds Fermeda of the sanction of having them all removed:

Fermeda: I've got an older sister, right, and she hasn't done any exams or anything but now she's going to college and doing a textile course and I'm really happy for her. She's taking driving lessons. 'Cause she didn't have that much freedom and she's got so much freedom now, more than me. I'm really really happy for her. But I don't know, they said I can go to college and everything and when we leave I don't know if they'll let me now. I'm just, you know, treading carefully.

Shabina: ... you've got to tread really carefully. Yeh, from the age of about 15 till about 17 or 18, tread very carefully. You go one way outside and they'd probably take you out of college and put you in a little house in cotton wool.

Two girls in the same group speak with obvious affection and respect for their fathers who encourage and support their education:

Nasrat: From the age of about 8 years old, my dad starting talking to me about college. You know, he started saying things 'What you gonna do?'. I didn't know anything about it. Gradually as I grew older he started telling me about A-levels and stuff like that so now I'm prepared for it but if I didn't do exams he'd be disappointed.

Farhat: Yeh, but every parent had a kind of like dream, don't they, 'My daughter's gonna become a certain person'. Like my dad wants me to become a doctor and, well, he wants me to have a proper education from college up to university. He didn't get the chance to.

Both girls indicate that their fathers would have wished for a fuller education themselves. Farhat speaks admiringly of her father giving up his education in order to support his brother and sisters when his own father became ill:

he had to support his younger brother 'cause something happened to my grandfather or something and he was taken ill. So being kind of like the eldest to the brother and sisters, it fell back on him so he had to come out of the country and he had to forget about his own education and support his family.

Nasrat speaks with pride of the determined way her father worked hard to educate himself:

My dad, right, he came over from Pakistan to England when he was 16 years old and he didn't know any English. Now what he used to do, he was that determined to learn English, was that every day (he got a job in the General Post Office) and every day he'd get the dictionary and learn five words out of it.

In these families traditional views have been modified in the light of experience and thus give us insight into the dynamic of attitude change as it affects the life and educational opportunities of different girls.

Understanding of Sex Roles

If the opportunities of these girls are given perspective by differences between and within families, their consciousness is even more heightened by perceived differences in treatment of males and females in their specific community. Frana and Tasim have different perceptions of limited choice in arranged marriages:

Frana: I ... arranged marriages aren't good. A boy and a girl, the girl doesn't get a choice. Usually it's the boy gets the choice ... Sometimes it's a boy or a girl ...

Tasim: They both get the choice.

So far as restriction of movement is concerned, the girls' perceptions are heightened by contrasting their restrictions with freedom allowed to their brothers:

Fermeda: No. Listen. Even if, even if they say you have to go out with somebody you know. You know when you want to go out you have to take your ... (brother) ... with you ...

Shabina: I feel really horrible.

Farhat: I don't.

Fermeda: You feel that they're interfering, but they really care about you but it's still interfer ...

Shabina: Yeh, but you know like the boys in the Asian community. They get the freedom of the world and the girls have to stick in the house. I don't like that. I think we should be treated equal.

The girls have somewhat different attitudes to the same situation with Shabina more acutely conscious of restriction and discrimination than Farhat, for example. Even within the home sex role differences are reinforced, as they go on to discuss:

Farhat: But it happens in some families, the boys are the men of the world and the women have to stay at home and do the cooking and the washing.

Nasrat: But if the girl's strong enough she can get her rights.

Shabina: But this one family I know, that the boys there they watch television and everything and their wives, or their sisters or something, comes into the room, off the telly. They think the telly's gonna disillusion the girl. That is so stupid ...

Even here Nasrat perceptively hints that one of the variables is the girl's own personality and that to some extent she can affect her own life style. The conversation continues to explore sex roles in relation to the hypothetical opportunity of choosing a husband:

Shabina: Well, he's got to be understanding. I mean, it's got to be a two-way system, give and take. He couldn't expect me to do the housework 24 hours a day. Couldn't expect to go out to a snooker club or something and just leave me at home. I would want to break out. I mean, I would like him to take me out occasionally.

Shemila: That's why you get married, isn't it?

Nasrat: I'd like my husband to have an education as well. I wouldn't really mind having looks as long as he's had an education as well.

Shabina: He's got to have a personality. I mean, what if he's a wife basher, what am I going to do? I'd probably batter him back so (laughter) That's me.

Nasrat: I'd get my husband if he did anything to me.

Fermeda: He's got to be loyal. I mean, he's got to let you have your rights as well.

These views express determination to strive within marriage for a balance of opportunity and responsibility between the sexes. By articulating these views the girls reveal they cannot be satisfied by mere re-enactment of traditional roles. Emphasis is placed upon personality, education and give and take:

Fermeda: He's got to let you do what you want to. You both have to, you know. You want to do something, you've got to talk it over first. He's got to listen to your point of view and you've got to listen to his and then sort it over like that.

Shabina: I mean, he can't have everything. I do this, I do that. You stay in the house. You cook for me. You wash my socks. You kiss my feet.

Nasrat: I'd like him to have a personality and have a sense of humour and a good education and let me do what I want.

It seems that differences between the sexes, so far as roles and responsibilities are concerned, may be narrowing in the succeeding generation, but we must remember that the situation remains hypothetical. Shabana in her group reflects on the situation her mother, a strong-willed woman experienced in her day:

Well I was thinking, what was she like when she was, say, my age and, um, if she'd fi ... if she'd stood up to what I believe in, or what she believed in then. I'm sure she had some problems as well, and, um, she's a really strong willed woman. She's, she's able to fight back and, er, you know, she was a, she didn't have much say in the families and if she wanted to stand up for her rights she could've. I, I feel that she should have stood up and fighted for her rights, but she didn't.

The possibility clearly exists that Shabana may not be able to influence sex roles as much as she would like. Nusrat, in a mixed group, reiterates the point that boys have more choice than girls.

Nusrat: When you say about Asians, right, and arranged marriages and stuff, nowadays usually the boys they get more choice on what they do and who they marry but a girl she doesn't have that choice. It's not right in the Asian community, they should have equal rights now, but usually it's the boys that get more freedom now in the Asian community, it's the girls, right, usually don't have that choice.

Darren: How do you go about trying to change that?

Nusrat: Well, we can't change that ...

Sajida: We can't change.

Nusrat: We can't change that. I mean, not now anyway. Well maybe when it comes to our times we might do.

The powerlessness felt by Nusrat and Sajida is reaffirmed in answer to Darren's question, but the possibility of making changes for a future generation is touched on. The girls clearly have a sense of evolutionary changes in attitude and behaviour from generation to generation. There is a difference between real choice for girls and constraint which does not amount to choice at all, because of social pressures. Hamida shows she recognises the fact:

Hamida: You know when we get marriages arranged ... You know in our family, right, that they arrange it and we get everything ready and the day set and everything and then from the other family the man comes, right, and he asks the girl, right, 'Do you want to marry my son?'. I mean, it's all arranged and you — everybody's sitting there. They're, waiting for you and they go ... I mean there's a lot of Asian families there. Everybody's there. If you say 'No', the family's respect is gone, right, and then, I mean, they say you have a choice, that isn't any choice for a girl.

Nusrat links the question of sex roles to the issue of opportunities for personal and social development, showing how much depends upon attitudes and expectations:

Nusrat: I think the parents are too over-protective of girls 'cause they think the girls can't do anything. They just got to sit at home, cook food, do the brushing up, washing up in the house and stuff. I don't think it's right. My brother, like, he gets the right to do what he wants and he can come back at any time he likes and he's only ten years old and I, I'm fifteen now, going on to sixteen and I, and I ain't allowed to come back at that time or I would get in trouble badly and I don't think that's right 'cause we should have equal opportunities. They think that we can't take care of ourselves but we're saying we're stronger than they think we are.

The issue of sex roles is returned to when the girls discuss education.

Attitudes to Education

Close to the girls' consciousness is the issue of single-sex schools. Whether or not girls themselves attend a single-sex school, the views they express are non-controversial. Farhat and Fermeda discuss differences in a typical manner:

Farhat: A lot of people think that single-sex schools and mixed schools are different, but when you come to think about it they're not different at all. My young sister goes to a mixed school and the girls and boys over there are separate. I, I mean the girls look at them as if they are aliens from out of space. They're just two different bands so it's like going to a single-sex school anyway.

Fermeda: When you go to a college, a sixth form and that, you're mixed in ... you're mixed in.

The girls at least have inside knowledge of education systems and how much depends upon their internal organisation. In secondary co-educational schools girls and boys choose frequently to sit in single-sex groups in class and to spend breaktime and lunchtime similarly. The talk proceeds with some nostalgia to discussion of primary school days when co-educational school was an accepted norm:

Farhat: In primary schools they made you sit next to a boy. Boy–girl–boy–girl system and I think that was good.
(Several speak together)

Nasrat: I really enjoyed my primary school days.

Shabina: Oh no, you know like when you used to sit ... (others speak) I would like to go back. You've got no worry there. Now you've got worry.

Nasrat: No worries, no exam.

Shabina: Just life, you know, one day at a time.

Nasrat: You don't have to think ahead, to think of all the problems that arise.

Fermeda: Not at junior school you didn't. You didn't have them say, 'Oh you can't go out without your brother' or something like that, you know 'cause you could go on your own.

Connections between education and their own roles and opportunities are already being made. Another group of Pakistani girls with Sarah, an indigenous English girl, discuss the value of secondary education.

Yasmin: Some people don't get anything out of going to school. I mean, they learn bad language but, apart from that, they don't learn anything else.

Shabina: Don't they? What do you mean? Don't you learn how to talk to people, how to write, how to read?

Yasmin: Yeh, you can't learn that at home.

Rifhat: Yes, but jobs are more easy to get.

Sarah: Yes, but some people have got O-levels and they still haven't got a job. That's just all them years down the drain.

Shabina: Yeh, but at least you've got them.

Yasmin: What do you do with a piece of paper when it says you've got your O-levels when you can't use them?

This is the crucial issue. The girls perceive there is no guarantee of jobs even if qualifications are gained. Yasmin takes the view that essentials are learned at home, but this is challenged:

Shabina: Could your father teach you at home?

Nida: Yeh, Urdu.

Shabina: Yeh. No, he couldn't give you O-level physics or something, could he?

Rifhat: But you're learning in this country. They are English, not Urdu ... Urdu won't do you much good here.

The limitations of education at home are rehearsed and Rifhat makes the claim that their mother tongue is of little value. Much depends on the encouragement that girls receive in pursuing their English education. We have seen that families can sometimes have a negative effect and the girls perceive the important role of teachers:

Sarah: Some teachers don't encourage you, do they?

Rifhat: They encourage just the brainy ones, right.

Nida: They pick their favourites in the class and encourage them and so you're left behind.

Nagina: No matter how hard you try some teachers don't encourage you and that's not fair.

Rifhat: If you want to learn it doesn't matter about the teacher. If you want to learn you can.

Rifhat valiantly tries to assert the independence of learners but the consensus is that these girls perceived a lack of encouragement in school. We must

remember that this is only one side of the story and the reality may be much
different; however, these perceptions of the girls must surely contribute to
their construction of reality and must affect their motivation and self image.
Nida adds:

> You just fall behind and go 'Forget it. I'm giving up'.

Possibly there is an interaction between the girls losing heart and teachers setting lower standards. Certainly it is a downward spiral that we should be aware
of and guard against.

A further limitation on progress can be the school curriculum itself. Many
girls touched on restrictions in the school system, bringing their attitudes to education into play with issues of equal opportunity and sex roles. In their group
Shabina and Nasrat both discover that they wanted to be engineers. Nasrat complains that her mother prevented her and Shabina discovers her prospects are not
hopeful.

Shabina: Yeh, but I mean, mechanical engineer, every boy can do it. I want to
choose something that boys — I want to be better than boys — I
don't want a boy to dominate me, ever saying 'Oh, you don't know
what this is'. I'd say, 'Yes, I do. I know what it is'.

Farhat: You'd be able to do that if we had subjects in this school. We haven't
got them subjects, we haven't got metal work, we haven't got woodwork ...

Fermeda: Say if this was a mixed school, we'd get metalwork and things like
that.

Shabina: Because we're a single-sex school, it means that we haven't got the
subjects that we would like but then if we were in a mixed school the
men would dominate over us.

Shabina can see both points of view, that in a single-sex school girls are not
dominated by boys; on the other hand their curriculum closes down certain
options which make equal opportunity impossible and reinforce the stereotyped
sex roles. A different group containing a different Shabina begin pessimistically
on the same issue:

Mafeez: I mean people who do A-levels don't get jobs. It's not worth the
bother.

Rifhat: It is if you want a career.

Shabina: How about if you don't try?

Nida: And you haven't got the right O-levels?

Rifhat: Keep your options open.

Shabina: Take a wide range of subjects and you might get somewhere.

This group perceives the value of an open, balanced curriculum with equal opportunity to choose from a wide range of options. Then in a heated discussion with girls talking at once, they make the comparison with their own school system:

Rifhat: If you got a good choice here ...
(Several speak together)

Nida: Even if you took the range of options ... Several voices: We didn't have TDK ... HE I wanted that subject ... we didn't have woodwork ... metalwork ... motor mechanics ...

Shabina: Listen, like Mrs S. she used to take us to all, you know, these women's equal rights and all that. Was there any equal rights in this school? There's no motor mechanics, no woodwork, nothing like that. Forget about typing, I mean, equal rights, they say everything's equal now, don't they?

Sarah: Technical drawing, not just art.

For these girls the opportunities to discover about woodwork, metalwork, technical drawing and motor mechanics do not exist and in this respect their school curriculum adds to the aspects of disadvantage already discussed. In this respect a National Curriculum is likely to ameliorate the situation by providing a scientific core, but some individual schools will still have to work towards providing equal access to appropriate options.

Only two groups discussed English teaching, focusing upon their work done for GCSE. The choice of books was criticised. In the words of Farhat, 'The books are just diabolical'. The main complaint seemed to be that the books were out of date, that subjects should be concerned with present-day situations. For example, girls saw *To Kill a Mockingbird* as old-fashioned and irrelevant, but enjoyed *Across the Barricade* as 'the only book that we could relate to'.

Shabina: *To Kill A Mockingbird* is about 50 years old and how are we supposed to go back 50 years and we've never been there. Now all we see is violence this, that, you know.

Nasrat: We seen it all before. Before the teacher should have set that book we should have been told about it. We should have, both of us, instead of being a one-way system, the teacher choose the book, the pupils do it. Both the teachers should have discussed it, what book, you know the pupil and the teacher to discuss what book we want and then we would have enjoyed reading it and doing work on it and the teacher would have enjoyed marking it.

It is possible that themes in *To Kill a Mockingbird* (racism, prejudice, intolerance, the individual standing up to society pressure) could have been shown relevant to the girls' own experience. However, this group have not been helped to make the connections. Interestingly they raise two crucial issues that English teachers should take notice of, i.e. involvement and enjoyment. Since readers play an important role in constructing the meaning of a text by bringing their own experience to bear on it, it is important to allow readers to take responsibility for their reading from the start. One way of doing this is to allow some choice of texts to be studied. Secondly, Nasrat highlights enjoyment (as does DES (1988) in the paragraphs on teaching literature) and seems to know the difference for all concerned, including the teachers, between barren, imposed study and involved participation in the text. She continues:

Nasrat: *Come to Mecca.* That was a really good book. That was about Asian
              people in today's society, what their parents thought of prejudice and
              there's another one ... *Magic*, that's a good book as well, there are
              good stories in there.

Nasrat appears to believe (wrongly) that Susan Gregory is an Asian writer, but admits she has little knowledge of what literature is available.:

Nasrat: There are a few books, I don't know what the names are, there are a
              few books in the library that have got to do with prejudice nowadays
              that I think would have been much better than *To Kill a Mockingbird.*
Shemila: Like that author of *My Mate Shafiq.*
              (Several speak)
Nasrat: That's really brilliant.
Shemila: They should have had that as a set book.

The girls show ability to make enthusiastic choices from the limited number of texts they have encountered, but what is glaringly apparent is the limitation of their experience of the range of literature in English that is now available. English teachers need to familiarise themselves with the diversity of challenging literature written in English by writers of differing ethnic origins. At the very least, students given choices and introduced to literature by writers from their own communities will be more at e and more willing to explore a novel like *To Kill a Mockingbird* with its American language and frame of reference difficulties and demands for British Asian readers.

We shall return to these issues in the next chapter which concentrates upon the girls' attitudes to English teaching as revealed by their questionnaire responses. What this chapter has shown is the way, for these girls at least, connections exist between our three areas of interest: life opportunities, sex roles and education. We too have separated them only for convenience of discussion, but we perceive strong links: for example, the need for education to develop awareness of roles as well as possibilities of modifying them; and for education to maximise opportunities in life. We end with an extract which affirms connections made by one group which begin with observations that one family has different expectations and establishes different opportunities for its children. This leads to a general point about educational discrimination at the macro level and Bushra's and Naila's realisations that such limitation and discrimination reinforces sex roles after school:

Rukhsana: What about this morning. That boy — them two boys at the bus stop. I don't think their father favours them or anything, but they got ... a taxi ... a private school and chauffeur and the two girls, they go to, er, ordinary school.

Ferhana: Yes, ... they get a chauffeur driving them to school.

Rukhsana: Every day.

Ferhana: They go to a private school and the girls go to this local one. (Several speak together) ... That's not fair, ... That's not right.

Ferhana: They just put their noses up in the air.

Naseem: In the whole of Birmingham there's six grammar schools. There's four for boys and two for girls and if a boy, say, gets 94% out of a hundred, the boy's going to pass that exam. So if a girl gets 94%, the girl's going to fail and that's not very fair, is it?

Bushra: The men just take it for granted that the women will do the housework at home and look after the children while they go out to work. Why can't it be the other way round?

Naila: Say when you're married, right, there is still a lot, you know, of sex discrimination, I think.

Discussion leads the girls to sensitive perception and intelligent reflection on their society and their positions in it. These qualities are further revealed in the questionnaire responses in the next chapter.

6 The Questionnaire Survey

Educational Backgrounds of Pupils

The sample, as outlined in Chapter 5, consisted of fifty girls, drawn from co-educational and single-sex schools in almost equal numbers, and covering four levels of abilities, from those in a top-ability stream to girls in a remedial group. Because of the small numbers we shall not use percentages, for this might misleadingly indicate conclusive rather than suggestive evidence. The numbers in the sample are too small to establish conclusive evidence on their own, but certain trends do emerge that are worth systematic investigation.and these trends are related to Whitehead's (Whitehead et al., 1975) much larger, national survey wherever possible.

The questionnaire revealed that forty-five of the fifty girls began their education in English primary schools, with twenty having attended nursery classes. Twenty-six girls remembered speaking some English prior to attending school, whilst eight had undertaken specialist EFL teaching in the primary school and nine in the secondary school.

Twenty-one of the girls anticipated gaining four or more GCSE (grade C) passes; twelve three passes, twelve one or two passes; five did not anticipate gaining any GCSE, or similar, examination qualifications. (The figures reflect pupils' expectations, but are reinforced by their positions in school groupings.) We remember that self-concept has a greater effect upon attainment than intelligence, (e.g. Brookover et al., 1964; Burns, 1979).

Of those pupils with the highest expectations of examination success, virtually all remembered speaking English before commencing primary school, with just over half having attended nursery school. At the other end of the scale, none of the pupils in the lowest ability group remembered speaking English in pre-school days, although a fifth of these had attended nursery school and all had attended English primary schools. In the middle range both pre-school English speaking and nursery education appeared to affect pupils' present achievements and expectations with those girls having these experiences having also noticeably higher attainments and expectations.

The provision of specialist English lessons did not appear to have redressed the balance for those who had not had the opportunity of early contact with the language. Only one of the able girls had received any specialist teaching. In Group 2, three had had EFL lessons in primary school and two in secondary school. In Group 3, a quarter had received specialist teaching in primary school and a quarter in secondary. In the least able group almost half had received special help in primary school and everyone had had help in secondary school.

There are unanswered questions here about the quality of help and the organisation of provision, but there is certainly no room for complacency. Possibly the girls with least ability in English and separated from the mainstream suffer through loss of self-image and subject content, falling further and further behind.

Attitudes to School

Almost two-thirds of the sample said that they liked school on the whole, but there were a number of criticisms made by them of school life.

Three-quarters said that they felt that the subjects they had studied were worthwhile, but that leaves a substantial proportion who did not answer positively. A number felt that they would have liked the opportunity of studying other subjects. Ten complained that they had been unable to study Home Economics because of other timetable commitments and a similar number made the same complaint about typewriting lessons. Four wished that Bengali or Gujarati were available; five had not had the opportunity of studying a European language as they had wished. Other subjects which girls had wanted to study were Art, Woodwork, Textiles, Sciences, Commerce (all of which were available, but clashed with other subjects on the timetable) and Mechanics and Football, which were not available to them.

Pupils complained of disliking particular subjects and were critical of other things commonly criticised by pupils such as 'soggy chips for school dinners', the state of toilets, school heating, assembly, and so on. Some girls complained about teachers, some because teachers expected too much work, a comment made by generations of schoolchildren, but others felt that certain teachers demonstrated racial bias. One child wrote,

> I hate the teacher, she is always nagging and talks about religion. She is prejudiced and she thinks that we shouldn't wear heels because we Pakistanis walk funny when we get old. She wants us to get married with whoever she says. I hate her!!!

Several girls wrote that they disliked a certain teacher because that teacher made them feel 'stupid'. One girl commented that she disliked a teacher because she 'keeps nagging us about our relationships, that you should not marry your cousins'. Several felt that certain teachers talked too much and did not give pupils sufficient opportunity of expressing their views in class.

Despite these criticisms, most pupils spoke of some teacher or teachers they liked or who had been helpful to them. A number of girls expressed views similar to that of the girl who wrote, 'I know in years to come that when I look back on my life, I will remember my school life and because I enjoyed it, the good times are the ones I will remember'.

Although the majority of pupils said that they liked school, only twenty, mainly from the able group, said that they hoped to go on to higher education, i.e. beyond GCSE.

When asked about their ambitions, five said that they wished to enter a profession; four wanted to work in offices, six wanted to become shop assistants or factory workers; three wished to have a career in entertainment; four wished to take up nursing or nursery work; three wanted to become writers; seven wished to marry; six said they wanted any sort of job; eight did not want any job; air hostess, engineer and dress designer were also mentioned.

The ambitions expressed were, however, what girls felt they would *like* to do; a number added that they did not expect to realise their ambition. Clearly the majority of pupils either wanted, or presumed that they would have, occupations that did not call for any advanced academic qualifications.

Influence of Family on English and Reading Habits

One of the conclusions drawn by Whitehead (1977) was that the amount of book reading carried out by children was positively associated with a number of variables, one of which was 'the smallness of family size' (p. 275). In his extensive survey, pupils were classified into those with 0–2 siblings, small families, and those with three or more siblings, labelled large families. In investigating the possible influence of family size on the reading habits of the girls in this survey, we found that only seven pupils came from what could be termed small families (one with one sibling, six with two), making a conclusion on the influence of small, as opposed to large families, difficult.

In the sample, no student was without siblings and more than half were members of families with six or more children, one pupil having fourteen brothers and sisters.

There did not appear to be any noticeable differences in the quantity of books read by each student over a period of four weeks in relation to the size of the student's family. The student from the smallest family, with one sibling, read four books in four weeks; the student with fourteen siblings read five plus books in the same period. Members of the sample averaged two books each in the four-week period, with children who read no books at all being members of families with three, four, five, six, and nine children, and those who had read five or more books belonging to families of three, five, six, seven, eight, and nine. The majority of the pupils were, of course, reading in their second language. Nor did there appear to be any evidence that family size had exerted any great influence upon pupils' expectations of success at GCSE level. The girl who was a member of the smallest family anticipated only two GCSE passes; the girl from the family of fifteen children was expected to pass in more than four subjects. Girls who did not expect any GCSE passes belonged to families ranging from those with four children to those with nine children; those anticipating four or more passes belonged to families of all sizes except the smallest and that with nine children.

There was no appreciable difference in the distribution of other expected passes in relation to family size. (In Whitehead's survey, the number of families with fewer than four children is higher amongst non-manual workers and the proportion of families with more than four children is higher amongst manual workers, so that the size of the family is seen to be related to the father's occupation and social class.) This may not be the case with Asian families. A 1963 study in Birmingham showed that Indian and Pakistani women at the age of 45 had had an average of between five and six pregnancies, whereas English women averaged three pregnancies, suggesting that in the Asian community as a whole, larger families are the norm (Krausz, 1971). If families of respondents are grouped in accordance with the five 'classes' devised by the census authorities, according to father's occupation, then the sample covered most classes as it included the daughters of men in Class II occupations (shopkeepers, a teacher, a manager); Class III (a foreman, a shop assistant) as well as unskilled, semi-skilled and unemployed persons. All children, however, live in similar areas of the city, sharing many experiences and values. The sample is too small to make more than tentative suggestions, but these trends and possible differences are worth further systematic investigation.

Reading Habits of the Family

Whitehead (1977) concluded that the family is the most important social institution in which the child participates and that 'we have undoubtedly found some grounds for believing that, in our sample, family circumstances exert an important influence on the child's amount of reading' (p. 77). It was suggested that the child brought up in a home where the father was employed in a non-manual occupation and in which more quality newspapers were probably read and parents would make use of public libraries, would lead to the child becoming more likely to read than the child of a manual worker. It would also result in the child enjoying a more successful school life with high achievement. We did not include questions about parental occupations; instead we questioned pupils about reading habits and availability of reading materials in the home.

The girls were asked to give: (a) the number of books which they owned; and (b) the total number of books they estimated were in their homes.

Seven said there were in excess of fifty books; sixteen said there were twenty-one to fifty, and twenty-six estimated that there were less than twenty in the home. (One girl did not know and was not prepared even to hazard a guess upon being questioned.) The respondents seemed less certain about their own ownership of books. Six girls said they did not know if they owned any books. The reason for this seemed to be that they had either only owned paperbacks of the Mills and Boon type and did not know if they had been disposed of, or they had owned children's books but were unsure if ownership had passed to a younger sibling once they had read them. Thirteen did not own any books while eighteen owned less than ten, with thirteen owning over ten books.

Only thirty-six were members of the public library and of these two borrowed books more than once a week, seven about once a week, fourteen visited the library once a month, the remaining thirteen visited the library only very occasionally. Some girls said that they would like to borrow books more frequently, but were not allowed to go out unaccompanied. A number of others used the library only as a source of material for projects and other school work. Very few spoke of the public library as a part of their leisure activities, most regarding it only as a source of information.

Reading of Periodicals and Newspapers

A number of homes had daily or Sunday newspapers regularly with only ten girls saying that they read a newspaper regularly. Few of the newspapers could be described as 'quality papers', with local newspapers and tabloids being the most popular.

No family read *The Guardian*, *The Telegraph* or *The Observer*. Only one family appeared to read a non-English newspaper, *The Daily Jang*. The popularity of *The Daily News* may be explained by the fact that it is a free newspaper delivered to most homes in the area, but it was interesting to note that similar numbers mentioned *The Birmingham Evening Mail* being taken by their families, showing that local news is more popular than national newspapers amongst this sample of families.

Sunday newspapers seemed to be less popular with thirty-one out of fifty families reading none.

Pupils' Leisure Reading Habits

Girls in our sample followed the pattern of those in Whitehead's survey, in enjoying reading of periodicals, with forty-six of the fifty questioned reading periodicals regularly, six girls reading more than four each week. Whitehead found that

> in general non-periodical reading tends to go hand-in-hand with non-book reading and heavy periodical reading tends to go hand-in-hand with heavy book reading; the only sub-group to whom this generalization does not apply is that of the 14+ girls. (Whitehead, 1977: 274)

We should therefore expect the sample to contain mainly enthusiastic periodical readers, who are non-book readers. In fact, the reading of periodicals was widespread amongst all reading groups, both heavy and light, with only four girls reading neither magazines nor comics. There are no discernible links between the amounts of book reading and periodical reading. Nine of those reading periodicals regularly had read no books in a four-week period; thirteen had read one book, eight had read two books, four had read three books, six had read four books and ten five or more books.

The periodicals mentioned are listed below in order of popularity. More than a quarter of the girls regularly read *Smash Hits*.

Smash Hits
Look in
Woman
No 1
Woman's Own
Bella
Beano
Marie
Newspaper Supplements
TV Times

Despite the popularity of this type of light reading, the girls were not without criticism of the contents of magazines and comics. Three-quarters felt that they did not cater for Asian readers and said that they wished for more appropriate articles about clothes, cosmetics and jewellery, music and other entertainment. Others criticised the lack of advice given in teenage magazines on coping with schoolwork and said there was insufficient attention paid by magazines to serious current problems such as AIDS and drug abuse. Only one girl expressed discontent with the literary content and then only to say that she wished there were more picture stories. It did not seem that fiction in the magazines was important, with girls buying them in order to read about entertainers or to read about trends in fashion.

The percentage of girls buying books is smaller than the percentage of girls reading periodicals. Almost half could not remember having bought a book. Ten said that the last book they bought was connected with GCSE study (non-literary) and only about one-third could remember ever buying fiction. Of these, only three mentioned could be described as 'quality narrative' in the sense used by Whitehead: *Huckleberry Finn, 101 Dalmations* and *Charley and the Chocolate Factory*. The others were teenage romantic paperbacks, Mills and Boon, and horror stories, such as *Vampire Junction*.

Books did not seem to be given frequently to the respondents as gifts. Only a quarter of the girls remembered ever getting a book as a present, although more than a third said that they felt that a book would make a good present.

Few of the pupils (only nineteen) were able to name a favourite author. Those names were:

Judith Krantz	M. V. Cary
Agatha Christie (twice)	Judy Blume (twice)
Graham Masterson	Penny Jordan
Enid Blyton (twice)	Mario Puzo
Daphne du Maurier (twice)	Rosa Guy
Roberta Forrest	Susan Gregory
A. Conan Doyle	Raold Dahl (twice)

Those pupils mentioning Dahl, du Maurier and Gregory had read books by these authors recently in class and may well have been merely writing down the only writers whose names came to mind at the time. None of the girls named an Asian author.

Romantic fiction was by far the most popular form of reading with all but one pupil listing it as enjoyable reading. Horror stories, murder mysteries and adventure tales were next in popularity, with science fiction, supernatural and fantasy stories also claiming mentions.

Whitehead quotes Terman's and Lima's view that children are motivated to read because of (a) curiosity; (b) desire for wishfulfilment; (c) the tendency to imitate, adding that

> The child does not read as the adult does for an hour's entertainment or instruction; he reads himself by a process of empathy into the book and finds there a satisfying fulfilment of his subconscious wishes. (Whitehead, 1977: 205)

For the pupils in this survey, romantic love and fear-provoking situations removed from their everyday lives seem to make the most appeal.

Television Viewing

Whitehead felt that 'the amount of television viewing accomplished by most children cannot help but reduce the amount of time they have available for reading', a view that was supported by the results of his investigation (p. 274). For those Pakistani girls whose families are reluctant to allow them to leave their homes unaccompanied, it seemed possible that their viewing hours could possibly exceed those of other children with more varied leisure activities.

We questioned the girls about the amount of time they had spent watching television in the previous seven days. Whitehead questioned his sample about the previous evening's viewing, but we wished to include the weekends when girls had the greatest amount of leisure and we had found, during the pilot study and preliminary interviews, that there seemed to be a tendency for children to follow a pattern of viewing, with the television being switched on and off at almost the same time each day. The girls were given sufficient time to calculate the amount of viewing they had done in one week and the answers to questions, put to them verbally in order to ensure accuracy, verified that the figures they gave reflected reasonably accurately the amount of time spent viewing.

Only six of the girls viewed for 10 or fewer hours in a week, with substantially more than half spending in excess of 30 hours a week viewing, an average of 4 hours a day. The average viewing per week for the whole group was 3.5 hours a day. This figure is higher than that of Whitehead's survey, in which the girls in the 14+ age group averaged 2.13 hours (p. 55) Whitehead's figure, however, relates to week-days only, whereas the girls in this study included weekend viewing.

It might have been expected that those girls reading four or more books in a four-week period would have been lighter television viewers than those who read nothing, but this did not appear to be the case. If anything, these girls also tended to watch more television with the majority watching 41–50+ hours per week. Non-readers were evenly spread over a range between 11–20 hours and 50+ hours per week. Similarly there was no discernible trend of relationship between ability grouping and television watching.

The group's preferences in television match their choice in periodical reading. Soap operas are by far the most popular, with the Australian *Neighbours* being watched regularly by virtually all the sample (except four girls), and the American *Dallas* and *Dynasty* regularly viewed by over one-third. Almost two-thirds also watched another Australian serial, *Prisoner in Cell Block H* despite the fact that it is often screened after midnight. Six girls named the British soap *Eastenders* among their favourite viewing.

Apart from *Top of the Pops* few other types of viewing attracted frequent mention. No one mentioned documentaries, news broadcasts or quality drama. When questioned about films and plays which they had seen, girls could remember only comedy films, such as *Ghost Busters*, or films such as those produced by Hammer Films about vampires and other horrors.

One-quarter of the girls regularly watched films in Urdu. These again were light, romantic entertainment of the 'Arabian Nights' variety, which in no way reflected the lives of the pupils.

English and Reading in School

More than two-thirds of the group said that they liked English as a school subject and all the sample considered it valuable. Asked to say what they liked about English lessons, girls specified such things as:

working with others;
being able to talk to other people;
the help in developing and speaking English language;
writing stories;
reading in lessons;
the projects when we had to do it all ourselves;
the chance to work out problems ourselves and write about them in our own way.

The main dislikes about English lessons were the overlong essays, the workload and the teaching techniques (i.e. teacher not fully explaining what was required or talking too much). The assignments which were carried out with most pleasure were those in which girls had greater control over the learning situation and felt that they were responsible for planning and carrying out the work, thus gaining a greater sense of achievement.

Although several pupils specifically mentioned reading as a reason for enjoying English, the numbers of pupils who said they enjoyed reading was lower than the number of those liking English lessons, with about one-third not enjoying reading. Only ten girls said they had read books in English by Asian writers, but even this low figure is probably overstated, since several of these girls named a book of short stories, *Magic*, as the book by an Asian author which they had read. This book was, in fact, written by Susan Gregory, although it featured stories about Asian girls living in Britain and the problems they encountered.

All girls belonged to schools with library facilities, though not all made frequent use of them. Somewhat more than three-quarters of the sample said that they used the school library, of whom only two borrowed books more than once a week, seven about once a week, nineteen about once a month, and 12% only occasionally.

A number of girls seemed unfamiliar with their school library. In the same school, pupils answered that books in Asian languages were available and were not available, that the library was freely available for use during any free time and that it was not available. Some girls revealed that they saw the library only as a source of reference material, but some of these pupils said that they would use the library if it was made more attractive.

The main opinions were: (a) their library needed new furniture, display material, redecorating; and (b) they wanted more teenage/romance novels. Only three girls said they wanted more books by Asian writers.

Both in class and in the school library, it was felt by a number of the girls that the books selected for them were inappropriate. Complaints were made that few books were about teenagers like themselves, but they did not necessarily mean Asian teenagers. Books mentioned as enjoyable reading were: *The Secret Diary of Adrian Mole*, *Nobody's Family Going to Change*, *Across the Barricades*, which all featured teenagers, but others spoke of enjoying fiction less obviously relevant to their own lives, such as *Of Mice and Men* and *Rebecca*. Girls were most critical of books which they felt were 'old fashioned' or 'out of date', mentioning as examples, *To Kill a Mockingbird*, *The Secret Garden* and *Oliver Twist* and those which they found 'boring', for example, *My Family and Other Animals* and *Kestrel for a Knave*. It was frequently remarked by the pupils that they felt they should be given more opportunity to select their own books for study purposes. These responses accord with the analysis of group discussions in Chapter 5.

Summary and Conclusions

In making conclusions from the evidence reviewed so far we must start with the reminder that the smallness of the sample and the absence of respondents from non-urban areas, preclude firm generalisations and conclusive statements being made about the results. In a more ambitious survey it would be useful to include more Asian girls from suburbs, those who attend schools in which the majority of pupils are white, and those from prosperous homes. The results of our investigations can only be said to apply to mainly Pakistani, Muslim girls from Inner-City areas whose parents are from the non-professional classes. The respondents did, however, represent a range of abilities, from those who expected to achieve four or more passes in GCSE to those who did not expect to achieve any external examinations passes. We therefore present the tentative findings as strands to be untangled further by subsequent investigation.

(1) The results of the questionnaire suggest that an important factor in academic achievement amongst the sample is the pre-school learning of English. The large majority of the ablest group and none of the least able group encountered and used English prior to schooling, with subsequent specialist English teaching failing to remedy the disadvantage suffered by those whose English learning began at school. This is a disappointing finding worth further investigation.

(2) The majority of pupils expressed a liking for school and for the teaching staff, with only a very small number suggesting that they had found any racial bias amongst teachers. Less than half of the pupils planned to undertake higher education, the majority anticipating marriage or employment not requiring academic qualifications.

(3) In order to compare the reading habits of the respondents with a wider group, girls were asked the number of books read in the previous four weeks for comparison with the 14+ girls in the survey by Whitehead. The answers showed that pupils averaged one book read voluntarily for each girl in the sample, whereas Whitehead's survey showed the average to be 2.15 (1.78 for 14+ boys) (p. 52). Earlier surveys by Jenkinson (1940) and Himmelweit et al. (1958) also showed average reading in excess of two books a month, suggesting that the voluntary reading for groups of pupils like those in our survey may well be far less than average.

(4) The size of the respondents' families appeared to have little bearing upon the amount of voluntary reading carried out, with children from smaller families reading similar numbers of books as those from larger families. Nor did size of pupils' families have any noticeable effect upon their expectations of examination success, with high and low expectations amongst children of most family sizes.

(5) It seemed probable that enjoyment of reading could be linked to a plentiful supply of books in the home and the girls were asked about the number of books owned by their families and themselves. Less than half said that there were over twenty books in their homes; about a third estimated that there were fewer than ten. The number of books owned by the pupils was smaller, with almost half owning no books (or not knowing if they owned any) and only about a quarter owning over ten books.

(6) Although more than two-thirds of the girls were members of the public library, only a third borrowed books at least once a week. Few borrowed books for pleasure, but regarded the library as an information resource centre. Of course, these findings may be influenced by the fact that these girls were not allowed to visit public libraries unaccompanied.

(7) Few girls appear to buy books, with about half not being able to remember ever having bought a book and a fifth saying that the last book they bought was in connection with non-literary GCSE study. Of those who had bought books only three books could be classified as 'quality narrative'. The most popular reading was romantic fiction followed by horror stories, murder mysteries and adventure stories.

(8) The amount of periodical reading recorded was extensive, even for those who were not heavy book readers. Pupils specified the number of periodicals (including comic papers) read in a four-week period. Only four had read no periodicals; almost half the sample had read in excess of eleven. Most girls named magazines about 'pop' music and personalities as the ones bought most frequently, with those about televison, fashion and homemaking slightly less popular. The fictional content appeared to be unimportant. The amount of periodical reading had little influence upon the amount of book reading.

(9) Few pupils had access to quality newspapers in their homes. About a fifth said that they regularly read newspapers, but with the exception of the two girls who read *The Sunday Times*, none of the pupils' families bought newspapers which were classified by Whitehead as 'quality papers' (p. 75). Local papers and a free local advertising newspaper were the main reading available. Only one family bought an Asian newspaper.

(10) The popularity of television and video viewing could well interfere with the amount of reading carried out for pleasure. Over half of the girls spent in excess of 30 hours a week watching television, the average viewing for the group being 24.5 hours (3.5 hours a day). From the results, it was not possible to conclude that television affects the reading habits of all the sample as the number of heavy and light viewers are spread throughout the heavy and light readers.

(11) The pressures of studying for examinations did not appear to have any influence upon the amount of voluntary reading, nor on the amount of

viewing, except that in the lower ability group (4), almost two-thirds were heavy viewers and light readers.

(12) The choice of viewing was, like book reading, mainly 'non-quality' with most girls showing a preference for 'soap operas' (*Neighbours, Dallas, Dynasty* and *Prisoner in Cell Block H*). A number of pupils watched video films, mainly romantic Asian films or 'video nasties' about murder and the supernatural.

(13) English was claimed to be a popular subject, with almost three-quarters saying that they liked it. Girls stated a preference for those English lessons in which they are given the opportunity of taking an active part and complained of the lack of involvement in the choice of topics and reading material. Some pupils disliked the amount of work they were expected to do, whilst others were critical of teachers' attitudes or tendency to talk too much.

(14) Reading was not regarded as a popular part of English lessons, with a third of the girls explicitly saying that they did not enjoy it. The amount of literature by ethnic minority writers studied in school was small, with few girls able to name Asian authors whose work they had read. Very few used the school library more than once a week, with two-thirds borrowing books monthly or less often. More than half the respondents were satisfied with school library provision, but others were critical about the stock of books, lack of comfort and inadequate furnishings.

(15) Criticism was made of the poor choice of reading material for the GCSE with pupils expressing the view that books chosen were often without relevance to their lives.

Having thus summarised the questionnaire findings, it is useful also to summarise here the information gathered from group discussions in Chapter 5, since issues raised there are likely to have an effect upon girls' motivation and attainment. Subjects which arose in each group, even in those discussions which were intended to deal with other topics, were those of sexual inequality and curtailed freedom. Some girls spoke of parents who supported their wish for a full education and career but, for others, the future appeared to be bleak with an arranged marriage as the only prospect for them after leaving school. It was clear that some girls felt strongly that they were being denied the freedom which girls from other ethnic groups, and Asian boys, are allowed. Some girls spoke of their resentment about being unable to complete their education, others of being allowed only to take up occupations approved by their relatives, such as factory work. For these girls, striving to achieve success in examinations must seem to be a waste of time. One girl made this point, describing how she became a troublesome pupil when, in the third year of secondary school, she learned that she would not be allowed to take part in post-16 education.

In several discussions, pupils argued about whether or not Asian girls were permitted to choose marriage and the marriage partner, with pupils sometimes denying that marriage was forced upon Asian women. There can be little doubt, however, that a number of girls firmly believe that no choice will be allowed them and this must inevitably lessen their motivation to work hard at school. On the other hand, the diversity of viewpoints and experiences warns against making unsupported generalisations about what might appear at first sight a homogeneous group.

7 The Way Forward

This final chapter returns to some of the findings discussed earlier, placing them in context and considering their implications. For reasons already mentioned blanket solutions and categorical policies are inappropriate. However, implications for change will be related to the trends discovered where these are supported by other research and some suggestions towards policy building are offered.

To begin with, in recording the views of a group of schoolgirls we have found these to be intelligent, honest and perceptive. There is clearly much to be gained from consulting pupils about their learning experiences, recognising that theirs is not the only viewpoint, but one which can illuminate and add to a school's ability to respond to needs.

We discovered also that a preconceived and stereotyped view of family influence is inadequate. For example, size of family does not appear to affect the amount of book reading. Also the girls' views reveal differences *between* households in a community as well as differences *within* households where one parent (not always the father) imposed more restrictions than the other. Attitudes are clearly in process of change with more support being given to education. Clearly, though, a girl's life chances depend upon the attitudes taken by her particular family. Her own life style and attitudes will be affected by the differences she perceives between her opportunities and those of her peers. However, her own personality is likely to influence the equation, since some girls are more conscious than others of restriction and discrimination.

Community Considerations

The strong feelings held by a number of girls about their lack of freedom to pursue higher education and careers were voiced repeatedly and, whether or not they are correct in their views about their future lives, the fact that they hold such views must influence their attitudes to schoolwork. Some made it clear that they saw no purpose in learning as they were destined to marry or take up a manual occupation upon leaving school. Mumtaz & Shaheed (1987) affirm women's rights to 'determine their lives according to their own aspirations' and to have the 'right to education, to work, to free choice of employment, to just and favourable conditions of work ... to participate in recreational activities, sports and aspects of cultural life'. These authors also spell out the method for realizing the aims:

> Through consciousness raising ... creating an awareness, primarily through women (a) of their existing rights and rights which are their due (b) of their equal status in society and their contribution to it (c) of the legal, economic, social, cultural and familial, discrimination against them. (p. 184)

'Culture' is not a clearly defined homogeneity and the problem for schools is that encouragement of such views may clash with the beliefs of many families. Classes in racial awareness and anti-racism do not provide the whole answer to this problem and efforts need to be made by educators, in consultation with religious and community leaders, to establish a policy which will overcome this dilemma, (including, for example, training courses, instruction of implementing policy and advisory services to assist teachers and pupils). Without positive action, some British Asian girls will continue to be denied opportunities open to most pupils of other cultures. If it is generally true, as the trends we reveal indicate, that children who are able to learn English in their pre-school days perform more successfully in school, then more children should be given this opportunity. Nursery school places could be made available for all children, with mother-and-child playgroup sessions, so that those mothers unable to speak English will also have the opportunity of learning with their children. As more children are born to Asian mothers who have themselves been educated in English schools (and who will, therefore be more fluent in English) fewer non-English-speaking children should enter the education system, but it is unlikely that the problem will disappear for some considerable time. Parents naturally will wish to retain their mother tongue, but having a strong competence in English also, they will be able to do much to help and encourage their children in both languages. The question which cannot be answered confidently is whether pre-school education is a critical factor in longer term educational success; or just one of a number of enabling features which may, however, be later overlaid or diminished by other factors such as parental attitudes to marriage. Our findings reveal the need for a larger, longitudinal study to clarify the issue.

It is important that British Asian parents are encouraged to become involved in their children's school activities as much as possible. Facilities, such as the library provided in one Birmingham school for the use of parents, with books in several languages, together with social events designed to bring parents into school, help to establish a good relationship between parents and staff and encourage parents to seek to improve their own English in order to help their children.

There is an urgent need for continuing research into attitudes and educational provision for ethnic minority groups in Britain. Using a sample of similar size to our own (50 girls) Shaikh & Kelly (1989) discovered differences between Pakistani-origin family members. Girls and their mothers 'were much more likely than the fathers to see the purpose of education for girls in terms of qualifications for getting a job'. This accords broadly with evidence presented from girls in our own study. Maybe fathers are content to apply traditional controls to their daughters. Maybe they are mindful that their daughters symbolize the honour and prestige of the family (the *izzat*) and so at all costs seek to avoid any risk to reputation or marriage prospects. These attitudes need further investigation. However, differences *within* a group have been highlighted by our study and these may be as significant as those discovered *between* Asian groups (e.g. Crishna, 1975).

Considerations for Language Teaching

One of the major concerns in the teaching of British Asian pupils has been the educational disadvantage suffered by those with a poor command of the English language. These pupils cannot hope to compete on equal terms with others, either in school or later when seeking employment. Some also find difficulty in coping with everyday aspects of life in England, passing on their disadvantage to their children.

The solution to this problem has traditionally been seen to be the placing of children in special classes, but the answers given by respondents in our survey indicate that such withdrawal does little to compensate for a lack of early English language learning. The withdrawal of pupils may also serve to develop a feeling of low ability to add to the lack of English language expertise. The separation of children from those in other classes may also lead to a feeling of isolation. Recent national reports (e.g. DES, 1985) have supported the view that the needs of E2L groups should be met by mainstream provision.

National policy on community languages in education is not as supportive. There has been a significant and regrettable falling away from the emphasis placed on community languages by the Bullock Report (DES, 1975). The recommendation there was explicit that every school should

> adopt a positive attitude to pupils' bilingualism and wherever possible should help maintain and deepen their knowledge of their mother-tongues. (20.17)

The Bullock Committee stressed the connection between language and learning, though without spelling out how exactly schools could encourage pupils to use their own languages to learn easily and naturally. (For practical suggestions as to how this may be done, see the chapters by Sylvia Winchester in Wade (1985).)

The Bullock policy was still reflected in the Swann Report ten years later in the statement that:

> ethnic minority community languages should form an integral part of the curriculum in secondary schools. (DES, 1985: 3.19)

Since then, however, the Kingman Report (DES, 1988a) appears to limit policy to the use of community languages as reference points and illustrations for teaching the study of language. We discussed in Chapter 4 how reports from the English Working Group also treat community languages as means to the end of 'Progress in English' (DES, 1988b: 12.9).

Considerations for Literature Teaching

It is clear from the discussions that some girls were being offered a restricted range of literature and were conscious of the fact. In British schools there are substantial numbers of children whose families have their origins in Pakistan and the New Commonwealth. The two problems (identified by Milner (1983)) of omission and stereotyping of black people seem to persist in some classrooms, even in areas where there is cultural diversity. The Cox Committee (DES, 1985) argue that

> literature in English in the classroom can — and should — be drawn from different countries. All pupils need to be aware of the richness of experience offered by such writing, so that they may be introduced to the ideas and feelings of cultures different from their own. (7.5)

Here the emphasis is upon the positive, enriching benefits of interacting with literature; not solely upon the functional 'correction of biases' that interests Milner. It is still important to avoid reinforcing stereotypes, for example, by introducing books which present black people in positive, admired roles; it is equally important to help children from minority cultures to gain access to books in which they find points of cultural contact with characters and situations. All readers profit from discovering in literature confirmation of their own experiences and cultural background as well as opportunity to enter different people's lives.

In this context there is concern that the words 'and from different cultures' were crossed out by Angela Rumbold from the National Curriculum statements of attainment in English. In a letter to the *Times Educational Supplement* (15th June, 1990), defending this excision, she claimed that the programmes of study already emphasise different cultures. One could argue that some literature teaching will always be limited to what is to be assessed. Certainly it means that programmes of study must not be forgotten; nor must the arguments that led to their development. It is a matter of regret that the two Cox reports are now unavailable, being regarded as ephemeral stages towards the National Curriculum in English. Readers who wish to supplement the published targets, programmes and non-statutory guidance with a rationale for the whole system are referred to Cox (1991).

Considerations for School Policy

There is no suggestion in our findings that schools have any right to change culture or parents' views. Yet many teachers find themselves in conflict or confusion when they discover pupils who may be denied educational opportunities. However, from the dilemmas described for us by the girls in this study there follow certain implications for school policy building. To begin with we have shown intra-cultural differences, so secondary teachers need to plan for learning activities which meet the needs of different individuals and groups in their classrooms. The English teacher has been highlighted throughout, but all teachers bear the responsibility for developing language abilities in their subjects. Even where pupils are monolingual there will be different varieties of language in use (accents and dialects, for example) and pupils will have different strengths and weaknesses in the four modes of listening, speaking, reading and writing. Since language is a main tool for learning, judgments based on prejudice will lessen learning opportunities and cause pupils to lose heart.

Every secondary teacher is equally affected by the need to recognise the value of the cultural background that pupils are part of. RE, History, Geography and Home Economics teachers, for example, will find ready ways of making significant connections with pupils' experiences. Ways of doing this are equally important in Mathematics and Sciences, subjects which have, in some schools, appeared unfriendly to girls at the outset.

Certain gender issues are particularly relevant to schools. For example, there is an increasing body of evidence that classroom talk is dominated by boys, that teachers direct more attention to boys and that this 'discrimination' often continues even when teachers are made aware of what they are doing (see for example, Delamont, 1980; Spender, 1982; Whyte, 1986). Changing attitudes and behaviour is not easy, but schools have a responsibility for taking initiative to effect change.

This responsibility arises not because schools create inequality and difference in race, gender and class. This study suggests that other powerful causes lie outside in society. If parents and other adults treat girls differently from boys then, long before they reach secondary school, pupils will have a clear idea of what behaviour is gender appropriate and what others expect of them. Their comparisons of their own families' life styles, living standards and employment prospects with others in affluent suburbs will have shown limits of attainment and the divisions of class. Newspapers, television and radio may well have presented stereotyped or negative images of certain ethnic groups, or else omitted them altogether.

The differences and equalities may therefore have been laid down by children's experiences outside secondary school, but teachers must take responsibility for ensuring that school systems do not perpetuate, reinforce or condone already serious divisions. There needs to be a positive and consistent effort for change. Neutrality is not sufficient for three reasons. First, prejudice, by its very nature, works insidiously through unawareness; only positive confrontation of the issues will effect change. We have documented the disinterest and disaffection caused by choosing teaching materials (e.g. *To Kill a Mockingbird*) without consultation, anticipation or awareness.

Secondly, teachers must work hard to counteract inequalities that develop within a system. They, like other members of society, can be influenced by prejudice, stereotypes, expectations and media images. They need a sensitive awareness of issues to ensure their response to pupils is not influenced by erroneous beliefs about gender, class or race. They need to understand, for example, that previous experiences may well have diminished some girls' confidence in their ability to succeed; much positive effort is required to restore self-concepts, build confidence, develop assertiveness and encourage appropriate selection of activities and option choices.

Thirdly, a special awareness and particular efforts are required to redress the balance when more than one source is found for inequality, loss of confidence and low attainment. For example, the girls in this study have limitations set on their performance by three factors: gender, race and class. When such factors operate together, the task of redress is obviously more difficult, but the responsiblity to allow pupils to achieve as much as possible is even greater.

We offer finally a number of positive suggestions which might form the basis of a policy for work in schools:

- welcome, value and use the linguistic repertoire that each pupil brings (as well as seeking to extend it) as a way of developing motivation and confidence as well as facilitating learning;

- support the use of talk and writing for learning in collaborative pairs and groups (as well as whole classes);
- ensure that girls have equal opportunity to participate, initiate, lead and control;
- challenge prejudice about gender, class, race or use of language varieties in classrooms;
- welcome, initiate and foster contacts with parents on an informal level (as well as through parents' evenings);
- use corridors and classrooms to reflect the positive images of female, working class and ethnic minority contributions to mathematics, science, humanities, arts, etc.;
- when assessing bilingual children try wherever possible to base results on competence in all varieties of language that they use;
- provide access to a wider range of literature written in English by Asian writers, both males and females;
- encourage the use of community languages where they facilitate learning (as well as the study of language).

Appendix

Thank you for taking part in this survey
* * *
Please answer ALL questions. The information
you give in this questionnaire is confidential
so please do not write your name on any of the
papers

DATE OF BIRTH ....

PLACE OF BIRTH ....

RELIGION ....

NUMBER OF BROTHERS ....NUMBER OF SISTERS ....

POSITION IN FAMILY (e.g. eldest, second eldest, etc) ....

PLEASE PLACE A TICK BESIDE ANY OF THE FOLLOWING YOU
HAVE ATTENDED:

NURSERY SCHOOL IN ENGLAND   ....

INFANT SCHOOL IN ENGLAND   ....

JUNIOR SCHOOL IN ENGLAND   ....

CO-EDUCATIONAL SECONDARY SCHOOL   ....

SINGLE-SEX SECONDARY   ....

SCHOOL IN A COUNTRY OTHER THAN BRITAIN   ....

WHEN YOU LEAVE SECONDARY SCHOOL WHAT QUALIFICATION
DO YOU EXPECT TO HAVE? (include any certificates earned in external
examinations)

....

....

....

DO YOU FEEL THAT THE SUBJECTS YOU HAVE TAKEN AT SCHOOL
HAVE BEEN WORTHWILE? (cross out yes or no)

Yes   No

WHAT SUBJECTS WOULD YOU HAVE LIKED TO HAVE TAKEN THAT
YOU WERE NOT ABLE TO STUDY?

....

WHAT LANGUAGE IS SPOKEN IN YOUR HOME? ....

DID YOU SPEAK ENGLISH BEFORE ATTENDING
SCHOOL?   yes   no

DID YOU HAVE SPECIAL ENGLISH LESSONS IN
INFANT/JUNIOR SCHOOL?   yes   no

HAVE YOU HAD SPECIAL ENGLISH LESSONS IN
SECONDARY SCHOOL?   yes   no

DO YOU LIKE ENGLISH LESSONS?   yes   no

WHAT DO YOU DISLIKE ABOUT ENGLISH LESSONS?

....

....

....

DO YOU STUDY OTHER LANGUAGES AT
SCHOOL?   yes   no

IF ANSWER TO ABOVE IS 'YES', WHICH
LANGUAGE   ....

DO YOU ENJOY THE STUDY OF OTHER
LANGUAGES?   yes   no

DO YOU LIKE READING?   yes   no

HOW MANY BOOKS HAVE YOU READ AT HOME
IN THE PAST FOUR WEEKS (DO NOT COUNT
BOOKS YOU HAVE BEEN TOLD TO READ FOR
HOMEWORK)   ....

HOW MANY MAGAZINES/COMICS DO YOU
USUALLY READ EACH WEEK   ....

HOW MANY BOOKS DO YOU OWN?   ....

DO YOU READ A NEWSPAPER AT LEAST ONCE
A WEEK?   yes   no

HAVE YOU GOT A FAVOURITE AUTHOR?   yes   no

IF ANSWER IS 'YES', WHO IS THE AUTHOR?   ....

WHAT WAS THE LAST BOOK YOU BOUGHT?   ....

DO YOU OFTEN GET BOOKS AS PRESENTS?   yes   no

DO YOU THINK A BOOK MAKES A GOOD
PRESENT?   yes   no

HOW MANY BOOKS DO YOU THINK ARE IN
YOUR HOME?

LESS THAN 10   ....

10 to 20   ....

20 to 50   ....

MORE THAN 50   ....

HAVE YOU READ ANY BOOKS IN SCHOOL BY:

(a) ASIAN WRITERS   yes   no

(b) AFRICAN WRITERS   yes   no

(c) WEST INDIAN WRITERS   yes   no

(d) AMERICAN WRITERS   yes   no

(e) NON-ENGLISH EUROPEAN WRITERS   yes   no

DO YOU BELONG TO THE PUBLIC LIBRARY?   yes   no

IF THE ANSWER IS 'YES', HOW OFTEN DO YOU BORROW BOOKS?

(a) ONCE A WEEK   ....

(b) MORE THAN ONCE A WEEK   ....

(c) ABOUT ONCE A MONTH   ....

(d) JUST OCCASIONALLY   ....

IS YOUR SCHOOL LIBRARY A COMFORTABLE,
ATTRACTIVE PLACE   yes   no

HOW OFTEN DO YOU BORROW BOOKS
FROM YOUR SCHOOL LIBRARY IN A MONTH?   ....

ARE YOU ALLOWED TO USE THE SCHOOL
LIBRARY WHENEVER YOU ARE FREE TO DO SO? yes   no

DO YOU HAVE TIMETABLED LIBRARY
LESSONS?   yes   no

DO YOU THINK YOUR SCHOOL LIBRARY HAS
A GOOD SELECTION OF INTERESTING BOOKS   yes   no
WHAT CHANGES, IF ANY, WOULD YOU LIKE TO SEE IN YOUR
SCHOOL LIBRARY?

....

....

DOES YOUR SCHOOL LIBRARY STOCK BOOKS
IN ASIAN LANGUAGES?   yes   no

WHICH OF THE FOLLOWING TYPES OF BOOKS DO YOU ENJOY
READING?

ROMANTIC STORIES.....................   HORROR STORIES ....

MURDER MYSTERIES...................   SCIENCE FICTION.............................

HISTORICAL NOVELS...................   BIOGRAPHIES...................................

WAR STORIES................................   ADVENTURE......................................

FANTASY STORIES........................   SUPERNATURAL...............................

SCHOOL STORIES.........................   STORIES ABOUT SPORT ....

OTHER (PLEASE SAY WHICH) ....

DOES YOUR FAMILY HAVE A DAILY
NEWSPAPER?   yes   no

IF SO, WHICH ONE?   ....

DOES YOUR FAMILY HAVE A SUNDAY
NEWSPAPER   yes   no

IF SO, WHICH ONE   ....

WHICH MAGAZINE/COMIC DO YOU
LIKE BEST?   ....

IS THERE ANYTHING ABOUT TEENAGE MAGAZINES THAT YOU
REALLY DISLIKE, IF SO WHAT?

....

....

DO YOU FEEL THAT TEENAGE MAGAZINES
CATER FOR ALL CULTURES?   yes   no

WHAT WOULD YOU LIKE TO SEE IN TEENAGE MAGAZINES THAT
THEY DO NOT HAVE NOW?

....

....

....

DURING THE PAST *SEVEN DAYS* APPROXIMATELY HOW MANY
HOURS HAVE YOU SPENT WATCHING TELEVISION?

........................HOURS

DURING THE PAST *SEVEN DAYS*, HOW MANY HOURS HAVE YOU
SPENT WATCHING:

(a) VIDEO FILMS IN ENGLISH   ....

(b) VIDEO FILMS IN URDU   ....

(c) FILMS AT THE CINEMA   ....

WHAT ARE YOUR FAVOURITE TELEVISION PROGRAMMES?

....

....

....

DO YOU HOPE TO STUDY AT A POLYTECHNIC
OR UNIVERSITY WHEN YOU ARE OLDER?   yes   no

WHAT IS YOUR AMBITION FOR THE FUTURE?

....

....

He glanced up at the clock on the mantelpiece. Nearly midnight. He was very tired, and the thought of climbing the stairs to his bedroom was making him feel even more tired. He was feeling his age these days, it wasn't to be denied. He would be asleep before his head hit the pillow. Tonight, he would sleep the sleep of the dead, his mind free at last from the horrors that had haunted it for so long.

But, as he climbed the stairs, he heard the clock chime the witching hour, and a shiver went up his spine.

THE BOCKHAMPTON ROAD MURDERS

A Reverend Paltoquet
Supernatural Murder Mystery

by

Pat Herbert

Sometimes we're not alone….

Prologue

Reverend Bernard Paltoquet sighed. It had taken him many years to discover the truth behind the tragic events in that insignificant South London terraced house, but at last his work was done.

The mystery behind the series of violent deaths in 57 Bockhampton Road which had taken place sporadically ever since the late 1890s, had finally been solved. Justice had failed to be done over the intervening years, and justice couldn't right the wrong, even now. He wanted, more than anything, to clear the names of the innocent and put the blame fairly and squarely where it belonged. But he knew he wouldn't be believed. He had found it hard to believe himself.

He put the file aside; the final sheets inserted. The sheets that supplied the missing information, that told everything. Dorothy Plunkett had lost none of her psychic powers, despite her advanced years. If it hadn't been for her, the truth would still be hidden. He owed her a great deal tonight.

Rising from his desk, he switched off the reading lamp and poured himself a brandy. He made his way from the study to the cosy living room where the fire was brightly, if artificially, burning. No more open coal fires these days; time and tide and smoke-free zones had seen to that. But it cast a warm glow around the room, nevertheless.

PART ONE

57 Bockhampton Road
London SW
August 1896

My dear Isabelle

Thank you for your letter of the 4th inst. I must apologise for the delay in replying but, as I am sure you can understand, I have been a trifle busy of late.

Your kind wishes and support mean very much to me, as I'm sure you know. They have supported me in this time of trial, and given me the strength to carry on. It has not been easy, and I know you are worried for me. I will not deny that it has crossed my mind, but I cannot accept that it is the only answer. There has been enough misery caused so far without my adding to it. Besides, it is a sin against God and my own vocation.

My grateful thanks to you for your kind suggestion that I come and stay with you all, but I must decline. You have enough to do with Arthur and the children. You do not need me to add to your burden.

I was sorry you had to say in your letter what you did about Edith. I do not believe she could be such a monster as you suggest. Until I find her and find out what happened, I will not judge her. What she has done or not done, we will not know until she can answer for herself. And I pray that one day I will see her again and learn the truth, however painful it may be.

I will close now. The shadows are longer, and the nights are beginning to draw in. I am expecting Sergeant Cobb shortly. He has become a dear friend to me. I believe he, too, thinks I will do away with myself and he comes in the evenings quite often now to make sure I am still in the land of the living. We play chess and drink whisky together, so I have some comfort.

Give my love to Arthur and the boys and tell them I am grateful to them for sending their kind wishes with your last letter. It has meant so much to me that you are all thinking of me.

Your loving brother,

Herbert

1

Edith Lomax sat at her dressing table, staring into the mirror. The face that stared back at her was very pleasing. She smiled as she brushed her abundant blonde hair. She never tired of admiring herself. Her blue eyes were deep, unfathomable pools and her heart-shaped face was perfectly symmetrical. In fact, the sort of woman the Pre-Raphaelite painters loved to paint. She had often regretted not being born some fifty years earlier because she was sure Rossetti would have been only too eager to put her down on canvas.

But she was born too late for the fame of her beauty to be immortalised in art galleries. Dante Gabriel Rossetti, John Everett Millais and all the others had long since ceased to paint. She was feeling sorry for herself. Never one to count her blessings, she could only see the negative things in her life: married to a respectable, but dull, man and required to live in a small, terraced house indistinguishable from all the others in the street. Her neighbours might be content to live such a squalid existence, but Edith Lomax considered herself above the run of the ordinary and, by that token, deserved something much better. At least, she supposed, Herbert was well-respected in the neighbourhood, being a doctor, which gave her some reflected kudos. But she couldn't forgive him for providing her with two daughters, grounding her completely in a humdrum existence she wasn't fitted for.

She had no means of escape. She was doomed to sit at home, waiting for her husband to return in the evenings for his supper and pipe, while she toiled over some senseless sampler that she had no interest in and didn't know what to do with when it was finished.

Their young parlour maid, Martha Finch, did most of the housework and cooking, so she didn't even have these mundane chores to keep her busy. She needed to get out of the house. It was summer, and she was young and beautiful. She wanted other people, especially the men amongst them, to appreciate her qualities. Her two little daughters were quite content in the care of Martha, so there was no need to stay cooped up with them all the time. Instead, she could leave them at home and parade up and down the high street, ostensibly looking in the shop windows to admire all the pretty things on display. She never had enough in her purse to buy anything, however, as Herbert, possibly aware of his wife's penchant for overspending, only gave her enough housekeeping money for daily essentials. He even made her keep a record of her expenditures. Every penny had to be accounted for in his house.

Martha didn't mind looking after her mistress's children, but couldn't understand how she could leave them all day long in her care. She never paid the poor mites any attention, only occasionally looking in at the nursery door to make sure they were playing properly and not making a nuisance of themselves. Dr Lomax was different. He loved his little girls. When he came home from visiting his patients, he would spend at least an hour in the nursery with them. But Edith never stayed longer than she could help. It was as if the poor little mites bored her which, Martha supposed, they probably did.

She had long ceased to be shocked by her mistress's callous behaviour, not only towards her children, but towards her husband who, thought Martha, didn't deserve it any more than the kids did.

"You going out on your own again, madam?" she would ask Edith when she saw that lady adjust her hat in front of the hall mirror. "Won't you take the girls with you? They could do with some exercise." Which was true if the cacophony from the nursery was anything to go by.

"Oh, don't be difficult, Martha. The children much prefer your company to mine. I'm just going to the park for a little constitutional. The weather is so fine. Then maybe I will have a look around the shops. You can take them out, can't you?"

"Very well, madam."

Martha supposed Edith's solo jaunts were innocent enough. Knowing how vain she was, her little maidservant assumed she just wanted people to admire her. Anyway, it was none of her business what her silly mistress got up to.

2

Abraham Smollett never failed to make an impression on the fairer sex. With his luxuriant moustaches, broad shoulders, handsome, leonine face, piercing grey eyes and dazzling smile, he was a romantic, almost Byronic figure. The only thing missing was the limp.

When Edith Lomax first met him, she was staring at a pretty hat in the haberdasher's window just off the high street. The sun was reflecting off the window glass, as a shadow loomed up behind her. She turned and, shielding her eyes, she saw a very handsome young man smiling at her. He raised his hat.

"Please excuse me," he said, politeness personified. "I believe I am blocking your path."

Edith blushed. "Oh no indeed. Not at all. It is I, I believe, who obstruct your way."

"Oh, but what a delightful obstruction!"

She twirled her parasol nervously. He was being all too familiar, and she tried very hard to be annoyed. But how grand he was, she thought. And rich! He looked the sort of man who wouldn't keep his wife short of money. He would take her to all the best West End shops and insist she bought whatever she wanted. She, of course, had no way of knowing if this was so but, her habit of comparing every man she met to her dull husband, always made him seem like a paragon of his sex.

"May I walk with you a little way?" she heard him ask, as she struggled to control her blushes. "I believe we are going in the same direction."

"Well, I...." she began. Then she managed to collect herself. "I believe we are not acquainted, sir?"

Abraham Smollett didn't seem in the least abashed. "I do apologise," he said at once. "I'm afraid I was so overcome by your dazzling beauty that I...."

"You forget yourself, sir!" declared Edith, feigning an anger she didn't in the least feel. She wondered how long she should keep up the pretence. Besides, she didn't want to put him off altogether.

"Oh dear, I seem to have offended you again," he said. "I did not intend to be so forward."

Edith, already tired of being an affronted female, allowed herself to mellow towards him a little. "I am not used to being accosted in this manner by strange men in the street."

Abraham acknowledged her scolding with a rueful smile. "I only wish we *were* acquainted. If I introduce myself and you do the same, then we won't be unacquainted anymore, will we?"

Edith hid a smile behind her fan. "There is no gainsaying that," she agreed.

"Abraham Smollett at your service," he informed her.

She responded in kind, and he lost no time in taking her gloved hand in his. Bending over it, he feigned a kiss. "Now that we are acquainted, will you do me the honour of taking tea with me?"

"Well..." she hesitated. "The day is quite warm, and I *am* a little thirsty. I was, in fact, thinking of resting awhile in the tea shop."

"Oh, yes," said Abraham happily. "That discreet little place just around the corner..."

Edith asserted herself once again. This man was really very trying. Did he have no sense of what was proper in good society?

"I cannot see why we need to be 'discreet'." The horse she was on now had never been higher.

"I only meant that it was secluded and quiet, where we can sit and take tea together unmolested. After all, it is a perfectly innocent pastime, don't you agree?"

"I only agreed to have tea with you because I am in need of refreshment and that is all."

"Then, please take my arm," said Abraham. He cocked his elbow, and she tentatively rested her hand on it. All this standing on ceremony had made her tired.

The little tea shop was, as Abraham Smollett had said, discreet, almost hidden as it was between a butcher's and a bookshop in a shady side street. But Edith's conscience once again asserted itself. She was having a cup of tea with this man because she was thirsty, and that was all. Of course, Martha could make her a perfectly good cup of tea at home. Martha, however, wasn't Abraham Smollett.

There were several other couples already seated in the tea shop as they entered. There were also some older women, enjoying a mid-morning chat over coffee and scones. Edith recognised two of them at once. As they sat down at a table by the window, Edith whispered to Abraham behind her fan. "That's Mrs Glossop and Mrs Redmayne over in the corner by the cake trolley," she told him. "They know who I am! You must act as if you are my brother or cousin or some such. On no account are you to behave as if you were courting me."

"I wouldn't dream of embarrassing you," he grinned. "As far as I am concerned I'm your long-lost brother returned from planting rubber in Malaya."

"Yes, that will do. Anyway, there's no help for it. They've seen me, so I must introduce you. Come." She led him to the older women's table.

"Hello, Mrs Glossop. Mrs Redmayne. I hope you're both well and have no need of my husband's ministrations," she said ingratiatingly.

Both ladies smiled at her. Were their smiles sincere? she wondered. "Hello, Mrs Lomax," said the one called Mrs Glossop. "We are both very well, thank you, dear. But tell me, who is this young gentleman? We don't believe we've seen him before?"

"This gentleman is my brother, er – Paul. He has just returned from Malaya. He has been planting rubber."

After politely shaking hands with the two women, Abraham led Edith back to their table. He raised an elegant eyebrow at the waitress who was staring straight at him in undisguised admiration, and she scuttled over to their table. He ordered tea and cakes for two, and she scuttled away again.

"Oh dear," sighed Edith. "I do not think those women believed you were my brother at all."

He only smiled as the waitress returned with the tea. He poured out the Earl Grey carefully, and the scent of bergamot seemed very heady to her at that moment. She sipped the tea slowly, looking into his eyes. What did it matter if they didn't believe he was her brother? She cared little for the Glossops and Redmaynes of this world, anyway. But she did care about her reputation all the same.

3

Edith lowered her gaze. She had been meeting Abraham surreptitiously for several weeks, always trying to avoid the places where she was likely to bump into people she knew. Her husband had looked at her strangely one evening but had said nothing. Edith had asked him coyly if he had seen any of their friends or acquaintances lately. She remembered how he had avoided her eyes as he answered that Mrs Glossop had consulted him the other day about a bad back. Something that was impossible to prove, she had thought grimly. "Apart from her back, was she all right?" she had then asked him.

"As right as she'll ever be," Herbert had laughed.

She hadn't pursued the conversation but knew Herbert had been made aware that his "brother-in-law" was back from Malaya, and probably how handsome he was. Perhaps he didn't believe what he had been told. Herbert despised gossip-mongers, she knew. Or, maybe, more likely, he didn't want to believe it. Either way, he hadn't raised the matter with her.

As the summer progressed, Edith was enjoying her meetings with Abraham more and more. It was all very innocent; they had held hands, taken tea together, strolled around the park, and he had even managed to steal a little kiss or two. But, lately, he was becoming more demanding. It was inevitable, she supposed. In her heart of hearts, she didn't want to take their relationship any further than this pleasant dalliance, but she knew she would be obliged to hold out some hope for him or lose him altogether.

❧

August was proving to be even warmer than July. But the flush in her face wasn't entirely due to the heat as she sat at her dressing table brushing her hair with vigour. She was vaguely aware her husband was talking to her.

"I'm taking the whole day off, dear. Why don't we take the children to the zoo?"

She had no intention of going anywhere near Regent's Park. She had other plans today. "You take them, Herbert," she said. "I have a headache."

"Oh dear, I am sorry. You do seem a little flushed," he said. He felt her forehead, which was indeed hot and clammy. "I'll make up a powder for you."

"Don't bother," she snapped tersely. Why was he always so *nice* to her? "I just need to rest."

"Yes, you must, dear," he said. "But I'll make up that powder for you, anyway. I'll leave it here by the bed so if you need it you will not have to go far for it."

"Thank you," she said through gritted teeth. Why couldn't he go and leave her alone?

"Come on Daddy," cried their little daughters, entering the master bedroom. They were jumping up and down in eager anticipation. "Are we going soon?"

"So you have already told them?" She looked at him askance.

"I did mention it. I thought you would be happy to come. I got Martha to make us up a picnic. I thought we'd make a day of it."

"Well, I hope you enjoy it," she said. "Please, Jemima," she said to her eldest child. "Stop pulling at my dress. I have a headache. Papa will take you to the zoo."

Ignoring both little girls' protests, she turned back to the mirror and continued to brush her hair.

"It's a pity it's Martha's day off," said Herbert, shooing the girls out of the room. "I'll ask her to change her day so that she can stay and look after you."

"You'll do no such thing!" She was more vehement than she needed to be, she realised. "I mean, I don't think it's fair to make her change her day. She probably has plans." She spoke more calmly now, but she could see her husband was taken aback by her outburst. She didn't blame him, because she had never bothered about how Martha was feeling before. Martha was there to do her bidding, and that was all. Any private life she might or might not have had was of no concern to Edith Lomax.

"Very well, dear. Whatever you say."

To her relief, he finally set off with the girls jumping and skipping around his heels. She could hear him protest as he unlatched the front gate. She watched from the bedroom window as she heard him say: "Do be careful, children. You'll make me drop the hamper."

She turned to the bedside table and saw the powder lying there. She picked it up and took it downstairs to the kitchen, dropping the contents of the paper packet down the sink and flushing it away. She smiled to herself as she turned off the tap. Headache? What headache?

She was almost ready to go out. She was to meet Abraham in the park as usual and bring him back to the house. Martha would be out by then and, luckily, her husband and children had already gone. When she had made the arrangement, she had expected Herbert would be on his rounds as usual. His announcement he was taking the day off had been a shock but, as it turned out, had proved more conducive to her purpose. A day at the zoo would serve very well to keep him out of the house, and the children too. That was the one thing she had been worried about. With Martha on her day off, the children would have been on her hands. She would have made them stay in the nursery, of course, but this was much better. Much, much better.

4

"I have never felt like this about any woman before. I love you, Edith Lomax, more than life itself," whispered Abraham Smollett.

He was holding her hand surreptitiously under the table as they sat in their favourite teashop, enjoying a buttered muffin and a pot of Earl Grey. The sun shone through the glass, warming them through.

"Please, Abraham," she protested, rather weakly. It was really much too hot to bother. "We can be seen, and I'm a married woman. Or had you forgotten?" She withdrew her hand.

"But you do love me, don't you?" he persisted.

"I'm not free to love you," she hissed at him. He was becoming tiresome now. "We are loving friends. Let us just remain so." She tried not to think what she had promised him at their last tryst as she stirred some honey into her fast-cooling tea. She looked around her. No one seemed concerned with them, to her relief. Although it wasn't very flattering as, in her opinion, there was no one more interesting than herself. Certainly not in this silly little teashop, anyway.

"That is not what you said at our last rendezvous," he pointed out. His manner was guarded now. He had lowered his voice, and she felt suddenly frightened. The promise had been made; it could not be broken.

"What do you mean?" She started to fan herself vigorously. It was suddenly very hot in the little tea shop. A waitress came over to her.

"Are you all right, madam? Can I get you a glass of water?" she asked solicitously.

"I'm feeling a little hot, that is all. But some water would be welcome," said Edith, relieved at the interruption. It gave her time to think. She was beginning to realise she knew nothing about the man who was sitting opposite her. She had confided her innermost feelings to him, but he had not responded in kind. He was probably just as married as she was. She swallowed the water the kind waitress had brought in a single draught.

"I think it is time we were going, don't you." It wasn't said with a question mark, even though he was smiling his most ingratiating smile.

"Go?" she enquired. "Go where?"

She couldn't go through with it, no matter what she had promised. It was the time to run away. If she broke off from him now, all would be well. She could go back to her stultifying life with her dull doctor husband and irritating daughters. Nobody would be any the wiser. But she knew she didn't want that. She craved excitement above all else. If she turned her back on him now, she would never see him again, and that thought terrified her.

"You know very well, dear. Please let's stop this play acting. I believe you live not far from here. We may as well go there as stop here. I have no more money for tea."

The menace in his eyes was unmistakable. Why was she unable to break away from him?

"But what about my husband?" she asked. "I have two children."

"So, you are saying you value your reputation above our love?" He seemed milder, kinder this time, but there was steel in his usually inexpressive grey eyes. If she broke her promise to him, what form would his revenge take? She was sure he would exact some penalty if she had the temerity to walk away. But she couldn't walk away, and she didn't want to. Danger was better than boredom. At least Abraham made her feel alive.

"It is easy for you. You have nothing to lose. It is harder for a woman, especially a married woman. You must give me time to think."

Abraham tried to reach for her hand again. But she rebuffed him. "Please, don't," she said.

"The time for prevaricating is past, Edith dear. You told me your husband has taken your daughters to the zoo for the day and your maid is out, too. We can be alone together where no prying eyes can see us. What could be better?"

Edith began fanning herself again. "We cannot be seen going back together, Abraham."

"But why not? I am your *brother* after all," he smiled.

She had to admit that he was right. If he was supposed to be her brother, there could be no harm in him coming back with her. But there were her nosy neighbours to consider. All they would see was a young man entering the house with her. She couldn't risk that.

"I know. But it would be less of a complication if my neighbours didn't see you."

"Very well," he said. "Whatever you say." She could tell he was impatient to go, but she delayed him by pretending she had lost a glove. It was soon recovered by Abraham who had noticed her deliberately dropping it on the floor in the first place.

She had no excuses left. He took her arm and led her gently out of the tea shop.

The waitress who had brought Edith the water turned to her companion. "I think there'll be tears before bedtime with them two. I bet they're not married. Well, not to each other, anyway."

Her companion giggled. "They've been coming here for nearly two months, you know, Gert. I always thought they looked like they were secret lovers. But for all we know, 'e could be 'er brother."

"Go on! Pull the other one. You know that's Dr Lomax's wife, don't you? 'E's your doctor ain't 'e, Rube?"

"Well, 'e's my mum's actually. I ain't never 'ad cause to consult 'im myself. 'E seems very nice, though. I don't like 'is wife much, though. A bit hoity-toity, if you ask me."

"Hmm, I know what you mean, but if she's being unfaithful, you can't really blame 'er, can you? I mean, wouldn't you like to 'ave someone like 'im? 'E's obviously well-off and you 'ave to admit 'e's ever so good looking."

"Yeah, well, 'andsome is as 'andsome does."

The waitress called Gert, who had never understood the meaning of that proverb, grinned at her. "Come on, Rube," she said. "Who are you kidding? Wouldn't you just swoon if 'e so much as winked at you?"

"Ruby, Gertrude," snapped a voice behind them. The tea shop manageress loomed from behind the counter. "Stop chattering and clear the tables. At once!"

5

Edith turned to watch Abraham as he sauntered slowly some way behind her, as she had asked him to. She had reached her garden gate and was looking nervously around for any prying eyes.

"I think you'd better go round the back," she said, darting glances up and down the street.

"Very well," he said, seemingly bored with the whole charade. "How do I approach from the back?"

Edith directed him to the corner of the street, instructing him to turn left and double-back down the parallel alley until he reached the back of her house. She would then let him in through the scullery door. She could see he didn't like the idea of this mode of entry, obviously unused to being treated as if he were a mere tradesman. He seemed about to protest, but fell in with her plan, if somewhat reluctantly.

"I will see you shortly," he said. "I will make sure no one sees me. Your reputation is safe with me."

Edith's hands shook as she unlocked the front door. She rested her back against it once inside and tried to focus her thoughts. For all her wish for adventures, she was strapped inside the corsetry of an England that frowned on adulterous affairs. She hadn't cheated on her husband so far, but now it looked as if she was set on the path that led poor Madame Bovary, in the racy novel she had just finished, to her destruction. If all went wrong for her, Edith made herself a vow. She wouldn't be taking arsenic to remedy the situation, not like poor Emma in the tragic Flaubert tale.

She made her way through the scullery to the back door, but just as she was about to open it, the front door bell rang. It was the sound of her salvation, even though she was unaware of it. Abraham was tapping gently on the scullery window, but she couldn't let him in now. She avoided looking into his eyes as she turned to answer the door. It was just as well because she would have seen something akin to hatred there.

She opened the front door slowly and peeked around it. It was her neighbour, Elsie Proudfoot, the nosiest woman in the street and the bane of her husband's life. She never let a week go by without consulting him about her back or her arthritis or her wretched bunions. And, if it wasn't her, it was one of her ever-burgeoning brood (all boys) who had gone down with some lurgy or other. She was a perfect nuisance, all round. However, today, Edith wasn't so annoyed at seeing her on the doorstep.

"Hello, love," said Elsie cheerily, wiping her hands on her apron. "I just thought you ought to know there's a strange man lurking in your back garden. 'Andsome devil, mind you. Wouldn't mind 'aving 'im lurking in *my* garden. Still, 'e looks a bit suspicious to me. D'you know who 'e is?"

"No, I do not," said Edith, giving her an imperious look. "My husband is not at home, so I am all alone at the moment. I will make sure I keep my door locked."

"You do, ducks. I wouldn't like nothing to 'appen to you. I'm sure the doc wouldn't neither, not to mention your two darling girls."

"I will be very careful, thank you, Mrs Proudfoot."

She tried to close the door, but her neighbour remained where she was. "Would you like to come next door for a nice cup of tea, love?"

"It's very kind of you, but I really must get on. I have a lot to do and my husband and children will be home soon."

"Why don't you leave it to your Martha? Don't she usually prepare the supper?"

"Not today, it's her day off."

"Oh, of course. I forgot. She was only telling me the other day she was planning to visit 'er sister in Bognor. Well she's got nice weather for it, I must say."

"Indeed. Now, please Mrs Proudfoot. I must get on." Edith made another attempt to close the door.

"All right, dear. I'll love you and leave you. Make sure that man isn't still lurking."

"I will. Thank you again. Goodbye."

Edith closed the door and rushed through to the scullery. She peeped through the window just in time to see Abraham's retreating back. She was about to shout after him, but realised this would draw attention, and she was sure Mrs Proudfoot would still be on the lookout.

It seemed her afternoon with Abraham was not to be, after all. Divine providence in the shape of the roly poly Mrs Proudfoot, had intervened at the last moment.

Maybe, she thought, someone was trying to tell her something.

❧

Edith walked up and down the living room, her mind a cauldron of conflicting emotions. Abraham Smollett had got under her skin and, although she didn't trust him or even like him now, she still wanted what she could get from him: a thrill. But she knew she was heading for disaster. The danger had been averted this time, but surely there would be a next time, if she wanted a next time. And that was what bothered her. She wasn't sure, anymore, what she wanted.

Questions raged in her head as she continued to pace the floor. Who was this man? What did he do with himself all day? Was he married? Did he have a family? Her thoughts were interrupted by her returning husband and daughters.

"We've had such a lovely time, Mama," said Georgina, her blonde ringlets bouncing up and down as she ran into the room. "We saw lions and tigers and heffalumps and monkeys and...."

"That's nice, dear," she said, brushing her daughter's hair lightly with her fingers. She wished she could feel the sort of affection for her that most mothers, so she was told, felt for their offspring. But all she could feel was a mild pity. "Now off you go and play, both of you. Supper will be ready soon."

"Yes, Mama," said Jemima and Georgina in unison. They were wise enough not presume on their mother's goodwill for too long. So, still excited by their trip to see the lions and tigers, they raced up the stairs, arguing who was going on the rocking horse first.

Edith felt her husband's eyes boring into her now that the children were out of the way. She felt herself flush as she tried to avoid looking at him.

"Edith, my dear, you appear somewhat distrait. Are you still feeling unwell? How is your headache? Let me make you another powder."

"I'm fine, Herbert, please don't fuss so." She waved his hand from her brow.

"But you still seem a little feverish. I do think you should let me prescribe something for you."

"Please.... I am feeling perfectly well. How was your day? I'm glad the girls enjoyed themselves."

Herbert strode over to the fireplace and took his favourite pipe from the rack on the mantelpiece. As he sucked it into life, he continued to study his wife with concern.

"Yes, we all had a lovely time. But we would have preferred it if you had been with us."

"Herbert, dear, you know the girls prefer your company to mine. I'm sure they had a much better time without me."

"How can you say that, Edith? You're their mother!"

"You know it is so. I don't seem to be able to inspire any affection in them. They even prefer Martha to me."

"Maybe if you spent more time with them," said Herbert, a look of reproach in his eyes, "they shouldn't prefer Martha. That worries me."

"It can't be helped," she said with a shrug. It was as if they were discussing a broken vase, not the misplaced affections of their children.

Herbert sighed and changed the subject. "Is Martha home yet?"

"No. She was due to catch the four o'clock train from Bognor Regis so she should be here soon," Edith informed him. "But I will start the supper."

"Are you sure, dear? I thought you might not be feeling up to it tonight."

"I'm feeling perfectly all right. I had a little headache, but now it has gone." It had never been there in the first place, she thought with irony, although it was there now.

"Very well, dear. You know best."

Having won that little battle, she turned and left the room. He drove her mad sometimes, always fussing over her. She wandered into the scullery and stared at the gas stove, but she couldn't concentrate on cooking now. To even thinking of peeling a potato made her head throb. She decided to wait for Martha's return, after all.

6

Dr Lomax lingered over breakfast reading his newspaper, much to Edith's annoyance. She was anxious for him to depart on his rounds as she had made another assignation with Abraham. After much debate with herself, she had decided to meet him once more. As long as they were in a public place, all would be well. Mrs Proudfoot had seen him and that had been too close for comfort. Edith would not be inviting him back to her home again. However, she was still anxious to see him, human nature being what it was. She had to ensure that Abraham was still as smitten with her as ever, even though he had been thwarted the last time.

"Shouldn't you be going, Herbert? The time is getting on, you know."

"In a minute, Edith. Just let me finish this article, it's very interesting."

Martha came into the parlour to clear away the breakfast things. Good, she thought. This was usually the signal for her husband to move himself. But he obstinately remained seated, reading intently.

"What is it that has caught your attention so, Herbert?" she asked him, trying to keep the impatience out of her voice.

"I'll tell you, my dear. I think both you and Martha should hear this."

Martha, in the act of picking up the full tray, put it down again, "Sir?"

"Yes, Martha, you must hear this, too. Please be seated."

Both women sat and looked at him expectantly. "Get on with it," said Edith, unable to conceal her annoyance. Who did he think he was? Tthe Pope? Sitting there, pontificating.

"Are you listening?" He seemed oblivious to Edith's ire this morning. In a funny sort of way, this made her respect him a little bit. Not much, just a little bit. He usually bowed to her wishes without a murmur, apart from increasing her allowance, of course. That was where he put his foot down. Heavily. He began to read from the paper.

"*Scotland Yard has issued a warning to young women in the South London area to be on their guard for a man in his early to mid-thirties who has been accosting women and ingratiating himself with them. These women are usually personable in appearance and of marriageable age. The police do not wish to unduly alarm the public, but it is believed this man, who uses several aliases, lures his victims to secluded trysting places and then strangles them. Three such murders have so far been identified as the work of this man. He is described as tall, with dark hair and eyes, and is considered by female witnesses to be uncommonly handsome in appearance. This man was last seen in the Clapham area on Sunday night. Anyone knowing the true identity or the current whereabouts of this gentleman should contact the police immediately. He should, on no account, be approached directly as he is considered highly dangerous.*"

"There," he said. "I thought you ought to know about this. I'm sure you are both sensible enough not to be taken in by this man, but it is best to be forewarned."

Edith looked at Martha and Martha looked at Edith. They both had a secret admirer who answered to this man's description. Pure coincidence, of course, thought Edith. There were many men who could fit the man the police were looking for. Abraham was tall, dark and handsome, true. But he was no strangler of women, of that she was sure. The idea was preposterous.

Dr Lomax folded his paper and tucked it under his arm as he stood up to leave. "So, just be careful. If either of you are approached by any gentlemen answering to this description, you should notify the police at once. I suggest neither of you goes out unaccompanied, for the time being at least."

"Excuse me," said Edith indignantly. "Do you expect me to accompany Martha on her shopping trips? I'm not a servant!"

"I just think it would be wise for neither of you to venture out alone at the moment. You are both very pretty, and I'm sure would attract the attention of a man such as this. Now I must be going." He kissed his wife lightly on the cheek and went to the front door. There on the doorstep was Mrs Proudfoot, brandishing the morning paper.

"'Ave you seen this about a young man going round strangling women?" she asked him without preamble. "I've seen a man like that 'anging around your 'ouse several times."

"Indeed?" said Herbert dismissively. He obviously wasn't taking her seriously, knowing what a notorious gossip she was. He turned to Edith and Martha, who stood in the hallway giggling behind their hands like a couple of schoolgirls. He raised his eyebrows at them and turned back to Mrs Proudfoot.

"Now, come along, Elsie," he said, in the familiar tone he used when treating her bunions, "you mustn't start rumours. You will make everyone frightened to go out at all."

He closed the front door and marched her down the path. "Good day," he said, raising his hat. It was clearly the end of the matter as far as Herbert Lomax was concerned. Edith and Martha continued to follow events from the front room window, united in their glee at seeing poor Mrs Proudfoot taken down a peg. They watched her, and she seemed stunned for a moment, then slowly walk back to her own front door.

"That's settled her hash," declared Edith with relish. "Now, Martha, do get on with the washing up. Then take the children to the park. They need to expend their energy. Can't you hear the noise they're making?"

They both listened to the hysterical screams and laughter of Edith's two lively daughters as their little feet padded up and down the nursery floor.

"Yes, madam," said Martha, returning to her kitchen domain. Edith smiled to herself. Although she didn't much like her pretty servant, possibly because she *was* too pretty, she had to acknowledge she was useful. Very useful where the children were concerned. Now she had to make herself presentable. Time was pressing.

She preened herself in the mirror. Yes, all was well. Her skin was glowing, and her eyes were glittering. No man with red blood in his veins would be able to resist her.

She could hear Martha chastising the children as they went out of the front door with a clatter. She made a final inventory of her face and hair, then stood to fetch her parasol and gloves. Five minutes later, she was walking down Bockhampton Road on her way to the park and Abraham Smollett.

It was another sunny day, so the park would be busy. That suited her fine. She thought about the man wanted by the police for killing young women. It wasn't Abraham, of course, but it didn't do to take any chances. Even in the unlikely event that he was a murderer, it didn't daunt her spirit in the slightest. It made her even more anxious to meet him, if anything. It was the danger and excitement she craved. You never knew, she thought, if he was the killer, she could expose him and then she'd be famous. The police would probably give her a medal.

Thinking these thoughts, she paused outside the newsagent's a few yards from the park. She took a newspaper from the rack and searched through it until she found what she was looking for. It was exactly as her husband had said. Only he hadn't read it all out to her. Her heart skipped a couple of beats when she read the name 'Abraham Smollett'. There it was in black and white.

Maybe she didn't want him to be the murderer after all. The theory was sound but, in practice, she wouldn't have a clue how to deal with him. She put the paper back in the rack with a shaking hand.

"So you've read it and now don't intend to buy it, I suppose? I have to make a living you know." The little bald-headed newsagent was at her elbow, looking very cross.

She looked down at him, aware there was an aggravating buzz at her elbow. "I beg your pardon?" she said. "Were you addressing me?"

"I can't see anyone else here, can you?" he retorted.

"Oh, do be quiet, you annoying little man," said Edith, not in the least bothered by his threatening tone and manner. After all, she'd been consorting with a mass murderer, so a scrawny under-sized tradesman held little fears for her. She pushed him aside, ignoring his protests, and flounced off down the high street without a backward glance.

The newsagent went back into his shop muttering under his breath that he wasn't a public lending library. Edith, however, was well out of earshot.

Sweeping on down the street, she felt her heart pounding nineteen to the dozen. She wouldn't, couldn't, believe her Abraham was a cold-blooded killer. The thought that the man she was about to meet might be contemplating adding her to his list of victims gave her palpitations. How could he deceive her so? She slowed her footsteps as she reached the park gates. Every fibre of her being was urging her to go in and face him. But, with every step, her bravado deserted her a little further. Did she really intend to meet him?

Whether she did or not, she simply had to. Of course, he would deny it. Say it was some other Abraham Smollett. It was possible, she supposed, but not very likely. It wasn't a common name. Except wasn't there an author called that? Oh no, that was Tobias Smollett, she then remembered. His books, like everything else, had bored her.

Very well, Mr Abraham Smollett, she thought entering the park, you'll have to work hard to convince me you're not a murderer. Maybe that feather boa she had her eye on in the haberdashers would be a start. Then a slap-up meal in the West End wouldn't go amiss, not just a cup of tea in the local tea shop. She'd had enough of that. Times would have to change to convince her not to hand Abraham Smollett over to the police.

~

She arrived at their appointed rendezvous by the bandstand a few minutes late. The band had not yet arrived, but there were plenty of people sauntering by. Her eyes scanned the crowds for Abraham but there was no sign of him. Usually, he was the first to arrive but today, he was nowhere to be seen. Although she was annoyed by his tardiness, she was also rather relieved as it gave her time to focus her thoughts more clearly.

Perhaps she had known all along he was too good to be true, she just hadn't wanted to admit it to herself. There had been odd times when his manner had iced over slightly, but these momentary flashes hadn't registered. Until now.

She had read, along with everyone else, about the salacious murders in the East End several years earlier. Some maniac had been going around in a leather apron and funny hat cutting up prostitutes. She had enjoyed reading all the gory details as they had become known, but she didn't equate these with real life. To her, Jack the Ripper was just sensationalist fiction, nothing more. The poor women who had been his victims wouldn't have seen it her way, of course, but, really, thought Edith Lomax, if they put themselves about in the way they did, then they deserved all they got.

The church clock chimed one o'clock, and she realised her beau was now an hour overdue. She began to suspect he was avoiding her. He would have seen that morning's newspaper article, of course, and had probably absconded altogether.

But where would he have gone? She didn't even know where he lived or, come to that, his real name.

At two o'clock she came to the obvious conclusion her lover wasn't going to keep their tryst. The sun bore down on her parasol as she walked up and down past the bandstand for the umpteenth time. The band had now arrived and was setting up their instruments. One of the musicians caught her eye and winked. She feigned indignation and turned abruptly on her heel. But it cheered her, nonetheless. There were other fish in the sea besides Abraham Smollett or whatever his name was.

As she let herself into number 57 Bockhampton Road, she saw her daughters listening at the parlour door. As soon as they saw her, they ran up the stairs as fast as their little legs would carry them. She opened her mouth to admonish them for making such a clatter but thought better of it. Why, she wondered, were they so interested in what was behind the closed parlour door? Was Martha up to something? Perhaps entertaining some rough young man who had taken her fancy? If so, she would teach her a lesson she'd never forget.

With this in mind, and the non-appearance of Abraham still rankling, she strode towards the parlour and reached for the door knob.

7

Martha sat at her mistress's dressing table, trying the various perfumes arrayed there. She had taken the children to the park that morning as instructed, but their delight at playing on the swings had been cut short. Usually, she had time for Jemima and Georgina, but not today. There was a more pressing engagement pending and she ignored their protests as she dragged them, protesting, homewards.

"Now, then," she had said crossly as they re-entered 57 Bockhampton Road. "Just you behave yourselves and stop whining. If you're good, I'll take you back to the park this afternoon."

That had shut them up, thank goodness. Now that both Edith and the kids were out of the way, she could attend to the matter in hand. A little dab of madam's perfume would do nicely, she thought, helping herself. That would set her off a treat. For Martha was expecting a gentleman caller in half-an-hour. And not just any old gentleman caller, either. Oh no. A *real* gentleman. A handsome, immaculately dressed individual who was going to marry her and make her into a lady. He didn't know it yet, but that's what she had planned for him. She pinched her cheeks to bring out their rosy flush and sprayed some more perfume behind her ears. Yes, she thought with satisfaction, that'll do.

Giles Fortescue had caught her eye one day while she was waiting outside the butcher's to be served. He had sauntered by and raised his hat to her. She hadn't been so conceited to think the greeting was for her. After all, she didn't know the man from Adam. But, it soon became clear she was the one he was addressing, and his eyes had danced with amusement. She had been so astonished that such an obvious gentleman would notice her, it had taken her some time to believe her luck.

"Pardon me," he had said. "I just had to say hello. You looked so pretty standing there, waiting patiently." Even though she was a mere servant, dressed in mere servant's clothes, she had her pride and dignity. She, just like any other lady, deserved to be treated with respect and not accosted in so forward a manner. But she had soon succumbed to the man's charm and had allowed him to escort her home. He had even carried her shopping basket for her.

Today he was coming to call on her in her own home. Well, it was her home as much as the Lomax's, wasn't it? She was allowed gentleman callers as long as they were kept in the kitchen and didn't overstay their welcome. That was the rule. Up until Giles Fortescue came on the scene, the only person who could be even vaguely described as a 'gentleman caller' had been Joshua Corbett, the butcher's boy. But she was finished with butchers' boys now. And wouldn't her mistress be jealous when she met Giles? That'd show Mrs Edith High-and-Mighty Lomax.

She finished pinning up her abundant brown hair into a more elaborate style than usual and gave herself a final admiring glance in her mistress's bedroom mirror.

Just then, the children ran into the room. "Why, you look ever so pretty! Better than Mama," said Jemima.

Georgina touched Martha's hair delicately. "Don't you look a picture? I wish you *were* our mama," said the littlest Lomax.

"Now then, girls. That's enough! I told you to keep to your room. Now, if you promise to be good, I'll buy you an ice cream each when we go to the park later."

"Ooh goody!" said little Georgina, clapping her hands.

Jemima, however, seemed less delighted. "Should you be in Mama's room?" she asked. "Should you be using her scent?"

"It's just a little dab, I'm sure she won't mind." She was having difficulty resisting slapping the child.

"So, you won't mind if I tell her then?" said Jemima, a knowing look on her face.

If ever the devil incarnate materialised in a child, that child was Jemima Lomax, or so thought Martha at that moment. "Well, I don't think we need tell 'er, do we dear? Let it be our little secret, eh?"

"What will you give me then?"

A blackmailer! And not even six yet. "I said I'd buy you an ice cream," said Martha, standing up and nudging them both out of the bedroom.

"I want more than that. I saw a skipping rope in the toy shop yesterday. It's ever so much better than the one I've got."

Martha kept her rising temper under control with some difficulty. She supposed she could just about afford to buy it for the little brat, as if she had any choice. But she'd get her come-uppance one day soon. When she was Mrs Fortescue, she'd be able to buy as many skipping ropes as would make a nice noose for the sweet little child.

"That's got rid of them at last!" thought Martha, as she listened to them arguing over the rocking horse as usual. Now, she must go and prepare some tea and put the cakes in the oven in readiness for her visitor. She would see what china she could find that would impress him.

The tea was in the pot and the cakes were on the silver cake stand when the doorbell rang. She resisted the temptation to run to the door, smoothing her hair and pinching her cheeks once more. Then, gliding elegantly along the passage, she opened the door to Mr Giles Fortescue.

The sunlight was in her eyes as she gazed up at the tall figure on the doorstep. Shielding her eyes, she smiled at the handsome gentleman who smiled back at her, displaying unnaturally white teeth. Funny, thought

Martha, she'd never noticed how white his teeth were before. They looked almost false.

"Please, to come in, Mr Fortescue," she said shyly, almost curtseying, but stopping herself just in time. She reminded herself she was meeting him on the same social footing today. There was no Edith Lomax to put her in her place.

"Giles, please. How many times do I have to ask you to call me by my Christian name? After all, you know me well enough by now, don't you, my dear?"

"Sorry, Giles. I've laid out the tea in the parlour."

She led him along the passage, looking up to see the two girls leaning over the banister, their eyes bulging with curiosity. "Get back to your room, you bad girls!" she said angrily. "I'm not to be disturbed while my friend is here."

Giles winked at the girls, much to their delight. "Please, my dear Martha, I don't mind the little ones. And so pretty, too."

Martha couldn't help feeling annoyed at his attention being diverted by the Lomax children. "They're a bit of an 'andful, though," she told him. "Their mother, my mistress, don't look after them properly. She leaves them with me most of the time."

"I am sorry to hear it," he said.

"The master is good to them, though." She smiled as she thought of Dr Lomax reading them bedtime stories.

"That is as it should be," smiled Giles as they entered the parlour. "They are lucky to have you, too, Martha."

"Do sit down, Mr – er, Giles," she said, blushing coyly.

He did as he was told, hitching up his trousers to reveal shiny white spats and intricately designed sock suspenders. She was both fascinated and embarrassed at seeing such intimate male apparel, and her hand shook as she held the tea strainer over his cup. The lid of the teapot rattled as she poured.

8

The late August weather had brought with it a promise of autumn, so Martha had banked up the parlour fire. Giles Fortescue watched it as it blazed and crackled in the grate, the flames reflecting off the trumpeting angels that adorned the side panels of the fireplace. For the first time in a long while, he felt content.

This lovely girl with her pretty manners had captured his heart. True, she lacked the poise and polish of the womankind he was used to, but she would make him a good and faithful spouse, of that he was sure. And she was kind to children, too. That was important. He had been searching for someone like her all his life. He would soon teach her how to conduct herself in polite society and how not to drop her aitches.

Maybe it was time he told her his real name, he thought. But then there would be too much explaining to do. And, although she was obviously a young woman who had a lot to put up with in her paltry little life, even she might not take kindly to knowing the truth about him. No, he couldn't take the risk.

Martha interrupted his reverie. "Would you like some more tea?"

"Thank you. And one more of those delicious scones, if you please."

Martha handed him his replenished cup and delicately split open another scone. "Butter? Jam?" she asked.

"Just butter – but lots of it," he replied. This was the life, he thought, lying back in the comfortable fireside chair, spreading his long legs before the blazing hearth.

While Martha and her guest were enjoying each other's company, Jemima and Georgina, were growing restless. They wanted their walk in the park and the ice creams they'd been promised, not to mention the skipping rope. Jemima had told her sister that Martha was going to buy them the one they'd seen in the toy shop the other day, and both children were beside themselves with impatience. It was nearly three o'clock, but there seemed to be no movement from the parlour. Finally, they decided to creep down the stairs and listen outside the parlour door. It would be much more interesting to find out what was going on in there with Martha and that man than doing their jigsaw puzzle yet again. And there were only so many times you could dress and undress a doll.

They were careful not to tread on the stair that always creaked and reached the parlour door without making a sound. The voices from inside the room were muffled, but their young ears were finely tuned, and they didn't miss a word.

"Martha, my love?"

"Yes, Giles?"

"I have grown very fond of you, you know that, don't you?"

"I – I don't know so much about that – "

"Well, my dear Martha, you may be sure it is so. Ever since we first met, I have thought of no one but you. Dare I think that you are not entirely indifferent to me?"

The children strained to hear Martha's reply as her voice was almost a whisper now.

"Please, Giles, I – "

"Darling, you are the one I've been waiting for all my life."

"Well, I – that is, I don't know. This is very sudden, like."

Georgina looked at Jemima and giggled. They knew enough of the world, despite being only four-and-a-half and five-and-three-quarters respectively, to know that what they were hearing was how the grown-ups made love. They pressed their tiny ears to the door once more.

"I know, my dear. But I would like to think that, in time, you would do me the very deepest honour of becoming my wife."

The children clapped their hands. So that's what getting married was like. Some handsome young man would ask for their 'honour'! They would be honoured! They couldn't wait. Lucky old Martha!

"We'll be bridesmaids, I bet," said Jemima. "I want to wear pink silk."

"I'll be prettier than you," asserted Georgina. She was younger than her sister but she knew, by the way people made more fuss of her, that she was the prettier of the two.

"No, you won't!" countered her sister, stamping her little foot.

"Will!"

"Won't!"

They giggled again. The rivalry between them was playful and not, as it was with many older sisters, malicious. The door had remained shut all this while as, unbeknownst to the little girls, their parlour maid was locked in a fervent embrace with George Arthur Hayter, sealing their pact.

They put their ears to the door again. "Can you see anything?" asked Georgina, as Jemima managed to reach the keyhole.

"Er, not much," replied Georgina, squinting through it. "I can only see the man's back and the table with the tea things on it. They're not saying anything."

"Oh, bother!"

It was just then that Edith Lomax came through the front door.

9

Edith stood at the open door, watching Abraham Smollett bending over her parlour maid. What was this? Were her eyes deceiving her? No, it was obvious what was going on. Her mind was clear now.

She had spent several fruitless hours in the park waiting for Abraham and, all the while he was here, in the parlour, with her maidservant of all people! Those hours had not been entirely wasted, however. She had had a lot of time to think and had finally, if reluctantly, come to the conclusion that Abraham Smollett must face the full force of the law. She had left the park with the intention of going straight to the police station but had arrived back home instead. Why she had changed her mind, she wasn't entirely sure, but now she realised it was lucky for Martha that she had.

Here was her Abraham just about to strangle the silly girl. Without stopping to think, she ran up behind him, reached for the fireside poker and smashed it down on his head. First, she heard the sound of his skull crack, then Martha's screams, as his body slumped to the floor.

"Oh, madam! What 'ave you done?" cried Martha, between screams.

Edith dropped the poker. As if in a trance, she bent down to examine her lover's body. She stroked his hair which was matted by a small seepage of blood. She saw, with horror, that the blow had also dislodged his teeth.

"You've killed 'im! And 'e'd just proposed to me! How could you?"

Edith looked up at her hysterical parlour maid, as if aware of her presence for the first time. "He proposed to you? Why on earth would he want to marry someone like you?" And, rising to her feet, she slapped Martha's face, partly to snap her out of her hysterics and partly just for the satisfaction of doing so.

Martha raised her hands to protect her from the blow and then slumped into the fireside chair, sobbing. "We was gonna be married!" she persisted. "'E'd asked me just before you come in, 'e did."

Edith sat down opposite her, Abraham's inert and toothless body between them. "Well he won't be marrying you now," she stated matter-of-factly.

"But – why – why did you do it?" Martha fumbled for her hanky and blew her nose loudly.

"Because he was about to strangle you, you silly girl. That's all the thanks I get for saving your life."

"What are you talking about? We was embracing!"

Edith sighed. "I hate to disillusion you, but I think you're quite wrong about that."

"Why do you say so? You know nothing about it. Giles...."

"Giles?" Edith gave a sardonic laugh. "Is that what he called himself?"

"Well, that's 'is name," said Martha defiantly. "Giles Fortescue." She started to blubber again. Edith took out her fan and flapped it violently. The room was suddenly very hot, even though the fire had long since gone out.

"I knew him as Abraham Smollett," she said, watching Martha's face as she took in this fact.

Martha stared at her. "What? You *knew* 'im?"

"Hasn't it penetrated your stupid head that this man has been deceiving both of us?"

"But you didn't 'ave to 'it 'im like that. Just because you was jealous."

Edith sighed in exasperation. "I just told you, Martha, I killed him because he was about to strangle you."

"It may 'ave looked like that when you come in," said Martha. "But you didn't even wait to find out what was 'appening, did you?"

"Look, Martha," Edith said, trying hard not to lose her patience. "Don't you remember what Dr Lomax read out to us this morning? About a man who is murdering women in this area? Didn't you take any notice of my husband's warning?" It didn't occur to Edith that she hadn't taken much notice of him either but, then, he was her husband and not taking notice of him was her privilege, and her privilege alone.

"That weren't nothing to do with my Giles."

"Oh, have it your own way," said Edith, putting her fan back in her reticule. She noticed Martha was studying something on the carpet not far from her feet. It was the man's false teeth.

"That wasn't the only false thing about him," said Edith.

It was an ironic statement, but Edith felt anything but light hearted at that moment. She was scared. She had killed a man, albeit in the heat of the moment. Still, he *was* a murderer, after all. But would the law take this into account when she went to the police? *If* she went to the police? No, she knew there would be no mercy for her. It would come out about her dalliance with the murder victim, and she was just as likely to be hanged for adultery as for murder.

Her dilemma, now, was either to give herself up to the police or run away. But, if she ran, where would she go?

10

Dr Herbert Lomax had always led a reasonably uneventful and blameless life and never, even in his most vivid nightmares, had he imagined what awaited him when he returned home to 57 Bockhampton Road that late summer evening. As he opened the front door, his eyes were greeted by the sight of his servant girl sitting blubbing on the bottom of the stairs. He then saw the blood on her skirt and hands.

"Why, Martha," he cried, putting his black bag down and going straight up to her. "What on earth's happened?"

Martha seemed deprived of speech, but she managed to point to the open parlour door. "In – in there," she sobbed.

He went through it and, at first, he couldn't see how many bodies there were, piled up by the fireplace. Before he could quite take in the scene of carnage before him, he slipped into blessed oblivion.

Martha's blood-stained hand touched his face, smearing his cheek. Her touch roused him, but his faculties had ceased to function properly and, for a few moments, he wondered who this pretty girl was who was bending over him so solicitously. Then realisation of what he had just witnessed flooded back to him.

He rose unsteadily to his feet, clutching on to Martha's arm as he slowly began to take in the scene.

There were three bodies lying on the hearth rug. It couldn't be true but, apparently, it was. Firstly, he saw a youngish man, devilishly handsome, but undoubtedly very dead. His skull had been smashed in and there was a pool of blood surrounding his dark head like a halo. Herbert Lomax wasn't possessed of a vivid imagination at the best of times, so what he was seeing had to be real. Even down to the macabre set of false teeth lying beside the body, saliva still clinging to them.

Then his eyes came to rest on the two other bodies lying there. They were piled one on top of the other, and he tried not to see who they were. Although he knew. It would have been hard to mistake a couple of dead children for a brace of pheasants. He blinked several times before slowly refocusing on them. There was no doubting the evidence of his own eyes and he had to believe it. There they were, his two beautiful little daughters, lying there with their skulls cracked open, blood oozing and seeping all around them.

"Georgie? Jemima?" he croaked, choking back his tears. He stretched out his fingers to stroke their dainty curls. They felt wet to the touch. He stood up shakily and put his hand on the mantelpiece to steady himself.

"Martha, Martha, what have you done?" he sobbed. "What have you done?" he repeated, like a mantra.

"What 'ave *I* done?" she screamed at him. "Do you think I could do all this?"

"But Martha, there's no one else here...." Then he suddenly remembered his wife. Where was Edith? Was she dead too? Had his maidservant gone out of her mind and been on a killing frenzy?

"Where's your mistress?" he asked her, gripping her by the shoulders.

"I ain't got no idea where Mrs Lomax is." She wriggled in his grasp. "Let me go!"

He released her without a murmur. "Isn't she here?" he asked, his mind a cauldron of emotions.

"No, sir," she informed him.

"Then, tell me, where is she?"

Martha was smirking at him. "She's gone."

"Gone? Gone where?"

"All I know is, after she struck this man with the poker, 'er poor little mites, your flesh and blood, wouldn't stop screaming, so she struck them too. She dropped the poker and ran upstairs. I 'eard 'er pacing the floor for a bit, then she came back down the stairs with a suitcase and told me she was leaving forever. She said not to try and find 'er, she was disappeared from the face of the earth. She said I was to look after you from now on."

"But why didn't you try to stop her?" Herbert stared at Martha, wondering whether to believe her. No, she was lying. She had to be lying, he told himself.

"I didn't know what to do, sir," cried Martha. "I was trying to revive the little ones. I was 'oping she 'adn't done for them. I thought they might be only stunned. But they're dead, all right. Then you come in, like."

"This is all too much to take in. My wife wouldn't do this – she couldn't!"

"I didn't believe it meself. But it's true. I bear witness. I cannot doubt my own two eyes."

Herbert slumped down into the fireside chair, noting with irony that his slippers were there, warming on the hearth. "When did you put these here, Martha?" he asked incredulously. How could his maidservant perform such a routine action after what had happened?

Martha smiled faintly. "I – I knew you would be 'ome soon, sir. I didn't think it my place not to perform my usual duties until you told me different."

Herbert shook his head in disbelief. "I hardly think I have need of warm slippers now, Martha."

"No sir." Martha bowed her head.

"Who – by the way – is this man?" He suddenly refocused his attention on the complete stranger lying dead on his hearth rug. Of course, Martha was mistaken. Edith must have killed him after he had killed her children. What mother wouldn't defend her children from such a fiend?

Martha looked triumphant suddenly. "'E was my fiancé. She killed 'im because she was jealous."

"Jealous?" He couldn't comprehend the word. "Why should she be jealous of him? That doesn't make any sense."

"No, sir. Not of 'im – of *me*. You see, 'e was courting me when she found us together. She killed 'im because she 'ad been 'is lover and now 'e preferred me and was going to marry *me*."

Herbert sighed. He had to believe it now. Martha wouldn't lie, she didn't have the wits. He had been a cuckold all along. The rumours he had heard and chosen to ignore were true. He supposed it didn't matter now. Nothing mattered now.

Just then, the doorbell chimed through the house. Herbert leapt to his feet. "Martha, what can we do? We can't answer it – not yet!"

"No, sir," she agreed, rushing over to the window to see who it was. She peered through the lace curtain and saw the bulky figure of Elsie Proudfoot. "It's Mrs Proudfoot!" she informed him. "We'd better open the door, otherwise she'll alert the whole street. You know what she's like."

"Yes, I know. But I can't face anyone yet, especially not that atrocious woman." The thought of her prying eyes was too much to bear. The doorbell rang again, this time more insistently and for longer.

"Oh dear!" he groaned. "She must be leaning on it. I suppose you'd better answer it, Martha."

"Yes, sir. If you think it's best." Then she looked down at her blood-stained clothes. "But, sir, I can't go like this, can I?"

"What do you mean, girl? Do as I bid."

"But the blood, sir...."

"What does it matter? People have got to know what happened some time. Besides, I'm sure she'll know what to do in this crisis. I seem to have lost all means of rational thought and I don't think I can face all this on my own."

"But you're not on your own, sir. You got me."

"Thank you, Martha. You're very loyal. But we need outside help. Let the woman in, please." The doorbell was still ringing. Elsie Proudfoot wasn't going to go away.

Martha moved slowly to the front door, wiping her soiled hands on her stained dress, patting her hair into place in front of the hall mirror before opening it.

"'Ello Martha dearie. Is your mistress at 'ome?" It didn't take the good woman long to notice the blood on Martha's clothes and hands.

Despite her dishevelled appearance, the little maidservant managed to reply with some shred of dignity. "No, she ain't, Mrs Proudfoot. Nor will she be for the foreseeable future."

"It's – it's just that my Tommy's gone down with something and I wondered if the doctor could come and look 'im over."

"Why not ask for the doc, then?" Martha asked archly. "The mistress knows nothing about medicine."

"I always ask Mrs Lomax to intervene on my be'alf with the doc. She usually gets 'im to attend my family as a favour, like. We 'aven't got much money, you know."

"That's none of my business," Martha pointed out.

Elsie was trying to see into the hall but Martha barred her view. "Is there something else you wanted?"

"Look, love, I can't 'elp noticing your clothes. Ain't that blood on your 'ands?" Mrs Proudfoot was obviously enjoying herself immensely.

"I been gutting a chicken, if you must know," said Martha, brushing a stray lock of hair away from her eyes.

Herbert Lomax came to the door as Martha said this.

Elsie was obviously in her element now. There was no hiding the whiteness of his complexion, the ghostly horror reflected in his eyes and, above all, the blood on his waistcoat and hands.

"Come in, Mrs Proudfoot," he said. "Something very tragic has happened here. We need your help. I don't know what to do. My little girls.... My wife has gone.... I – I...."

He swayed against the wall as Mrs Proudfoot waddled through the front door. She managed to prop him up before he collapsed altogether. "Come on, doc. Don't give way. Let's see what we can do. The world ain't come to an end."

"Oh yes, Mrs Proudfoot," he muttered. "I think you'll find it definitely has."

11

The carnage Elsie Proudfoot witnessed on entering the parlour of number 57 Bockhampton Road rendered her almost speechless, a condition she had rarely suffered from in all her forty-four years. What she had expected to find was the body of the handsome young man she had seen loitering outside number 57 on several occasions. She had seen him being let in by Martha earlier that day, so it wasn't hard for her to put two and two together. But, on seeing not one, but three, bodies, and two of them the lovely Lomax daughters lying in their own blood, even Mrs Proudfoot was lost for words. She prided herself on being a woman of the world and took most things in her stride. But there were limits and, for Elsie Proudfoot, on seeing the dead bodies of the little Lomax children, she had reached those limits.

"Where's your good lady wife, Doc?" she asked, once her power of speech had fully returned.

Dr Lomax shook his head, seemingly robbed of all his wits. Martha was at his elbow, resting her hand on his arm in a proprietorial manner which did not go unnoticed by their gimlet-eyed next-door neighbour.

"Will someone tell me what's 'appened 'ere?" Elsie realised, with a certain amount of glee, she was going to have to take charge of the situation.

At first, neither Herbert nor Martha were making much sense to her, but gradually she began to piece together what each of them was telling her.

"So, you, Doc, 'ave come 'ome to find these dead bodies?" She shied away from mentioning the two little ones by name. "And you, Martha, you was a witness and saw Mrs Lomax do this lot in?"

"I – I saw it all, Mrs Proudfoot. You need to call the police right away. They need to find Mrs Lomax –"

Elsie Proudfoot stared at Martha now. She was a pretty little thing, but she wasn't as innocent as she painted herself, she could bet her last penny on that. "But, missy," she said, "I saw you. I saw you let that man there on the 'earthrug in the front door this morning."

Martha didn't seem abashed by this statement, even though Herbert was eyeing her with suspicion now. "What are you saying, Mrs Proudfoot?" he asked her.

"She's right, sir," said Martha meekly. "'E was my gentleman caller. I'm allowed to 'ave them. You said so. And she was jealous. Mrs Lomax was jealous, that's why she killed 'im."

Elsie realised she had been put in her place by this whippersnapper of a servant girl. Defy her would she? She'd see about that. "I've seen that same man there going about with Mrs Lomax. You saying 'e was going about with you, too, girl?"

Martha, for answer, gave her a glare. If Elsie had had X-ray eyes, she would have seen the rude gesture she was making with her fingers behind her back.

Herbert broke in now, seemingly in charge of his faculties once more. "I think I begin to see what's happened. I suspect that man is the one the police are looking for. Edith killed him because she found out who he was." He looked almost happy for a moment.

"But what about your poor kids?" pointed out Mrs Proudfoot.

"*He* killed them, so she killed *him*," said Herbert without hesitation.

"That's not what 'appened," whined Martha.

"Well, we shall see, missy, shan't we?" said Elsie. "Now, if you ain't got no objection, Doc, I think I'd better fetch the police."

❧

Sergeant Jack Cobb stroked his moustache thoughtfully. He had been called to 57 Bockhampton Road the evening before and, although he was an experienced copper, the carnage he found in that house surpassed almost anything he had witnessed before. And his experienced and jaundiced eyes had been party to most of the dreadful things that people were capable of.

The man of the house, Dr Lomax, had seemed genuinely distraught. According to that hussy of a parlour maid, he hadn't been on the scene when the murders took place, but *she* had. And, according to Miss Finch, it was her mistress, the doctor's wife, who was responsible for the murders. Naturally, she'd disappeared without trace, so there was no gainsaying the parlour maid's version of events. A search operation had been mounted at once, but Sergeant Cobb was not hopeful of finding her. How could a mother murder her own children in cold blood? It beggared belief.

Cobb had made short work of his interview with Mrs Proudfoot. A well-meaning body, but hearsay and gossip were no use in a matter as serious as this. Dr Lomax was still waiting to be interviewed, as Martha Finch sat before him now. He looked at his only witness as she sat there demurely, butter daring not to melt in that impudent little mouth. He knew her type, he had her number, all right. All fluttering eyelashes and innocent smiles, but underneath a ruthless streak buttoned down until such time as it was needed. He didn't entirely blame the Martha Finch of this world. They had to survive somehow, he supposed. Attack was the best form of defence for people like her.

There was no way to know if she was telling the truth, but it seemed Edith Lomax was implicated simply by not being there to answer questions. But, like all good coppers, he was keeping an open mind.

"Now, Martha. I want the truth now. You're telling me that your mistress killed her lover and then her children because they wouldn't stop screaming? And then she ran away? Have I got that right?"

"Yes, sir. It's the truth, more's the pity."

"So can you tell me what you think made her do these awful things, Martha?"

"Jealousy, plain and simple." Martha stared straight into Sergeant Cobb's eyes. There was defiance in her attitude, daring him to contradict her.

"Jealousy? To kill her own children? She was jealous of her own children?"

"No, 'course not. I meant she was jealous of 'er lover and me."

"Now, Martha, you know that we have established the identity of the dead man, don't you?"

She seemed disinclined to answer his question, looking everywhere around the little interview room but at her interlocutor's face. "Do I?" she said at last.

"He was George Arthur Hayter, alias Abraham Smollett, alias Giles Fortescue et cetera, et cetera. He was responsible for killing three women and would certainly have gone on to murder again."

Martha was looking down at her hands in her lap. There was still a trace of blood on them, despite the application of carbolic soap. "All I know is, she told me 'e 'ad been keeping company with 'er. 'E wasn't, 'cos 'e was keeping company with *me* and was gonna marry *me*."

"He may have married you, Miss Finch," said Cobb, "but I wouldn't have given you much chance of survival if you displeased him in any way."

"What d'you mean? I wouldn't 'ave displeased 'im 'cos 'e loved me."

"Very well, we'll let that pass for now." Sergeant Cobb felt sorry for the girl. So desperate was she to believe George Arthur Hayter would have married her, she wasn't going to admit he was the notorious woman strangler of Clapham. Not for all the tea in China.

"Let us return to Mrs Lomax. You assert that she killed this man you say you were to marry through jealousy and then killed her children because they wouldn't stop screaming?"

"That's what I said," said Martha, her expression sullen, marring her looks for a moment. "It's the God's 'onest truth, so 'elp me."

He looked at her closely. He was sure she was lying, but without Mrs Lomax to deny it, there was nothing to be done but get her statement written up and signed. Where it would take him was another matter.

Dr Herbert Lomax looked a sorry sight. Red-eyed and unshaven, Sergeant Cobb had no doubt he was suffering deeply. The loss of his daughters and the possibility (remote, in Cobb's opinion) that his wife had murdered them would have broken the spirit of the hardest of men. And Lomax, Cobb could see, wasn't the hardest of men. Far from it.

"I'm sorry to have to put you through all this, Dr Lomax. But I need to get at the true facts," said Cobb, giving Herbert an encouraging smile. "Can you tell me what happened when you arrived home yesterday evening?"

"It was just like any other evening," Herbert Lomax replied. "I got home about six and – no – it wasn't quite like any other evening." Cobb watched as the bereaved doctor seemed to be struggling with a recollection.

"Take your time," he said kindly. "There's no hurry."

"Well, as I said, it was just like any other evening, only Martha, our parlour maid, was sitting on the stairs when I came through the front door. She was crying and I could see blood on her clothes."

Cobb poured him some water and noticed the man's hand shake as he picked up the glass. It took Herbert a long time to recount what he had witnessed, as the good policeman allowed him to break off every time he saw the doctor getting too emotional.

"Thank you, Dr Lomax," said Cobb finally. "We will need you to sign your statement before you go."

"All right," said Herbert, getting unsteadily to his feet.

"Have you no idea where your wife could have gone?" Cobb asked, collecting up the notes he had just made.

"Well, her family live in Wimbledon. She may have gone there, I suppose...." said Herbert, sitting down again. The effort to stand had evidently been too much for him.

"She isn't there. We've already tried. We got the address from your neighbour, Mrs Proudfoot."

"Oh, I see. Then, I don't really know. I can't imagine what she is doing for money. I gave her the week's housekeeping yesterday, but that won't last for long...."

"No. Do you have any idea at all where else she could have gone? Any other relations or close friends? We really must find her – as much for her sake as anything."

"I told you, I don't know. I would tell you if I did. She – my wife – wasn't someone who made friends easily."

Cobb could see Herbert hadn't enjoyed admitting this. To Cobb, though, this Edith Lomax sounded like a fascinating creature, and he sincerely hoped he would meet her soon. For all sorts of reasons but, included among them, the chance to thank her for ridding the world of a psychotic killer.

"Make no mistake, Sergeant," said Herbert quickly, "I love my wife. But I know her faults, and murdering little children isn't one of them."

"Let's hope we find her soon," said Cobb, standing up. "Until she can answer for herself, this case is far from closed. Now if you would be good enough to wait there, I will get these notes in some semblance of order so that you can sign them."

"All right," said Herbert. He looked resigned sitting there, but, Sergeant Cobb supposed, sitting in a police station was probably infinitely preferable to sitting by his own fireside after what had happened there.

12

Sergeant Cobb closed the file with a sigh. The triple murders in 57 Bockhampton Road had occupied his mind and actions for almost three months with little result. A countrywide search for Edith Lomax had proved fruitless; it was as if she had vanished from the face of the earth. Scotland Yard had been called in but, so far, even the best brains and resources of that establishment hadn't managed to find her either.

Cobb had fallen in love with her shadow. He was both repelled and attracted by her. He stared at the photograph which had fallen out of the file. It was a head and shoulders portrait of a very beautiful young woman. The face of an angel? Definitely. The heart of a devil? Possibly.

Then there was that parlour maid, Martha Finch. He couldn't rid himself of the feeling she wasn't all she seemed. There wasn't anything he could put his finger on. To all intents and purposes she was what she appeared to be. A young parlour maid, serving her master and mistress faithfully and caring for their children. What could be wrong with that? Except – what? Whatever was bothering him about the girl, he realised it amounted to plain dislike. But there was something else about her that was nagging away at him. It was his copper's nose, his intuition. He didn't trust her. He didn't believe a single word that came out of her mouth.

On the other hand, he liked Dr Lomax the more he saw of him. The poor chap was heartbroken and clearly having trouble holding on to his wits. There was no possibility that he had carried out the murders. So that brought him back to Edith Lomax. Until she was found, the jigsaw would remain unfinished. Edith was all the blue bits of sky that obstinately wouldn't fit together.

The theory at Scotland Yard was that, filled with remorse, she had drowned herself. To that end, they had dragged the local reservoir, being the handiest place for a would-be suicide. No body was found, however. A couple of old perambulators and a cast-iron sink were all they could come up with. Cobb wasn't convinced by this theory, anyway. He was convinced she was still alive. But where?

Her parents hadn't heard from her and now, of course, did not wish to hear from her ever again. The last he heard was that Edith's mother was continually reaching for the smelling salts, her middle-class existence blighted forever. So much for parental love, thought Cobb. At least the legal system assumed a person was innocent until proven guilty.

What a world we live in, thought Cobb, as he put the case file away, carefully returning Edith's photo to it as he did so. The 'unsolved' stamp was ready to hand, but he still refrained from using it. He would give it a few more weeks. You never knew when something would turn up. And as long as it wasn't Edith's toes, he wouldn't give up looking for her.

∽

Herbert Lomax looked across the dining table at Martha as she laid out his cutlery for the evening meal and dutifully placed a steaming plate of food in front of him. What was it? he wondered. All food tasted the same to him these days, or rather of nothing. No matter how tasty the dish, he could have been eating ashes for all he knew or cared.

Martha did her best, poor girl. What she must have suffered, he thought. Seeing his wife go berserk with the fireside poker and murdering his innocent darlings. He had tried not to believe her capable of such atrocity, but the longer she stayed away, the more he could only assume the worst. He had ignored Martha's continued assertions that she was the guilty party for as long as he could, but what else was he to think? It was beyond all endurance to go on believing in her innocence. The fact that she had been unfaithful to him didn't help, of course. If she was capable of such deceit, wasn't she just as capable of murder? The two seemed to go hand in hand in Lomax's view.

"Sir?" Martha interrupted his thoughts.

"Sorry, Martha? Were you saying something?"

"I just asked you if you would like some bread and butter, sir."

"Oh, no thanks, Martha. And please, take this plate away. I can't eat it."

"Oh, but sir, I made it 'specially nice for you. A stew to build you up. You'll be wasting away if you ain't careful."

"That will suit me fine, Martha. I don't see the point of carrying on anyway."

"But your patients need you, sir. What will they do if you don't look after them?"

"Dr Greaves is quite capable of dealing with them. They prefer him now, anyway. They don't need me. Nobody needs me."

"But, sir, life 'as to go on...."

"Has it?"

Without another word, Martha removed his untouched plate and took it to the kitchen. After she had disposed of it, she took the apple pie out of the oven. It was done to a turn and smelt delicious. She cut him a generous slice and smothered it in piping hot custard. Herbert's stomach turned over at the sight of it.

"I'm sorry, Martha, but I can't eat anything at the moment. Please take it away and bring me the brandy."

Martha did as she was bid, placing the decanter and glass beside his chair in front of the fire. The evenings were decidedly chilly now that winter was taking hold, and she had got a friendly fire going. He sat there, gazing into the flames, as she poured him a generous tot.

"'Ere, sir. This'll cheer your cockles," she said, handing him the glass.

Herbert took it from her and, as he did so, his hand accidentally brushed hers. Something snapped inside him, something he had kept coiled up but ready to spring at the slightest touch. And that touch was Martha's. He started to weep copiously. As she put her soft arms around him, he let the coil unwind as fast as it could and he sobbed his heart out.

13

Martha, tears streaming down her face, watched him as he took her blood pressure with calm, professional precision.

"There's no doubt about it, Martha. I'm sorry, but you are going to have a baby," said Herbert Lomax, looking at her with a serious expression. He knew it was hard for unmarried mothers to be told such news, but he didn't feel sorry for her, only for himself. He was about to lose a good servant girl.

"But, I ain't been with no one – except you."

He coughed to hide his embarrassment. "We shouldn't have done it. I don't blame you, I should have had more control." He really should have, he thought. But he had been at such a low ebb that evening.

"Well, we did and now I'm up a gum tree." She tapped her belly, which already looked rounder and plumper.

"You are lying to me, Martha," he said, more assertive now. He knew the ground he was on was firm enough. "I'm not the father of your child, Martha."

"But you must be. I never done it with no one else!"

"You're at least three months pregnant, so there is no way the baby could be mine."

Martha hung her head. "But, sir, I don't know what to do! You've got to 'elp me!"

"I'll do everything I can to see you safely through your confinement, Martha. In the meantime, you must tell the father. He must do right by you and marry you."

"'E won't do that. 'E's hardly earning anything. I don't see 'ow 'e'll be able to support me and my baby."

Dr Lomax shrugged coldly. The detachment he felt was uncharacteristic, but he could feel no genuine concern for Martha's predicament, only relief that he wasn't responsible. It so easily could have been his. "That is not my concern. If he won't, or can't, marry you, then you'll have to rely on your parents or the workhouse."

"But can't I stay 'ere? I can still do everything for you – cook your meals, clean the 'ouse...."

"And let everyone think that the baby is mine? Edith's only been gone for three months."

"You didn't think about then when you bedded me though, did you?" Martha faced him boldly. "Anyway, your precious Edith's a murderess. Why'd you keep bringing 'er up? She's gone for good."

"I'd thank you not to speak of your mistress in that way," he said, even more coldly now. She was going to make a nuisance of herself, and he was beginning to worry. "Please adjust your clothing and get my supper."

Martha got up off her bed where she had lain while Herbert Lomax had examined her. She wriggled into her scattered garments. "Oh, so you still expect me to get your supper, then?" she said, snivelling.

"You can continue with your duties for another week or two," he said, looking away from her. The sight of her partially naked body wasn't helping. He was just a man, after all. "After that, I'm sorry, but you'll have to go. Before you start showing. You're already putting on weight, you know."

Martha's snivels turned into full-scale blubbering now. "So it was all right for you to take advantage of me, but not all right now I'm expecting!"

Herbert eyed her sternly. "If the baby had been mine, it would have been a different matter. Anyway, I think the boot was very much on the other foot. You took advantage of my unhappiness that night. I admit that I slept with you, but I wouldn't have done if you hadn't encouraged me. I can hardly be blamed for accepting something so freely offered. You must learn to behave with more decorum, Martha, if you want to get on in this world."

"But what am I going to do? I can't get another position in my condition. Can't you 'elp me get rid of it?"

He was shocked by her brutal request. "I shall pretend I didn't hear that. I would not dream of taking the life of a helpless unborn child. It's against everything I stand for."

She slipped past him and out of the room. "Now, please hurry with the supper, Martha," he called after her. "I'm hungry."

❧

The next day, Martha refused to stir from her bed. Herbert called through her door, concerned that his breakfast had not been prepared. "I can't go on my rounds with nothing inside me," he complained.

But Martha remained supine. "I ain't well," she said.

"A certain amount of vomiting in the early mornings is to be expected in your condition," he told her. "But you're a healthy young woman and it shouldn't prevent you from doing your duties."

"I ain't getting up," she asserted.

"I think you shall, Martha," came his stern disembodied voice through the door. She had taken the precaution of locking it.

"Shan't!"

He finally left the house, but not before he had told her to pack her bags and leave. He did not want to find her there when he got home. No more prevarication. He meant what he said. She hid her head under the blankets and sobbed quietly.

An hour later, she slowly rose and got dressed. She was an automaton, smoothing her apron and adjusting her mob cap. But she wasn't preparing for a day's household chores. She had come to a decision.

He had told her to go, to not be there when he returned that evening. Well, that didn't suit her at all. She *would* still be there when he got home and, despite what he had said, he wouldn't be turning her out of the house.

As Dr Lomax walked slowly along Bockhampton Road that evening, he reflected on what a mess his life had become. A wife absconded, believed to have killed three times, and now a maidservant accusing him of getting her in the family way. Herbert had never harmed a fly. He was a dedicated doctor, caring for the sick. Why had all this horror landed squarely on his none too sturdy shoulders?

He missed his wife more and more as each day passed. Sergeant Cobb had told him what Scotland Yard thought, that Edith had committed suicide because she couldn't face up to her crimes. But Herbert, like Cobb, didn't believe it for a single second. She was still alive, but under what conditions? If only he knew where she was. All he wanted to do was find her and help her, no matter what crimes she had committed.

The lamps were lit in the parlour as he let himself into number 57 Bockhampton Road. Not a good sign. Where was Martha? Had she lit them as a last service for him? It was possible, he thought, remembering how, in the midst of tragedy, she had placed his slippers to warm on the blood-stained hearth.

He went towards the light and opened the parlour door. The fire was lit in the grate and, yes, there they were: his slippers warming on the hearth as usual. However, there was no sign of Martha.

He sat down by the fire and pondered. He couldn't help staring at the stained rug. He couldn't bear it. How could he go on living here, with the reminder of what had happened staring him in the face every day? It was beyond all human endurance. His sister had written, begging him to come and stay with her and her family. But he couldn't impose himself. She had her hands full, as it was.

He got up after about five minutes and walked into the kitchen. It was in darkness. Although everything had been normal in the parlour, the kitchen was anything but. And there was a strange smell. It wasn't the usual smell of Martha's cooking tonight. Perhaps he shouldn't have been so harsh. He needn't have ordered her to go just yet.

Then he saw her. She was lying limply with her head in the gas oven. He had told her to go, and she had gone. He pulled her gently from the oven, turning off the taps as he did so. He checked for a pulse, but he was far too late. His practised eye could see she had been dead for over an hour.

The poor child, he thought bitterly. He had been a beast to her, and he was suddenly overwhelmed with pity and remorse. Where was his charity? She had been right. He *had* taken advantage of her. He had used her and then flung her aside as if she had been poison. He should have looked after her and seen that she got through her confinement safely. Who cared what the neighbours thought?

But he had no second chance to say sorry. It would have served no purpose, anyway. After all, he wasn't the baby's father. Why hadn't she sought *his* help? Oh,

Martha, he cried, hugging her lifeless body, what have I done?

So, once again, he would have to undergo a police investigation. The house was cursed. Another unnatural death had taken place within its walls. It was too much. But at least it wasn't murder this time. Martha had killed herself, so he was in the clear. He looked around for a suicide note and, finding none, wondered if she could even write.

He wandered back into the parlour and looked around. Then he noticed the envelope on the mantelpiece addressed to him in an unformed, childish hand. He tore it open with a shaking hand. The scrap of note inside read:

Dear doctor,

I'm sorry for what I am about to do, but I can't see no other way. Don't blame yourself I want to die really its best. I only wanted to serve you, but I know you still love the mistress. I can't face the shame of the baby neither.

Goodby, Martha.

The first thing that struck him was how good her spelling was. Apart from the lack of punctuation, she was quite erudite. What an irrelevant thing to think at a time like this, he chastised himself, folding up the pathetic note that provided a meagre postscript to such a short, tragic life.

14

Elsie Proudfoot was cock of the walk. Living next door to a house where first three, then four, deaths had occurred in quick succession, gave her respect and standing in the neighbourhood. She had always been the first to know what was going on but had never had such thrilling news to impart before. Press reports were redundant in Elsie's neck of the woods. People found out the latest titbits much sooner from her good self. The *Daily Bugle* and the *South London Recorder* might just as well have saved their ink, as far as the close-knit community surrounding Bockhampton Road was concerned.

After blackening the name of Edith Lomax forever, the local gossips turned their attention to her poor, benighted husband. They had been going to him for years with their petty ailments, but not anymore. Especially now that that nice parlour maid, Martha, was dead, and by her own hand apparently. Even though there had been a suicide note, many people had furnished it with extra salacious details straight out of their own imaginations. There was no doubt that Martha had been the doctor's mistress and the baby she was expecting was definitely his. Joshua Corbett, the butcher's boy, was particularly eager to ensure that everyone knew that.

Elsie, however, didn't believe anything so bad of the doctor. However, despite her protestations, other people weren't so charitable. Once they knew the bare facts, they lost no time in putting their own interpretation on them, the general assumption being that there was no smoke without fire.

Herbert, meanwhile, had more or less become a recluse, confined to the 'house of death'. His patients had deserted him, and he could think of no other reason to venture out just to be stared and pointed at by the outraged neighbours. So he went on from one dreary day to another, his life crumbling around him as he did so.

After the initial shock of poor Martha's suicide, his thoughts returned to his missing wife. Everyone had already tried, found her guilty and hanged her. Were they right? Was he being a fool to think her incapable of such inhumanity? He hadn't been blind to Edith's faults. She was a difficult, snobbish and often uncharitable woman. But he had never thought her so evil as to kill her own children. He looked at her photograph regularly, familiarising himself with her charming features as if he needed to remind himself what she looked like. No one with such a face could be a killer, he was convinced.

Since Martha's sad demise, Elsie Proudfoot had proved herself indispensable to Herbert. He began to rely on his neighbour heavily to feed him and do other chores for him. As he didn't leave the house for days on end, there was little need for much laundry. What little there was, the good lady was more than glad to oblige.

But Elsie wasn't the only person to show concern for his wellbeing. He also received intermittent visits from Sergeant Jack Cobb. He would call on him after his day's work was done, and the two men often whiled away the long winter evenings together over a game of chess. Herbert found himself not merely grateful for the man's company, but also growing rather fond of him. A confirmed bachelor, Cobb also looked forward to visiting Herbert, in preference to returning to his rather austere lodgings and indifferent supper provided by the surly housekeeper he couldn't quite find it in his heart to dismiss.

The death of Martha Finch had caused some ripples at the station, but Jack Cobb wasn't having any of it. He knew in his bones that Martha had been a jumped up little hussy who, while not exactly deserving her fate, hadn't done herself any favours by her loose behaviour. The note she had left, mentioning the baby, did not trouble him one jot. Dr Lomax had given his side of the story, even admitting to the good Sergeant that he had foolishly succumbed to her charms just once, and once only, he was more than ever convinced the man was blameless. And it was soon clear to him just who, in fact, was responsible for Martha's unfortunate condition.

Joshua Corbett had come into the station in high dudgeon shortly after the news of Martha's suicide had spread, demanding that Dr Lomax be put behind bars for causing her to do away with herself. Cobb had no means of proving it, of course, but it didn't take a genius to work it out. Corbett was there to make sure the blame for Martha's pregnancy was laid firmly at Herbert Lomax's door, and not at his own. Cobb had a sneaking pity for the young lad, as he knew he lived in fear of his brutal father's belt and, if he found out that his son had got Martha into trouble, he would be thrashed within an inch of his life. Well, he thought, old man Corbett wouldn't find out from Sergeant Jack Cobb.

One evening, Dr Lomax and the good Sergeant were playing a peaceful game of chess when the front door bell of 57 Bockhampton Road rang through the house. It was after ten o'clock, not a time when casual visitors called. Lomax had received a few unwelcome visitors following Martha's suicide, but lately he hadn't been troubled so much. A brick had been hurled through the parlour window with a threatening note wrapped around it but, so far, that threat hadn't been carried out.

Herbert rose to his feet and, going over to the window, peeked through the curtains. He saw a young, scruffy-looking individual, with a scowl on his face, standing on the doorstep. His fists were clenched, his nose was red, and his whole demeanour suggested a long and fulfilling night at a nearby hostelry. He recognised him at once.

"It's Joshua Corbett, the butcher's boy," he whispered to Cobb.

"That little tyke," grunted Sergeant Cobb. "He's been making a nuisance of himself down at the station, blaming you for Martha's predicament and suicide."

"Hmmm! It's not a social call then," said Herbert in an ironic tone.

"Hardly. Better let him in, though, or he'll disturb the whole neighbourhood." They could hear him yelling through the letterbox now.

"Come out 'ere and face me like a man! I know what you done to Martha! You made 'er kill 'erself! Now come out and get what's coming to yer!"

"I really don't think I could face him at the moment," sighed Herbert. "There's been enough trouble in this household without adding to it unnecessarily."

"I think you might find his visit illuminating, nevertheless," advised the Sergeant.

"Oh, very well, if you think so."

All this time, Joshua had been pulling the bell handle with impatience. He was still shouting through the letterbox: "I know you're in there, Lomax! Come 'ere before I break your blinking door in!"

"He means business, old fellow," smiled Cobb. "But I'd hazard his bark will be far worse than his bite."

Herbert moved reluctantly to the front door and opened it, causing Joshua to tumble into the hall.

"About time, you rotten swine," said the young lad, swaying unsteadily. There was no doubt that most of his bravado was as a result of the liquor he had consumed.

Lomax, seeing the true state of things, grabbed him by the collar and yanked him into the parlour where Sergeant Cobb was standing before the fireplace, hands behind his back, rocking backwards and forwards on his heels.

"Now, young sir," said Cobb, "What is the meaning of calling at this late hour and making a nuisance of yourself with the good doctor?"

"I've every right, I 'ave. You lot down the nick won't listen to me so I ain't got no choice, 'ave I? 'E might escape the hangman's rope, but 'e won't escape my fists!" With that, he lunged out at Lomax who sidestepped gracefully, causing the young man to topple over and hit his head on the mantelpiece.

"Take what's coming to yer, can't yer!" Joshua yelled, undaunted by the blood oozing from his forehead.

"Just sit down, you stupid boy," said Cobb, grasping him by the collar, while Joshua hit out with his fists, only making contact with the air between them. "The doctor has something to tell you, and you are going to listen whether you like it or not. Failing that, I'll march you home to your father who no doubt will be interested to hear what you have been doing with poor Martha down back alleys late at night. I don't think he'll take very kindly to that information, do you?"

It was clear that this threat had scared Joshua, for he unclenched his fists and sagged like a punctured balloon.

"Don't tell me dad, for Gawd's sake," he pleaded, beginning to sniffle.

All this while, Herbert had remained silent, gazing at the scene before him, trying to make some sense of it. He now decided to speak up for himself.

"Joshua, I can assure you that I wasn't responsible for Martha's condition. She took her own life because she was scared of having to bring up a fatherless child."

"Says you!" snarled Joshua. But it was clear all the stuffing had gone out of him.

"Look here, young fellow-me-lad," said Cobb. "I will say this only once. If you don't stop making a nuisance of yourself with Dr Lomax, I can make life very uncomfortable for you. Now get out and don't let me catch you here again."

"Very well, I'm going. But you ain't 'eard the last of this...." Joshua was slurring his words and beginning to look decidedly unwell.

"I sincerely hope we have, otherwise Mr Corbett will find out what sort of a son he has spawned, if you get my drift?"

The young man sniffed and wiped his nose with his grubby sleeve. It seemed that Cobb's drift had gone home, as he allowed himself to be escorted to the front door by the stern, but kindly, copper.

"What an unpleasant individual," commented Herbert when Cobb returned, smiling.

"Not altogether someone whose company you'd seek out," replied his friend with a grin. "But he has a lot to put up with."

"You mean his father? He certainly seemed scared when you threatened to tell him was he'd been up to."

"I'm sure that brute gives that young lad and his other kids the strap at the least provocation."

"Oh dear, I didn't know."

"Well, why should you? Anyway, I think Corbett Junior has learned a valuable lesson tonight, at any rate," said Cobb, still smiling.

"What's that? And why are you grinning like the Cheshire cat?"

"Not to drink too much, for a start. I left him spewing all over your geraniums."

"Oh, well," sighed Herbert. "I never did like those particular flowers very much."

Both men laughed.

15

It was one of those balmy early summer afternoons that promise so much when Dr Herbert Lomax decided his family deserved a little treat. He would take his family to the British Empire Exhibition at Wembley. The weather was perfect and he could think of nothing better than to spend time with his wife and little daughter, not to mention his two stepsons, who were whooping around the parlour with joy at the prospect. Apparently the Exhibition was a great success and had attracted millions of visitors. It included an amusement park and boasted the world's first omnibus station. The whole family was very excited.

Herbert, now in his early sixties, had never found Edith. Time had moved on, the courts of the land had long since declared her legally dead. It was his old friend, Sergeant Jack Cobb, now retired, who had introduced him to Miranda Harcourt, his recently widowed sister. It was an instant mutual attraction, even though she was some twenty-five years younger than Herbert and had two small sons. But, far from putting him off, he had welcomed the boys with open arms. They were the family he thought he'd never have again, and his joy was complete when his own little daughter, Florence, came along. He was sad sometimes, though, when he looked at her. She reminded him so much of the two he had lost.

But today was a happy day for Herbert's second family. The bus put them down outside the Wembley venue and they joined the queues of people waiting patiently to enter the British Empire Exhibition. Once inside, they made their way through the milling crowds, the two boys setting off at a fast pace and soon disappearing into the throng of visitors going into the amusements arcade. Little Florence clung to her mother's hand, a look of wonderment on her small, pretty face.

"Oh dear, Herbert. Those two will get lost in there. Will you go and find them, while I take Florence to the ice cream stall?" said Miranda.

"Of course, dear. But I'm sure the boys will be fine. They can look after themselves."

Miranda gave her husband a stern look. "Herbert!"

He smiled. "Sorry, pet. I'm on my way." Obediently, he left his wife and daughter and headed into the arcade. It wasn't easy getting through the crowds, but he managed to steer a path towards one of the main attractions: a huge laughing clown that dispensed liquorice sweets with each penny inserted into the slot beneath it. There were plenty of other, more expensive, gifts to be had, even a wrist watch, but somehow the metal claw never seemed able to hang on to any of them long enough to dispense them to the eagerly waiting public.

"What a swindle," thought Dr Lomax. He wondered if any of the prizes were ever won or if the metal claw was set so that it could only hold a few jelly beans at a time.

He scanned the throng of people for his stepsons but to no avail. Each time he saw a boy of about the right age, he turned out to be a stranger. After about fifteen minutes of fruitless searching, he came to a stall selling fluffy toys and decided that a pink teddy bear would be just the thing for Florence. As his hand went to pick it up, another hand, small, delicate, feminine and covered in a white lace glove, reached out for it at the same time. Both hands took an arm each of the teddy bear. Dr Lomax looked up to see an elegant, still beautiful woman in late middle age staring straight back at him.

The jolt he received on seeing Edith's face sent him reeling back against the wall. Edith clung on to the teddy bear as she lost her balance and started to fall to the floor. Herbert put his arm around her waist to steady her. He could hear someone in the crowd suggesting he took 'his good lady wife' to the tea booth outside the arcade. "Give her a cup of strong, sweet tea," came the advice. "She'll soon be right as rain."

He led Edith to the tea booth that the man had pointed out and sat her down while he went to get the beverages. When he returned some time later (he apologised for the long wait, but there was a queue), he found her fanning herself furiously, her eyes not quite meeting his.

"Here, drink this while it's hot. I've put three sugars in."

Edith put away her fan and raised her eyes to meet his. She smiled as she stirred her tea. "Thank you."

"You're – you're looking very well," he observed. "And hardly a day older." It was a lie, of course. But she was still beautiful, even if that beauty had hardened with the passing years.

"It's good to see you, Herbert," she said. "I've often wondered how you've been getting on."

"I was very unhappy for a while after – after what happened...."

Edith put her hand on his. "You know why I had to go. I didn't want to, but I had no other choice. I couldn't stay after I'd killed that man. I would have been hanged for sure."

Herbert sipped his tea, while he continued to admire his wife. "You are still so beautiful, Edith. I'm so glad that you seem to have prospered so well."

"Even after – even after – well, you must hate me – our daughters?"

"Yes – well. There was a nationwide search for you. I wanted to hear your side of the story. I still find it hard to believe you could have killed them in cold blood like that."

Edith stared at him. "You really believed I could have killed them?"

"I – I didn't want to believe it – but what was I to think?"

"Did Martha tell you that I'd killed them?"

"Well, yes, she did..."

"And you believed her, rather than defend me?"

"But what could I do? You'd disappeared. I wanted more than anything in the world to find you and get at the truth."

She was looking right into his eyes now. "I don't think I'll ever forgive you for believing that of me," she said.

"That's a cruel thing to say. I never wanted to believe it – but you never really had much time for them, did you?"

"No, I confess I didn't. They bored me." She finished her tea and gathered up her belongings. "Now, I think we'd better forget that this meeting ever took place between us. Don't you?" She rose to leave, the haughtiness in her manner that he remembered so well asserting itself.

"Please, Edith, please sit down. I need to know what happened to you after.... Please Edith, I need this...."

"Do you?" She was inspecting her parasol. "Isn't it best to leave things as they are? Whatever I tell you now will be mistrusted, anyway."

"Of course it won't!" Herbert felt the ground slipping away from him. She had walked into his life a little over half-an-hour ago after a space of nearly thirty years, and she was now about to walk out of it again. Forever. "You just vanished and, for all I knew, you could have been lying at the bottom of some river. Don't you understand what that did to me? Not knowing what had happened to you?"

Edith was looking at him with a softer expression now, and she sat down again. "Do you think I could have one of those nice sugar buns, Herbert?" she asked him.

He leapt up and went to the counter, eager to do her bidding. Whatever happened, he must keep her with him until he knew the truth. If Miranda and the children were wondering where he was, he couldn't help it. He would explain everything to them later. Miranda knew all about Edith Lomax and the tragedy that had befallen Herbert. She would understand.

The cakes provided, Herbert watched her select one and proceed to cut it into tiny slices. She had always been a fastidious eater, he remembered.

"Well?" he queried, impatience getting the better of him.

"Well, Herbert?" she echoed.

"Please, Edith, tell me what happened to you. I know you have managed very well by your appearance. Your clothes are well made and you are well in yourself."

"The practised eye of the doctor. Thank you, Herbert," she smiled. "Is there more tea in the pot?"

He poured her another cup of tea, having difficulty keeping his temper. He began to remember how she had always irritated him in this way, delighting in making him feel uncomfortable even when, as was so often the case, she was in the wrong.

"And you, Herbert, you are looking prosperous too. I'm glad life has been kind to you, despite everything."

"No thanks to you, Edith."

She glared at him over her tea cup. "Very well, Herbert. You want to know the truth. Well, I will tell you. Whether you will be edified by my story is another matter."

"After I'd hit that awful man, I realised I couldn't stay to face the consequences. Martha would inform against me, of that I was certain, so there would be no point in denying it. So I just went and packed a small suitcase – just a few essentials. But, as I was leaving, the girls followed me and asked me where I was going. I hadn't reckoned with trying to explain to them what I'd just done.

"It was the worst moment of my life, Herbert. Worse, even, than the murder of that vile man. For the first time, ever, I felt a twinge of maternal instinct. I was hugging them and they were crying. All of a sudden, I knew they loved me and that I loved them.

"But I had to leave them, so I told them to be good girls for their mama and to go to their room. I told them you would be home soon and that Martha would make them their tea. Of course, I knew that was unlikely, given the state she was in and the body on the hearth. I did feel bad about leaving her with all that, but what else could I do?

"So I left the house, but I was worried about the children now. So I decided to make sure they were all right. After all, I couldn't trust them to Martha's care, not now. As I came back through the front door, I saw the children were going into the parlour. Jemima was just tall enough to reach the door handle. Then I heard the screams. So I turned and left. I admit it was a cowardly thing to do, but I knew they had discovered what I'd done. I just couldn't stay to face them. Anyway, it was better for them that I was out of their lives. I knew you wouldn't let any harm come to them. Please, Herbert. Let me tell this in my own way. Don't interrupt, it's hard enough as it is.

"Anyway, I felt completely disoriented now. But I was determined to go. I remember looking in my purse at that point and saw that I still had most of the housekeeping money that you'd given me just the day before. That would tide me over for a few days at least, and I started walking along the street, walking as fast as I could without drawing attention to myself. I was prepared to run if I saw a policeman.

"I got to the cab rank by the station without incident and hired the first one that came along. But as I took a seat inside, I realised I had no idea where I was going. I couldn't go to my parents. They would have asked all sorts of questions and, besides, that would be the first place the police would look. So, when the cab driver asked me where I was going, I said the first thing that came into my head. King's Cross station.

"The journey seemed to take forever, and I kept fearing the police were following me. But when it seemed they weren't on my tail, I had time to reflect on my circumstances. Then it occurred to me. I could get a train to Luton where an old friend of mine lived. Lavinia Reynolds, you may remember her? Anyway, she'd married a parson and moved with him to Luton some years ago. But we still kept in touch. We wrote to each other about once every two months. Her letters were usually very boring. I always wondered why I bothered to read them, let alone reply. But I was glad now. Glad that I'd kept in touch, because now, I realised, she was the only friend I had left in the world.

"When I got to King's Cross, I found I had a long wait for the Luton train, so I decided to while away the time in the station buffet. I remember studying the menu card to avoid looking into the eyes of strangers. It was as if they knew what I'd done. Of course, they didn't, but my guilty conscience was playing tricks on me, and I think I was a little feverish.

"Then this soldier appeared out of nowhere. He was balancing a teacup and plate of sandwiches in one hand, while holding on to his kitbag with the other. He asked if he could share my table, as all the other tables were taken. They actually weren't, and I knew he was attracted to me. I wasn't sure, at first, that I wanted his attention, but it seemed churlish to refuse.

"He introduced himself as Sergeant Ernest Hayward. He told me he'd just come on leave. Said he'd served in the Boer War. To be honest, Herbert, he could have served in her local greengrocers, for all I cared. But he seemed so proud of himself, and he was very good looking. Don't look at me like that, Herbert. I didn't have anything like that on my mind. Not then.

"When he asked my name, I had to think quickly. The only name I could think of was my own. Before I married you, I mean. So Starling I became or, rather, reverted to. I was Edith Starling again, from that moment. My wedding ring was hidden by my glove, so that posed no difficulty.

"He asked me where I was going and, when I told him, he said that was where he was going too. I thought he was lying at first, but I found out afterwards that his family really did live in Luton. He asked if he might impose himself as my travelling companion, and I agreed. By then, I'd realised it would have been unwise to travel alone. A young woman travelling on her own would surely have attracted attention and that was the last thing I wanted.

"At that point, I excused myself to go to the Ladies where I removed the ring – your ring, Herbert. I'm sorry, but I had no choice. I wanted to keep it, but knew that I daren't, so I dropped it down the sink plug hole. I knew, from that moment, my new life was starting. Yes, Herbert, I married my good looking soldier and I have been very happy, by and large. He's been good to me, better than I deserve."

Herbert eyed the teddy bear Edith was still clutching. "I don't think we've paid for that, by the way," he said. "I'll go and make amends. Is it for your daughter?"

Edith smiled wistfully. "No. I have a young niece by my second marriage."

When Herbert returned after paying for the bear, she asked him who he wanted the toy for. "My daughter, Florence. Yes, I remarried. It was a long while after you walked out of my life," he added, as if by way of apology.

"I'm glad," she said.

"Is – is your husband here with you today?" asked Herbert, looking around.

"Somewhere. He's practising his rifle shooting skills in the arcade. There's a stall that's offering prizes for shooting wooden ducks, I believe."

"He must be wondering where you've got to," he pointed out.

"Oh no. He knows I like to be on my own sometimes. He'll come and find me soon, I've no doubt. But you must have the teddy bear. For Florence, you said? How old is she?"

"She's just five and as pretty as a picture. So you never had any more children?" Herbert asked tentatively.

"No, I don't have any children. Which I think is a blessing, don't you?" The irony in her tone wasn't lost on him. "It's all right, Herbert," she said, pre-empting his protest. "It's fine. I understand how you feel. After all, as you said, what else were you to think? I just wish I knew who really did kill them."

That hadn't crossed his mind until now. But, she was right. If Edith hadn't killed them, then someone else had. Martha had been mistaken, after all. She must have jumped to the conclusion that, as there was no one else in the house at the time, her mistress must have been the guilty party.

"Now, I've got a husband to find," she was saying, "and I believe your wife will soon be missing you, too. Not to mention your daughter."

"Er, yes. I've two stepsons too," he told her.

"My, my. Quite a brood."

He took her arm and led her out of the tea booth. "Thanks for the teddy bear, by the way," he said as they prepared to take their leave of each other. "Florence will be thrilled. But I'm sorry to deny your niece."

"Oh, don't worry," smiled Edith, "she's probably a little too old for it now, anyway."

Herbert watched her departing back, reflecting that she could be a young girl, her figure was still as trim as ever. It was hard to realise just what had happened. The door to the past had been opened to him after almost thirty years, and he now knew what had become of her. Their meeting, the one he had wished for, for so long, was over all too soon and there were still so many questions left unanswered.

16

Why did he have to suck on his pipe in that annoying manner? she wondered.

It was the day after her reunion with Herbert, and she had been thinking about him ever since. There was some truth, she reflected, in the old adage 'absence makes the heart grow fonder' for, to her now, Herbert seemed a cut well above her second husband. Another adage popped into her mind now. 'Familiarity breeds contempt'. Why could she never be satisfied with what she had? Ernest Hayward was a decent enough man but, as the years passed, he had proved himself just as boring as Herbert, if not a little more so. Still, she had to admit, she didn't know where she would be today without his intervention. Her real past was unknown to Ernest; the past she had made up had satisfied his mild curiosity only too easily. Her beauty had dazzled him, numbing that part of his brain that should have asked a few more questions. She had sometimes wondered what would have become of her if she hadn't been so beautiful. She would, most likely, have ended up in the river as Herbert had imagined.

She sat opposite Ernest this evening, in the same chair by the same fireside as every other evening. She had her knitting, as usual, to while away the time. Ernest's favoured pastime was reading detective fiction. She couldn't resist the thought that nothing in the novels he so avidly devoured could compare with the real life events she had lived through. But, of course, she could never tell him.

She paused her knitting and tutted pointedly as her husband continued to suck on his pipe. "Either fill it up and light it or put it away, Ernest," she said crossly.

"Sorry, dear," he said, dutifully putting it down.

He turned the page of his book. The clock chimed eight o'clock. At least two more hours before it was time to go to bed, she thought. It was no life for someone like herself. Maybe the gallows would have been preferable, after all. A short life, but a gay one, wasn't that how it went?

Her thoughts returned to Herbert Lomax. She wondered if he still lived in Bockhampton Road. Why hadn't she asked him? She suddenly realised she wanted to see the house again, whether Herbert was still in it or not. That would be an adventure, at least. She would take a trip to Wandsworth, she decided. If the weather continued fine, it would be a pleasant outing.

However, living in Primrose Hill meant a complicated journey which would have been much easier if her husband drove her there. But she couldn't ask him to do that. What would he think? Would he start to put two and two together? No, she thought. He wasn't the sharpest knife in the drawer, but it wasn't worth taking the risk.

She would hire a cab to take her all the way there. Money was no object these days and, she would say one thing for Ernest, he wasn't as mean with his money as

Herbert had been. They enjoyed most of life's little luxuries and always had enough money to take holidays when they liked, as well as eating out when the fancy took them. Ernest had also acquired a car, a Model T Ford. They were the first in the neighbourhood to own a motor vehicle. She could bet Herbert didn't have one.

The day she decided to make the journey back to her past and 57 Bockhampton Road had turned out fine, with the merest hint of a breeze. The clouds scudded across the sky, as she stepped down from the cab outside her destination. It didn't take more than a single glance to realise that Herbert no longer lived there. It was obvious that no one lived there. The house stood out from the rest of the terrace by its very neglect and dilapidation. She suddenly felt scared. Could she face going in there alone? She still had the key but, of course, the locks could have been changed.

She paid off the cab driver and gingerly opened the gate. He called to her. "I don't think anyone's lived there for years, madam. Are you sure you've got the right address?"

"Quite sure, thank you," she replied and began walking up the overgrown path to the front door. She looked around her as she walked, wondering if any of the neighbours she knew then could still be around. Elsie Proudfoot had been in her forties, so would be in her mid-sixties now. Could she still be living next door? she suddenly wondered. If so, the nosey old so-and-so would be bound to be looking out of her window and would surely recognise her.

Her heart leapt into her mouth when she saw the lace curtain twitch in Elsie Proudfoot's front room window. She sighed with relief when the head that poked out didn't belong to that good woman, but to a much younger person. A man, in fact.

"'Ello?" he called to her. "Did you make a mistake? There's no one living at number 57. Not for years and years. There was a triple murder there, you know," he said. "And a suicide," he added with relish.

Edith gave him an old-fashioned look. Was he trying to scare her off? "I see this neighbourhood hasn't changed much in that time. There's always someone watching you."

The young man was taken aback. "I'm sorry, I'm sure. I was only trying to be 'elpful."

Edith cleared her throat and addressed him again. "I see. Well, I have just come from the estate agents. They have given me a key to have a look round. I might buy it."

"You'll be very silly if you do," said the man. "My old mum, God rest 'er soul, told me that the murders put people off from buying the place. She thought she'd never live to see the day when it was occupied again. And she was right."

So Mrs Proudfoot was dead. That was a relief, thought Edith. "Was your mother living here when the murders took place?" Although she knew full well, it would be interesting to hear another version of what had happened from a neutral outsider.

"Yeah. She used to keep an eye on the family that lived there then. She liked them very much. It was a doctor and 'is wife and their two girls, plus a parlour maid. A looker, by all accounts. Mum consulted the doc about me and my brothers often – we were always getting ill as children, you see. Not enough vitamins, apparently."

"Do you know what happened to the doctor after that? Did he move right away?"

"I don't know. I was only small when 'e left. I remember Mum was sad that 'e was going but that 'e 'ad no choice 'cos the parlour maid 'ad killed 'erself in there."

"Killed herself? Do you know why?"

"God, no. It was a long time ago. Although Mum did say there was some scandal about a baby, and that the doctor could 'ave been the father." The young man was obviously enjoying himself relating all the lurid details to her. A chip off the block, she thought with an inward smile.

"Well, I mustn't keep you, young man. I'll just take a quick look around and get the key back to the estate agent. After what you've told me I doubt I shall be buying it."

"I shouldn't think so. Anyway, good luck, Mrs…?"

"Hayward," she said quickly. "And you are?"

"Bob Proudfoot, at your service," he grinned cheekily.

She remembered little Bobby, the youngest of the Proudfoot brood. He was usually on the front doorstep whenever she went out in the summer, playing marbles or some such game. She remembered he often seemed bored without anyone else to play with, his brothers all being a good deal older. Bobby had obviously been an afterthought. She had felt sorry for him then, but he seemed happy enough now.

She continued on up the path and came to the front door with its peeling paint and letter '5' hanging upside down by one nail. She thrust the key in the lock and tried turning it. Nothing happened. It was as she feared; the lock had been changed. However, she gave it another go and this time she could feel it give a little. It was just rust, she realised. After a couple more turns the door creaked slowly open. It smelt strongly of damp inside, mixed with other even more unpleasant odours.

Oh well, she thought. Here goes. She put her handkerchief over her mouth and nose and proceeded slowly down the hall. The first door on the right had been the parlour, she remembered. She opened the door which gave with an even louder creak than the front door and entered. There was mould on the walls in great patches and she saw that the front window had several cracks in it. She noticed a spider had made its home there. Well, good luck to him, she thought. That's the only living creature that could live here, that's for sure.

She turned towards the fireplace and gasped. It had always been an adornment to the room, but now it looked wrong. The whole surround looked as if it had just been polished, and the andirons positively gleamed at her. The ornate panels with their trumpeting angels could have been installed yesterday, their colour was so vivid. The whole structure seemed to be beckoning to her.

Filled with wonder, she moved towards it.

PART TWO

St Stephen's Vicarage
Wandsworth SW
March 1953

Dear Mr and Mrs Maltravers,

I hope you will forgive my writing to you, a perfect stranger, but I wanted to introduce myself to you. Now that little Henry has settled in with you, I would very much like to be allowed news of him from time to time, as one who helped him through the first few hours and days after the tragedy. If I may even be permitted to visit you in Cambridge when everything has settled down, I would very much appreciate that too.

I have no doubt that you will care for Henry far better than I could, being his maternal grandparents. I am only sorry there was a little unpleasantness between you and Mr and Mrs Freeman as to who would get to keep the child. I do hope the rift will soon be healed and that little Henry will be able to see them often. At a time like this, as I'm sure you will understand, it is important that he has the support of everyone in his family now that he is an orphan.

I have known Henry almost from the day he was born. I christened him here at St Stephen's, and his parents were staunch churchgoers, never missing a Sunday service, and often attending on Wednesday evenings too. Henry had just joined the Sunday School and had quite endeared himself to Mrs Wagstaff who

113

teaches the Bible to the little ones. She sends her warm wishes to you, and I enclose a small gift from her to Henry. It is a New Testament, which I hope will give him comfort in these dark days.

Please do let me know how he progresses and if there is any small service I can render to him or you in the meanwhile.

Yours sincerely,

Bernard Paltoquet (Rev.)

17

John and Carol Freeman had just the one child, Henry. He was a good little boy, always happy to play on his own when his mother was busy. He never bothered her to come and play with him, quite content to keep himself amused with his colouring books, toy soldiers and jigsaw puzzles.

Then, one day, Carol heard him talking to himself in his bedroom. She smiled. He was an imaginative child and had probably invented a little brother or sister to play with. She knocked gently on his bedroom door and peeped in. Henry was sitting on the bed with his arms around two invisible companions.

"Hello, Mummy. This is Georgie, and this is Jemima. They're my bestest friends in all the world. They live here with us."

"Hello, Georgie. Hello, Jemima," Carol said, playing along. "What are you all doing?"

"We're playing 'I Spy'," replied Henry, "and I'm winning."

"Good for you," laughed his mother. "Now it's time for tea, dear. Have you washed your hands?"

"Not yet, Mummy. Can Georgie and Jemima have tea with us?"

"Of course." Carol was quite happy to feed them as it wouldn't cost her a penny.

"They need to ask the pretty lady first," said Henry.

Carol was a bit surprised by this. Most children invented imaginary companions but didn't often invent adults to go with them. Her son was a very unusual child, she thought with pride. Such intelligence in one so young.

While Henry ran to the bathroom to wash his hands, Carol went back downstairs and set out the tea plates, careful to add two extra. She also set two more chairs at the table, and then waited for Henry to come down the stairs. When he didn't appear after five minutes, she went to the bottom of the stairs and called up to him.

"Come on, Henry. Your tea's getting cold!"

Henry's face peered over the landing banister, tears streaming down his cheeks.

"Whatever's the matter, sweetheart?" Carol ran up to him and hugged him tightly.

"She – she....," he stuttered between sobs.

"What, darling?"

"The-the lady – she won't let them come to tea with me!"

Carol was concerned by her son's apparent despair. How could he get himself so worked up about his imaginary friends? But, to him, they probably seemed real. "Please, Henry. What do you mean?"

"*She* doesn't like us," sobbed the little boy.

"Oh, darling, don't be so silly." She didn't know what else to say. If the lady he was talking about *had* been real, she would have had a few things to say to her.

Henry stamped his little foot. "I'm not being silly! The pretty lady said she didn't want the girls to have tea with us because she didn't like *you*!"

Carol was taken aback at this. What kind of a fertile imagination had Henry got? "Doesn't like *me*? Did she say why not?"

"No."

That, then, seemed to be that. "Never mind what the pretty lady says, darling. She is being very unkind. Let's have tea without them. We don't need them."

"But they're my friends! Mummy, why doesn't she like you? I like you. Daddy likes you...."

"I should hope so," laughed Carol. "Now, dry your eyes and come and have your tea."

As she said this, she felt the air around her turn suddenly very cold and had the eeriest sensation she was being watched. She turned around swiftly, but there was no one there. She hugged him tighter, as she felt the eyes upon her again.

The house had been very dilapidated when they had first moved in, and she remembered all the dark corners that had long since been banished by paint and wallpaper. The eyes had seemed to be hidden in those dark corners then, but now they were here again, boring into her. The hairs on the back of her neck were standing on end.

"I don't want to live here anymore with that horrid lady!" he cried.

"Don't be silly, Henry. It's only you, me and Daddy live here. No one else."

"What about the girls? And the horrid lady?"

"There's no one else here, darling. We live on our own."

"But the girls always play with me," Henry protested. "They say that this is their home. They've lived here for ever so long – long before we came."

Carol was scared now. The cold atmosphere, the feeling of being watched and her distressed son all added up to something she couldn't explain, not to herself, and certainly not to her son.

"I'm going to call Daddy," she said suddenly. She rushed to the telephone in the hall and dialled her husband's office number. As she heard it ring, she wondered what she was going to say to him. That her son was upset by imaginary companions? That she felt that someone was watching her? He would think she was mad. He had a very important job as a civil servant with the Ministry of Transport, and he wouldn't thank her for disturbing him with such trivia. She slammed the phone down before he could answer. Damn him! she cursed, rather unfairly.

Henry was sobbing quietly beside her, but the atmosphere had lightened considerably now. She no longer felt cold or that she was being watched. She hugged him again and wiped his eyes with her hanky. Thank goodness, she thought.

"There, there, darling. Let's not think anymore about the nasty lady. Let's just have tea by ourselves, shall we?"

Henry nodded and sniffed. "We don't need them, do we, Mummy?"

Carol smiled. "No, we certainly don't. Come on, there's jelly and ice cream for a special treat. And, tomorrow, I'll let you in to a little secret. Daddy is taking us to the zoo!"

That cheered him up considerably. "Can Georgie and Jemima come too?" he asked.

"We'll see," she said. Over my dead body, she thought.

Later that evening, after Henry was tucked up in bed, Carol told her husband what had happened. As she predicted, he dismissed the whole incident as a storm in a teacup. She knew it wasn't, but there was no one more pragmatic than John, and any suggestion of a ghost in the rafters would have set him off laughing. But it wasn't a laughing matter, it really wasn't.

They sat comfortably beside the ornate fireplace, a cosy fire burning brightly in the grate. Suddenly, she felt the room grow very cold, and she looked up to see Henry standing in the doorway, his teddy bear clutched to his chest. He was sobbing his heart out. John, it seemed, had felt nothing and still sat there reading his evening paper. It was as if a mist was surrounding him. He wasn't in the same time zone anymore.

Then, as Carol got up to go to her little son, the poker came down on her head. She fell into the grate and cracked her skull on the fender. She died instantly.

John was standing up now, seemingly aware for the first time that something was wrong. Where was Carol? He didn't even have time to find her body before he felt a crack on the side of his head. Bleeding profusely from the temple, he started to crawl towards his son.

18

The notorious double murder in 57 Bockhampton Road had shocked the nation. The police had drawn a blank, the only witness being the five-year-old son of the victims. They hadn't known how to approach the child, and the scant information they could glean from him added up to precisely nothing. It wasn't to be wondered at. How could so young a child even understand what had happened to his parents, let alone provide the clue to their killer?

The mystery of the deaths had deepened when the murder weapon disappeared. It had been brought to the station, bagged and labelled, but the next time they went to examine it, it was gone. The bag and the label remained, but no blood-stained poker was to be found.

All little Henry Freeman could tell them was that a 'pretty lady' had hit his parents with a poker. The bit about the poker had been true, except it was no longer in police possession to corroborate his story. Someone had managed to remove it without anyone knowing. Maybe it was the 'pretty lady' herself. But how a person answering this description could have got past the police security to steal the murder weapon was a mystery.

The usual painstaking enquiries had got the police no further forward. Not one of the Freemans' neighbours, friends and family could shed any light on a motive for killing them. According to everyone, they had been a perfectly nice, ordinary couple. John's drinking pals, as well as his colleagues at the Ministry of Transport, all said what a nice chap he was, a happy extrovert who was always the first to get a round in. Carol's friends said exactly the same about her, except she generally left the round getting-in to her husband.

However, there was one inconsistency that told against John Freeman. It wasn't a reason for killing him, or at least the police couldn't think of one, but apparently, he had told a close friend he had often felt strangely moody and irritable when he got home at night. He was always fine until he got through the front door of 57 Bockhampton Road, and then fine again when he left it the next morning. It didn't mean anything, of course. If he had murdered his wife, then there would be a motive, a reason of some sort. But he had been killed himself, and he would hardly have done that in a fit of pique. At least not with the fireside poker.

The police had asked Henry about his father's moods but, as the little boy was usually in bed by the time his father got home from work, he couldn't really throw any light on the subject. He did say, however that his daddy was always happier when he took him out at weekends, but that didn't lead the police anywhere except up a blind alley. And it seemed that, unless either the 'pretty lady' or the blood-stained poker turned up, the murder investigation was more or less at an impasse.

The Freemans' parish vicar, Reverend Bernard Paltoquet, was more concerned about the fate of their son than the identity of their murderer. He had become involved from the first, being the one to discover the bodies and on hand to console little Henry before he went to live with his maternal grandparents in Cambridge.

Bernard had promised to visit the little boy as soon as he was settled in his new home, and so, on a cold, grey day in early March, several months after the murders, he arrived at Cambridge train station. He had been looking forward to meeting the grandparents, Mr and Mrs Maltravers, but had also been a little nervous. Would they know how to deal with such a traumatised child? he had wondered. But his fears were soon put to rest at the sight of the pleasant couple who, although in their early sixties, seemed at least ten years younger. They both ran up to him on the platform, waving as they approached. Alf Maltravers shook him firmly by the hand, while Winnie Maltravers hugged him and started to cry.

"Sorry, Reverend," said Alf with some embarrassment. "It doesn't take much to set Winnie off these days. We're still very much in shock over our daughter's senseless death. And John's too, of course. He was such a good, kind man. We were so happy when Carol told us they were getting married. He had a good job in the Civil Service, so we knew that she was set up for life. And when Henry came along we were so happy for them."

Alf was chatting away while they drove the two miles from Cambridge to Long Stanton where the couple had a small bungalow in a quiet cul-de-sac.

"Where's Henry now, by the way?" Bernard asked.

"He's at school. He's just started at the local infants this week," said Alf. "We kept him at home for a few months because we didn't think he was up to being with other children yet. But we thought it was about time he had something like a normal life again. We'd hate to think he'd suffer because of what happened. He's a bright little boy, and we think he'll get over this terrible time once he's settled in here."

"I'm so glad he's going to school. And I'm sure he'll be able to come to terms with the loss of his parents with you two to take care of him," said Bernard.

Winnie, who was sitting in the back of the car, started to cry again. "Thank you, Vicar. We do our best, but our house hasn't been the happiest of places lately, and I'm afraid Henry must have felt this pretty badly. He cried himself to sleep night after night when he first came here, but we gave him the best Christmas we could and, since then, he has started to improve. They say that children are resilient, but can any child ever really get over the violent deaths of his parents? Especially when the poor little mite saw it all happen."

Bernard sincerely hoped that Henry was young enough to put it all behind him and grow up to be a well-balanced, contented human being. He said as much to Winnie and hoped it didn't sound too glib. He trotted out platitudes to his parishioners when needed, often not knowing the answers himself, and sometimes not even believing in his own propaganda.

When they reached home, Winnie took Bernard into the well-appointed kitchen and sat him down with a cup of tea and a plate of chocolate biscuits.

"Alf has gone to fetch Henry from school, so you'll soon see if he's made any progress since you last saw him. We hope we're doing the right thing, sending him to school. He's quite reserved these days, and I'm worried that he won't make friends very easily."

"It's bound to take him time to come out of his shell, Mrs Maltravers – "

"Winnie, please – "

"Winnie. And you must call me Bernard. Has Henry told you anything more about what happened?"

"We haven't ever brought the subject up. We feel it's up to him to say if he wants to talk about it."

"Do you think you're right not to encourage him to talk about it? I'm wondering if it would help him – it might get the horror out of his system more quickly. I'm not an expert, and you're his grandparents and responsible for him, but it might be an idea to try and bring him out of himself."

Winnie sat down at the kitchen table and took her hanky from her apron pocket. As her tears started to fall, she looked imploringly into Bernard's gentle eyes. "The truth is, Bernard, I'm being selfish. I don't think I could stand to hear about what happened to my Carol, and I couldn't bear to see Henry go through all that trauma again. It would break his little heart. He's fragile enough as it is."

"I'm sorry, Winnie. You're right, of course. I'm just an interfering old fool."

"Oh no, of course you're not! I think you're probably right and I *should* encourage Henry to talk about my Carol and John – not just about the murders, but about his relationship with them before that. I believe he'd be happy to remember the good times." She dabbed at her eyes, but the tears still managed to escape down her cheeks.

"Please try not to upset yourself so. Henry will be here soon, it wouldn't be good for him to see you like this." Bernard put his arm around her shoulders.

"No, no. I always try to hide my sadness in front of Henry. He has enough to put up with as it is." Winnie blew her nose as they heard the key turn in the lock. The little boy ran into the room and hugged his grandmother fondly. As he turned and saw Bernard, his little face screwed up and tears welled in his eyes.

"Granny, please! Tell that man to go away. I don't want to talk to him!"

"But you remember Reverend Paltoquet, don't you?" said Winnie. "He looked after you for a little while. You said you liked him."

The little boy looked at the vicar out of the side of his eyes. "I remember. He saw what happened. He thinks I killed them, but it was the pretty lady!"

Bernard got up and went over to him, the last of his chocolate biscuits in his hand. "Of course, I don't," he said, "and, to prove it, I'm going to give you my last chocolate biscuit. There!"

Henry took it from him slowly and began to munch.

"What do you say to the kind man, Henry?" asked Winnie, watching him with amusement.

"Thank you," said Henry, through a mouthful of crumbs.

19

Henry finished the biscuit, all the while staring at Bernard. It was a truce of sorts, but the adults could see it was a precarious one. A word out of place at that moment could tip him over the edge.

"Come on, Henry love," Winnie said gently. "This gentleman is your friend. He only wants to comfort and help you now, if he can."

Henry's tears had dried now, and the look on his face had changed from suspicion to curiosity.

Bernard said, "Henry, would you like to go for a little walk with me round the garden?"

"No!" Henry screamed. "No. Go away!" The chocolate biscuit hadn't quite done the trick.

"Look," said Bernard, reaching into pocket. "I've got a nice sherbet sweet for you. Would you like it?"

Henry blinked and looked at him. "Yes, please." Bernard wondered if his grandparents were concerned he was bribing Henry with teeth-rotting sweets, but it was in a good cause.

Bernard bent down to him and ruffled his hair. "Here you are," he said, unwrapping the sweet and popping it in his mouth. "Come on, let's go into the garden, shall we?"

"All right," said the boy. "Is it all right, Granny?"

"Yes, of course," said Winnie. "Now put this on and wrap this round you."

An extra layer of coat and scarf, and Henry was ready to go. Bernard held out his hand and the boy took it without protest. It felt warm to the reverend's touch. But tiny, frail. Bernard thought his heart would break.

They walked among the carefully tended flowerbeds. Daffodils and narcissi were thriving, despite the cold March wind and, although the afternoon was overcast, a promise of spring was in the air. He sat the boy down on the bench by the greenhouse. Henry was calmer now and seemed content to be in his company.

"How do you like your new school, Henry?" Bernard began.

The child didn't reply immediately but continued to suck on his sweet thoughtfully.

Bernard persevered. "Have you made any friends yet?" he asked.

This question seemed to animate him slightly. "I met a boy today called Trevor. He says he wants to be my best friend."

"That's very good. I'm pleased," said Bernard, smiling. "Is he a nice boy?"

"I think so. He gave me his second-best marble. Look." Henry pulled a large, multi-coloured, round piece of glass out of his trouser pocket and showed it to him proudly.

Bernard admired it dutifully. He was relieved to see the little boy doing the things that little boys did. "Henry?" he said gently.

The boy looked up from his marble. "I'm gonna give Trevor my Nigerian stamp in exchange. It's a double."

"I'm sure he'll be pleased. You'll make good friends, you two."

"Yes, we will." Henry put his marble back in his pocket and patted it gently.

"Henry?" Bernard tried again. "What made you think that I thought you'd killed your parents?"

Henry's eyes began to brim with tears. Bernard gave him a hug.

"I don't want to upset you by making you talk about that terrible time again. But you know I never believed such a wicked thing of you, don't you?"

"I thought I did. But the lady told me that people will think I did it because she wasn't a real person and they wouldn't believe me."

"When did she tell you that?" Bernard was intrigued.

"When I came into the room after she'd killed them. She was standing there with the poker in her hand. She was in a sort of mist, like not really there."

"Henry, do you mean like a ghost?"

"I suppose so. She looked furry."

"Furry?"

"Well, there was like a furry ring round her. She was dressed in a long frock, and her hair was all piled up on top of her head."

"Did she look like an old-fashioned lady? Like you sometimes see in history books?"

"Sort of. She was pretty, but I didn't like her."

"Had you ever seen her before?" Bernard asked. Henry was beginning to come out of his shell now, and he seemed to be at ease with the vicar, as they sat side by side in the garden. A few drops of rain began to fall, and Bernard took off his coat and wrapped it around the boy.

"Yes. I'd seen her lots of times. Except she sometimes looked different."

"Different?" asked Bernard, unwrapping another sweet for Henry, as well as one for himself. "In what way?"

"Just – different frock. Different hair."

"I see. Could there have been two pretty ladies?"

"Two? No, I don't think so. There were two little girls, though."

"Two little girls? What girls?"

"Two little girls that were there all the time. They were dressed funnily too. They had lacy knickers on. They peeked out from under their frocks and they had curly hair. They were very pretty, and we played together lots. Well, until that lady told them they couldn't have tea with me."

"So, the lady who you say killed your mummy and daddy was there before that day then?"

"Oh yes, she and the girls had lived there for ever so long. Years and years and years, they said."

"Henry, did you ever think that, if that were so, why weren't they any older?"

"No. I never thought of that. I'm silly."

"Of course, you're not, Henry. The reason they weren't any older was because they were no longer living in the way we are. We get older all the time, but they had already died. They were the age they were when they died. Do you understand what I'm saying?"

Henry's little face was a picture of bewilderment. "I – I'm not sure. Sort of. They were haunting our house?"

"Yes, Henry, I think so. Was the pretty lady their mother, do you think?"

"I don't know. I suppose so. They seemed to do what she told them and belong to her. But I never really saw them together. And they never spoke to her when I was in the room."

"I see. Henry, I believe this old-fashioned lady and the two little girls you played with were in your house because of something that happened to them there many years ago."

This was all too much for Henry and he returned to his marble. Bernard smiled. "I'm sorry, Henry, you mustn't mind me. I get carried away. I read too many ghost stories."

Henry looked up at him with concern. "You needn't worry. I was never afraid of them – well, not until that day." Bernard could see that he was about to cry again.

"Let's get back to the house. It's starting to rain quite hard now."

They raced back into the kitchen where Winnie had made them mugs of steaming hot chocolate.

"You'll stay to supper, Reverend?" asked Winnie, when they were sitting in front of the living room fire with their drinks. "Alf and I would love you to stay the night as well."

Bernard looked around the cosy room and at the two adults and small child. What a serene picture they made. No one would think, coming upon them now, of what manner of horror they had all lived, and were still living, through.

"If it's not too much trouble, I would be delighted to stay." Bernard could smell the stew simmering on the stove, and he realised he was very hungry.

Later, after supper, Bernard was sitting with Henry's grandparents in front of the fire, a large brandy by his side. The boy had long since gone to bed.

"I think Henry is a very bright little boy," said Bernard.

Winnie and Alf looked proud. "Oh, yes he is," said Winnie eagerly. "His schoolteacher said so only last week. One of the brightest in her class, she said. Already, and he's only been there a week."

"Yes, and I believe he's telling the truth about what happened to Carol and John," said Bernard. "He doesn't quite understand, but I believe he's beginning to, that their deaths were caused by something – " he paused.

"Something?" queried Alf, pouring him another brandy.

"Something not of this Earth."

"Are you trying to say they were killed by a ghost?" Alf looked bewildered, Winnie less so.

"I think you're right, Bernard," said Winnie. "I know you don't believe in ghosts, Alf, but I do. And, anyway, what other explanation is there?"

"Well, not ghosts, for God's sake, pardon me, Vicar," said Alf, grumpily. "A load of twaddle!"

"So, would you prefer to believe your grandson is a liar?"

"No, of course not. Just that he's mistaken, that's all. He was traumatised by what he saw."

"Well, if it wasn't ghosts," said Bernard calmly, "what or, rather, who do you think did kill them?"

Alf shrugged. "I don't know. A burglar caught in the act, probably."

Bernard sighed. "You're probably right. It's the more rational explanation, of course."

"Good," said Alf, obviously satisfied he had got his point across. Bernard could see who ruled the roost in that household, although he wouldn't have been surprised if Winnie wasn't the one who got her own way most of the time.

"Any more brandy in the bottle?" asked Bernard.

Alf laughed and poured him another generous measure.

PART THREE

136

MILES & CROSBY CONTRACTORS LTD
Wood Lane, Enfield
Tel: Enfield 6401

Mr B. Allardyce
18 Potters Way
Stevenage, Hertfordshire

15th January 1966

Dear Mr Allardyce,

This is to confirm your appointment as Site Supervisor for the project currently in progress at the Grenville site in Coldharbour Way, Earlsfield. We feel you are eminently suited to this role and have therefore agreed to the following:

1. You will reside at 57 Bockhampton Road, Wandsworth, being a suitable domicile for yourself and your family and being within travelling distance of the Grenville site. Miles & Crosby will be responsible for paying the first three months' rental, after which the responsibility will revert to yourself. If you then decide to remain in London after the project is finished, we will ensure that the property can be rented on to you afterwards. We would also hope that you remain in our employ as we have several more projects in the pipeline in the

South West London area which we would like you to oversee.

2. We will provide a car for you to travel to and from the site, and you may also use it for domestic purposes for as long as you are in our employ.

3. In addition to the increase in salary (please see attached contract for details), you will also receive luncheon vouchers to the value of two shillings daily.

Please read the enclosed contract carefully. Once you are satisfied with the conditions stipulated therein, please sign and date it, and return it to us in the s.a.e. provided.

May we take this opportunity to wish you every success in this new venture you are undertaking with us. We are a rapidly expanding company and are pleased to promote staff who we feel deserve it. As a valued member of our team, therefore, we are pleased to offer you this opportunity, which we trust will give you job satisfaction and security for the foreseeable future.

In the meantime, please do not hesitate to contact our Personnel Manager, Arthur Spinks, who will be happy to answer any queries or concerns you may have.

Yours faithfully,

Ronald Campbell Miles
Managing Director
Miles & Crosby Contractors Ltd

20

Mary and Bert Allardyce moved into 57 Bockhampton Road with their three young sons in February 1966. They had been married for five years when they moved from their Hertfordshire home to South London following Bert's promotion to Site Supervisor for a big building project his firm had undertaken. Miles & Crosby had been more than generous to him and his family, finding them a place to live and paying the first three months' rent. He had also received a large increase in salary and the offer of a company car. Bert had to turn this down, however, as he couldn't drive.

"Why don't you learn?" Mary had asked him, but Bert had come up with various unconvincing excuses for not doing so. It finally transpired that he wasn't confident behind the wheel, having crashed his father's car when he was sixteen. Having a car didn't matter anyway, they both agreed, as the site he had been put in charge of was within easy reach by public transport.

They had been content up until the move, living in a small, but adequate, cottage in Hertfordshire, but their burgeoning family soon made it necessary to find somewhere larger. So, Bert's promotion came at just the right time.

Mary was disappointed, however, when she first saw the house chosen for them by Bert's company. It was one of a mundane-looking terrace in a similarly mundane-looking street. There were no trees to be seen and, what greenery there was, was provided by the privet hedges uniformly allocated in the front gardens of each house. But at least their new house was a lot bigger than their little Hertfordshire cottage, even if 57 Bockhampton Road wasn't exactly her ideal home. It was nothing like the ones she coveted in her *House and Garden* magazine, but she supposed that was expecting too much.

The first thing that impressed itself on her the day they moved in, was the ornamental fireplace in the front room. Even though the whole place was filthy and needed cleaning out from top to bottom, there wasn't a speck of dirt on it anywhere. It seemed to give off an almost artificial glow, as if it was backlit somehow. But she didn't much like it, being far too ornate for her taste. She suggested to Bert they got rid of it and replace it with a plain stone or tiled hearth. Just like the ones in *House and Garden*. They were all the rage. But, as Bert pointed out, they were only renting the place, so they probably wouldn't be able to remove it.

That was another thing about the house she didn't like. The place was theirs, yet it wasn't. All her life she'd lived in rented accommodation. Wasn't it time they had a place of their own? she asked Bert. "We could afford a mortgage on the money you're earning now," she pointed out.

"Maybe one day, love," he had said. "When we've got a bit of capital behind us. Be patient for a few more years, eh? This'll do us, for now."

Bert Allardyce had been thrilled to get the promotion he knew he richly deserved. He had joined Miles & Crosby when they were just starting up, and it was mainly through his diligence and strong work ethic that the building company had thrived.

However, the new job had its drawbacks, the main one being the longer hours. The extra money and the new house were godsends, but Bert sometimes wondered if he had bitten off more than he could chew. He was so tired when he returned from the building site in the evenings, it was all he could do to keep a civil tongue in his head. Wasn't it enough that he slaved his guts out all day without having to come home to the kids screaming around the place, and his wife nagging the socks of him? He loved them all, of course he did, but didn't they realise that, when he got home, he deserved a bit of peace?

They had only been in the house a matter of weeks, but Mary was gradually warming to her new surroundings, even to the weird fireplace. It wasn't so bad, she decided, when you came to think about it. A fresh coat of paint here and there and a thorough clean out, that was all that was really needed. And it was roomy enough for the boys to run about in without getting under her feet. All in all, it wasn't such a bad bargain.

However, Bert's irritation with the kids surprised her. In their old home, they had crawled all over their doting father when he got home from work and he'd loved it. Since moving to Wandsworth, he was a changed man. Always biting her head off and telling the boys to be quiet. Maybe he'd taken on too much with this new job, she reasoned, but he'd soon get used to it and be back to his old self.

In the meantime, he was earning enough money for them to afford a few little luxuries, as well as being able to put a bit by for the mortgage. Maybe they could actually buy 57 Bockhampton Road eventually! She found she rather liked the idea. There were worse places.

The twins were already settled into the local infants' school and Terry, who was still too young for proper school, was taken off her hands by a nearby day nursery for a couple of hours, three times a week. That gave her plenty of time to fuss about the home, although sometimes she wondered if it was enough. She mentioned to her husband that she might take on some sort of part-time work when the boys were old enough, but he was dead set against it. Even the extra money didn't sway him.

In fact, it made him very angry. His moods seemed to be getting worse and Mary, who had always looked forward to Bert's return home from work each evening, began to dread hearing his key in the lock. Nothing seemed to please him. Either the potatoes weren't cooked properly, or the meat was too tough, or he'd tripped over one of the boys' toys in the hall. She began to worry that there was something seriously wrong with him but banished the idea as quickly as it came. He was just tired, that was all.

Then, one evening, as she was dishing up the evening meal, she noticed a strange look on his face. She had got used to seeing him frown at her over his evening paper, but this was something different. Something much more worrying. A dark shadow seemed to spread across his features and his eyes took on a flint-like hardness.

Her hand shook as she poured out the gravy.

"Careful, you silly cow," he muttered. "You're spilling it."

"Sorry, Bert," she said.

"Don't I have enough to contend with without you throwing my supper at me?"

Mary, smarting from the injustice of this remark, was about to point out to him that spilling a drop of gravy was hardly akin to throwing the whole meal at him, when she realised he was gripping the table cloth and twisting it in his hands. It was like he was imagining throttling her.

She was suddenly very afraid.

❦

Mary Allardyce's body lay in a crumpled heap by the fireplace. Bert, still holding the blood-stained poker, stared down at her. "Who is that woman lying there?" he wondered. He rested his free hand on the mantelpiece and tried to regain his breath. There was a mutilated corpse where his wife had just been standing. He couldn't understand what had happened.

He tottered over to the table and collapsed onto a chair. He threw the poker down and covered his face with his shaking hands. Tentatively, he looked through his fingers. Then he rubbed his eyes and looked again.

His wife was calling from the kitchen. "Do you want custard on your crumble, Bert?"

21

Mary put the crumble down in front of her husband. She had the sauce boat in her hand, and it was shaking. Would he accuse her of throwing the custard in his face? she wondered. But then she stopped. He was looking even more scared than she felt at that moment.

"Hey, Bert, what's wrong?" she said, carefully putting the sauce boat down on the table. "You look as if you've seen a ghost."

He turned his gaze towards her. "Mary, I've just had the weirdest experience."

"Are you all right? Shall I call the doctor?" She felt his brow. He didn't seem feverish.

"No, not that sort of experience. I'm not ill. I – I don't really know how to tell you this, but I just saw your dead body over by the fireplace. And I was standing over you with the murder weapon in my hand – that poker."

"Oh, Bert, how horrible!" she cried. Wish fulfilment, no doubt. Things were worse than she thought. However, she tried a reassuring smile. "You must have dozed off for a minute," she said. "You know how tired you are when you get home from work these days. Not a nice dream – but only a dream, for God's sake."

"No, you don't understand. It was *real*. You really *were* dead. I'd clobbered the life out of you with that poker. There was blood all over your face and head."

"Don't be silly, how is that possible? I've been in the kitchen clearing away the supper things and taking the crumble out of the oven. Look, it's done to a turn. I would have noticed if you'd hit me with the poker." She tried to make a joke of it but didn't really feel like laughing.

Bert took her hand. "Oh Mary, I must be going mad. Perhaps I need to see a doctor or something."

"Don't worry, love. You just had a particularly vivid nightmare, that's all." The sort of doctor he needed, she began to think, wasn't a bog standard GP. The sort he needed, he wouldn't go near if you paid him. She knew her Bert. She stroked his hair and kissed his bald spot. "Don't worry anymore. Eat your crumble."

Bert's appetite seemed to have completely deserted him. He poured the custard over the crumble and moved the food around with his spoon. His wife could certainly cook a good crumble, but he couldn't touch it now. What had happened was not easily explained away. He knew what he had seen. It was real. Could it have been some sort of premonition?

She annoyed the life out of him when he came home each evening, which he couldn't understand, because, all day long, he thought about her and couldn't wait to see her again. He loved her so much. And the boys. They were his pride and joy. He bored them silly on the building site with his family snaps. So why did he feel such animosity when he came home to them? He really must be going mad.

And now this latest incident, or whatever it was. He'd definitely hit his wife. He had heard her skull crack as he smashed the poker down on her head, not once, not even twice, but three times. The relief he'd felt when he realised she was still alive, had been tempered with the knowledge that something almost outside of his natural experience had happened to him. And was still happening to him.

❧

Mary didn't know what to do to reassure him. There seemed to be only one thing to do. "Okay, Mr Allardyce. It's the doctors for you. Get your coat."

It was a rainy Friday morning and they were sitting at breakfast. "But I've got to get to the site before lunch. There's some scaffolding problems apparently."

"They're nothing to the problems inside your head, Bert. You're going to the doctor's first, I want no arguments or excuses. I've got Mrs Franklin to take the twins to school and look after Terry, so we can go right now as soon as you've finished your cornflakes."

"But what's supposed to be wrong with me?"

"I don't know, but something certainly is. You've not been yourself for ages, Bert, you know you haven't."

"But what can the doctor do? I haven't got a pain. No pill can get rid of what I'm feeling."

"I know, dear. But maybe he can refer you to someone who knows about these things." Mary began clearing the breakfast things from the table, all the while watching his reaction. What she had just said, she knew, would set him off at once.

"You mean a trick cyclist," he muttered. "Why don't you just come right out and say it? You think I'm going mad."

"No, Bert, of course I don't. But something's wrong and maybe a psychiatrist can get to the bottom of what's worrying you."

"I won't see one of them quacks," he stated. "I'll go and see MacTavish, if you like. But there's an end of it."

Well, she thought, that's a start. Perhaps their local GP, Robert MacTavish, could persuade him to see a psychiatrist. "All right. Have it your own way. We need to get going if we're going to be seen this side of Christmas as it is. You know how full his surgery gets."

"Okay," said Bert, chasing an obstinate cornflake around his dish. "I'd better call the site to let them know I'll be late."

They left the house ten minutes later and set off to the surgery two streets away. The rain was beating down heavily on their umbrella, and the grey skies seemed to match their mood. But, despite the weather, almost immediately Bert cheered up. He turned to his wife and smiled.

"Look, Mary, there's really nothing wrong with me. I was just tired and fell asleep for a minute and had that awful nightmare. We don't need to trouble the doctor."

"But that's the whole point," Mary said in exasperation. "You keep telling me you feel okay at work, it's only when you're at home you get moody and irritable. With us. Yet when we all went out last weekend to the pictures you were fine. Bought the boys ice creams and everything. You enjoyed the film, remember?"

"Of course, I remember. But I wasn't tired then. It was Saturday."

"Yes, I know," she said. "But then you got into a bad mood the minute we all got home. I think it's something to do with the house that sets you off."

"The house? How can it be the house? It's just bricks and mortar."

"Is it though? I think maybe we need an exorcist, not a medical opinion."

Bert stopped in his tracks. "What the hell are you talking about?"

"I'm just saying that, it's very queer that you feel all right away from the house. You just get in a mood when you're indoors with me and the kids. It's either the idea of living with us is depressing you or you feel some kind of negative force in there. That's what I think."

"For goodness sake, Mary," he grumbled, as the rain started to seep down the back of his neck. His wife was hogging the umbrella as usual. "You've been watching too many late night horror films."

Mary shrugged. "I don't know about that. All I know is something's not quite right about that house. I felt it almost from the beginning, although now I really like it. But, what's more to the point, I don't think you do."

"What you're really getting round to saying, in your usual long-winded way, is that you think our house is haunted or I'm possessed or something."

"Well, I'm not quite saying that, but there doesn't appear to be an easy rational explanation for the way you feel. You've also told me you keep feeling cold, when the central heating is on full blast, and I've usually stripped down to my vest and knickers! I tell you, Bert, the temperature's much too high for me and the boys. Either you're ill or there's another reason. Anyway, we're here now, so at least we can see if you're really ill or not."

They entered the surgery, glad to get out of the rain. Their relief from the weather was dampened when they saw the room was depressingly full of patients. Many were old and obviously unwell, if the constant coughing and phlegm-clearing were anything to go by. MacTavish certainly had his work cut out that morning.

"We'll be here forever, Mary," said Bert in despair. "These people look much more in need than me. Let's leave it for now."

But Mary was adamant. "We're staying. I'm not leaving here without something being sorted out for you. I can't stand another evening of you sitting there brooding and taking it out on me and the kids. And now you're having hallucinations – that's got to be the last straw!"

"I'm sorry, Mary. But just look at all these people. We'll be here forever. I really can't wait now. Let's come back this evening."

Mary sighed. "Oh, well, I suppose you're right. It doesn't look as if we'll be seen for ages yet. There ought to be an appointment system. But you'd better be home early. We need to get here before the crowd builds up again tonight."

As they huddled under the umbrella once more, Bert assured his wife that he would get away from work as soon as he could. "Now I must get to the building site before the scaffolding collapses," he told her, relinquishing the brolly to her as they parted company at the traffic lights. "See you later," he said as he pecked her on the cheek.

Mary watched her husband dash across the road after the disappearing bus. She just couldn't understand it. He was behaving quite normally now, but at least he was acknowledging something was wrong, which was a start. What was bothering now, however, was the nagging conviction that a doctor wasn't the answer to Bert's problem.

Then she had an idea. She would pay a visit to that nice vicar, the one who preached at St Stephen's Church, and ask him what he thought was the matter with Bert. There was something very unhealthy in her home, and it might be worth asking a man of the cloth what he thought could be done about it. In her mind, she had a picture of a fiery priest yelling at the unseen presence in her house, probably in Latin.

Maybe she had been reading too many horror stories and watching too many late night movies. But it wouldn't hurt to confide in someone whose job it was to listen, offer advice and, above all, wouldn't pour scorn on her theory. After all, if a religion based on a Virgin birth could be believed in, then surely a vicar would be open to other spiritual ideas.

She wasn't a regular churchgoer – just Christmas and Easter as a general rule. She had never been to one of Reverend Paltoquet's services, although they had all planned to go to the Easter Sunday service in a week's time. After all, they had only moved to Wandsworth a few weeks ago. Anyway, she would introduce herself to him now. Thinking this, she retraced her steps in the direction of the St Stephen's vicarage.

22

Mary needn't have worried. Reverend Bernard Paltoquet welcomed her warmly and instructed his housekeeper to bring them some tea. While she sipped the scalding brew, he went to his filing cabinet and withdrew a battered brown file, stuffed full of press cuttings and photocopies.

"This is my research into your house's history," he told her. "I think you need to know all about it, Mrs Allardyce."

Mary looked puzzled and just a little scared.

"Please, I can see I'm making you worry. I'm sorry," he said. He paused before continuing. "This file contains detailed information about what happened to the family who lived there before you."

Mary replaced her teacup in the saucer with a shaky hand. "Please, Vicar, tell me all you know. Don't hold anything back because you're afraid it will upset or scare me. You see, I'm very worried about my husband. He thinks I'm making a fuss, but I know there's something wrong with him, and I'm sure it's connected to the house."

"How long have you lived there, Mrs Allardyce?"

"Mary – please. Only a few weeks. Bert's firm found him the accommodation in Bockhampton Road when he got offered promotion. Before that we lived in Stevenage."

"And how long has Bert been feeling depressed?"

"He began feeling unhappy almost straightaway. But we put it down to the stress of the work he's involved in. He's been given more responsibility than he's ever had before and he's very tired when he comes home in the evenings. But he only seems to be moody and irritable when he's at home. The minute he's outside he feels all right again. It happened like that this morning. We went out to go to the doctor's, and then he said there was nothing wrong with him. He felt fine."

"Could that just have been an excuse because he didn't want to visit the doctor?" asked Bernard.

"Oh, no, I'm sure it wasn't. Anyway, he came with me to the doctors without complaining."

"And what did the doctor say?"

"We didn't stay to see him. His surgery was full to bursting, and Bert had to get to the site. There's a scaffolding problem, apparently."

"Are you patients of Rob- er, Dr MacTavish? He's a very popular doctor in these parts." Bernard was smiling.

"Yes, so I understand. We joined his panel when we moved here, but haven't had cause to consult him until now, of course."

"Oh, quite. So, are you going to see him this evening instead?"

"Yes, that's the plan."

"Good idea. Now, where was I? Oh, yes. I was telling you about the family who had the house before you. They were living there in the early fifties. I had just taken up my incumbency here at St Stephen's about a year before they moved into Bockhampton Road. They were a nice couple. Mr and Mrs Freeman, and their son, Henry. He was about four or five at the time.

"They were regular churchgoers which endeared me to them straightaway." He smiled at Mary who looked embarrassed. "However, it soon became clear that all was not right with them. Mr Freeman was an extrovert character, hail-fellow-well-met type. The life and soul of the party, not to mention the local pub. He was at The Feathers most evenings, much to his wife's annoyance. But, despite that, they were a very loving couple and doted on little Henry.

"Then one Sunday they didn't come to church. I didn't think much of it at the time, but then I wondered if one of them was ill. They always attended, rain or shine, so I thought probably that was the case. Anyway, I decided to pay them a visit."

Bernard sat down opposite Mary and stirred his tea. "I'll never forget that day," he continued, munching a chocolate digestive. "It was cold and very wet. It was mid-November, and there was nothing to relieve the gloom. I knocked at the door and waited. It was eerily silent, so I thought that nobody was home. It then dawned on me that perhaps they had gone away for the weekend. I knew they sometimes visited their in-laws in Hoxton or Cambridge, but they usually told me the preceding Sunday if they wouldn't be there the next week. I thought they must just have forgotten to tell me, so I didn't feel worried then.

"But I felt something was wrong, nevertheless. The rain was incessant, and it was pitch-dark at two in the afternoon. However, I decided to return to the vicarage and get Mrs Harper to make me some tea. I'd never felt so depressed.

"But as I turned to walk back up the path, the door opened a crack and I saw little Henry hiding behind it. He was sobbing his heart out.

"'What's wrong, Henry?' I asked him. But he just cried even harder. I gently pushed past him and called out for his parents. But there was no answer. I walked into the living room and nearly passed out at what I saw. The bodies of Mr and Mrs Freeman were lying in front of the fireplace. Beside them was a blood-stained poker."

"When I finally got the boy to speak, all he said was: 'it was the pretty lady'."

"'The pretty lady'?" Mary repeated, puzzled.

"That's what he kept saying. Obviously, he was in deep shock, so I didn't think a lot of it at the time. I took him back to the vicarage with me and left him with Mrs Harper. I thought it best to call the police from my study as I didn't want to alarm the child any more than he already was. I suppose that was silly as the boy knew his parents were dead, although one never quite knows what goes on in a child's head, does one?"

"Certainly not in my boys' heads, that's for sure," smiled Mary.

"Ah, you have boys. How many?" asked Bernard.

"Three. The twins, who've just started school and a two-year-old. We all plan to come to the Easter service next week, by the way."

"Jolly good," said Bernard. "You will be most welcome. Anyway, I thought the boy might have thought his parents were pretending or something, so I called the police out of his earshot."

"Poor child," Mary said, blinking back a tear. "What a thing to happen to a little boy. So, what happened when the police arrived?"

"Well, apparently the only witness to the double slaying was Henry. I told the police that he was in no fit state to be interviewed then, but I relayed what he had told me about the 'pretty lady'. This got them off on a false trail, of course, although no one knew that at the time. It became clearer when I talked to Henry later on."

"Did you look after Henry then?"

"Yes. Mrs Harper and I refused to let him go with the social workers. As far as we were concerned, we were his foster parents until other members of his family had been informed.

"Anyway, from what Henry had been saying, I knew the chances of finding his 'pretty lady' in this world were not high. I didn't exactly believe in ghosts then, although I've always believed there are forces of evil as well as good at work everywhere, and always have been. Being a man of the cloth, you would expect me to believe that, wouldn't you?"

"So, did the police just give up in the end?"

"Yes. Well, there was nothing else they could do. Without any other witness to the murders, only Henry, they were stuck."

"What a terrible story," said Mary, shuddering.

Bernard Paltoquet stood to refill her teacup. "Yes," he said, "It is a terrible story, as you say. The double murder of Mr and Mrs John Freeman remains unsolved to this day."

Mary's hand shook as she tried to take a sip from her freshly filled cup. She set it down, her hand visibly shaking, making the saucer clatter against the milk jug on the little table, and spilling some of its contents.

"I – I'm sorry, Reverend," she said, taking out her hanky to mop up the milk. "I seem to make a habit of spilling things lately."

"Don't worry, Mary. Mrs Harper will see to it later."

"But what does it all mean?" she asked. "Did the little boy tell you all this? About his parents' murder, I mean."

"Well, after a fashion. It wasn't easy to work out what the child was saying, as I'm sure you can appreciate. He was in deep shock, and he was only about five at the time."

"Do you know what happened to him?" she asked.

"He went to stay with his mother's parents in Cambridge, where I understand he spent the rest of his childhood. He must be in his late teens now."

"Did you go and see him after?"

"Yes, I went once. About three months after the murders. He was being well looked after by his grandparents, and I think he was in the best place to recover from such a terrible experience. If one could ever recover from it, that is."

"He must have nightmares about it all the time."

"Yes, I'm sure. But time is a great healer and he was very young. The young are more resilient than we think sometimes. And self-preservation also comes into play here. His mind would probably have blocked out the worst aspects of what he saw, I should think."

"I hope you're right. But, Reverend, do you really think that the murders were as a result of supernatural causes? Are you telling me that you think my house is haunted?"

"I can only tell you what happened, Mary. The police couldn't find any motive for the murders, and no suspects either. They interviewed all the people the Freemans knew, but nothing of any use came to light."

Mary sat, stunned into silence. If, indeed, her house was haunted, would she or her husband, or even her children be safe? Could such a tragedy happen again? Bert was certainly acting very strangely and the reason for his behaviour could only be put down to the house. Of that much she was more certain than ever, after what Bernard had told her.

"What happened to the house after the Freemans' murder? Did it get sold on?"

"Eventually, yes. It was sold to the Council for a very nominal sum, I understand. The reputation of a house where two unexplained murders had taken place would have made it unsalable. I think they had the idea of demolishing it and rebuilding a new house in its place. But somehow they never got round to it, probably through lack of funds. It's been empty for about fourteen or fifteen years – until you and your family moved in, in fact."

"Did you find out anything about the history of the house?" asked Mary as she rose to leave.

"Actually, I've more or less made it my life's work. I've been researching the house's history for some time now, and can trace it back to around the 1890s, when a doctor and his wife lived there."

"What did you find out about them?"

"Oh, it's all very patchy so far," he said. "I hope to uncover some more information soon, though. If I'm right in my suspicions, I think the story of the doctor's wife will reveal the key to the whole mystery."

"Do you think it's safe to stay there, Reverend?"

"Where else can you go, my dear Mary?"

"Well, that's the problem. I'm more worried about my children than anything else. Do you think they're safe?"

"I wish I knew," sighed Bernard Paltoquet. "I really wish I knew."

23

Mary was waiting for Bert at the front door when he returned that evening. She hadn't long come back from visiting Bernard, and the idea of going to see the doctor didn't seem such a good one now. What would be the point? MacTavish might be good at curing aches and pains, but he wasn't equipped to banish ghosts. On the other hand, until Bert was convinced he wasn't ill and that there was something wrong with the house, they might just as well go and see him.

"Hello, Bert," she greeted him. "Shall we just get straight round to MacTavish? Before you change your mind."

"But I'd like a cup of tea before we go, Mary love."

"Sorry, Bert. Not now. When we get back. I've got your favourite for supper – steak and kidney pudding."

"That's nice," he said. "But I'm spitting feathers. Surely a quick cup of tea's okay?"

"Look, Bert. I've got something to tell you, and I'd rather you didn't go in the house yet."

Bert looked at her quizzically. "Why ever not? Oh, I suppose you think I'll go all moody again. Well, I won't. I feel fine. Now give us a kiss and then a cup of tea."

Mary could almost believe her Bert was his normal self again. And, of course, he was. But the minute he got inside the house, he'd be sure to go downhill again and, long before the supper was on the table, he'd be carping and moaning his head off as usual. She just couldn't stand much more of it.

"Where are the boys?" he asked, as Mary still barred his way inside the house.

"Next door," she told him. Mrs Franklin had been surprised when Mary had asked her to look after them again so soon after asking the same favour that morning. But she was a good-hearted soul, having two of her own, and agreed.

"They'll think they live there at this rate," he laughed.

"She knows I'd do the same for her," said Mary. "Now, listen, Bert, I saw the vicar today. I told him about the effect the house was having on you."

"You did what? Why on earth did you tell the vicar? We don't even know him! What's it to do with him, anyway?"

"Well, more than you think, Bert. He knows us, and he knows about our house."

"He does? What about our house?"

"Well, I think you'll find it very interesting. He basically thinks that there's nothing wrong with you. That's the good news."

"Okay. So, what's the bad?"

"Look, try not to be so sceptical."

"You're going to tell me that he thinks our house is haunted, aren't you?"

"Well, yes, as a matter of fact I am. He knows a bit about the history of this house and what's happened here in the past."

"What a load of rubbish! I'm not falling for that one. And if I'm supposed to be being haunted, why not you too? Or the kids?"

"I don't know, Bert," she sighed. That was something that had been puzzling her, too. "But, listen, he said that there's a history of hauntings in this house dating back to the late 1890s."

"How does he know all this?"

"Apparently, he got quite interested in the history of this house because of the people who lived here before us. He was quite close to them."

"What happened to them? Did he tell you?"

"Yes, he did. And I think you need to know all about them before you go back into the house. I'll tell you on the way to the doctors."

"But, according to you, I don't need to see the doctor as I'm not ill after all. Just possessed." He gave an ironic laugh.

Mary put her arm through his as they set off down the path. "It's best to make sure you're not ill first, before we have to accept that it's something more sinister," she said.

By the time they reached the doctor's surgery, Bert was fully apprised of what Bernard had told Mary. It was a load of bunkum, wasn't it? Not about the awful murders, of course, but how such events could be affecting him, which was what his wife, not to mention the vicar, was implying. Still, it would certainly explain why he felt so cold all the time and why he only felt depressed when in the house.

The surgery wasn't so full as earlier that day, but they would have at least a half-hour wait. Mary flicked through her favourite *House and Garden* magazine, while Bert paced impatiently up and down.

"Please calm down, Bert. The doctor won't be long," said Mary, looking up from an 18th century-style bathroom on page 56 of the magazine. "Here, Bert, look at this. Wouldn't you like to wallow in a bath like this?"

"Not in our house, I wouldn't. It's cold enough without sitting for hours in a steel bath," he grumbled.

"Come on, Bert. Don't think about the house now. We'll beat it, don't worry. After all, ghosts can't physically harm you, can they?"

"God knows, Mary. I wish you hadn't told me all that about that poor little boy in our house. To think he saw his parents murdered in our very front room. And not so long ago, either."

They were speaking in low tones, but they noticed that one or two of the waiting patients were eyeing them curiously.

Mary pulled him down into the seat beside her. "Sit still, for God's sake. We're being stared at."

Dr MacTavish finally came out to usher them into his surgery. It was a comfortable, well-furnished room, designed to put people at their ease. There was a fire in the hearth and, above it, the mantelpiece was arrayed with empty miniature whisky bottles. The doctor himself was a tall, weather-beaten Scotsman in his early fifties, with sandy, slicked-down hair and spectacles perched precariously on a hawk-like nose. His naturally severe expression melted into a surprisingly pleasant welcoming smile as he greeted the Allardyces.

"So, what brings you to my surgery today?" He spoke in a soft, vaguely Scots burr, designed to soothe. Although a Scotsman by birth, his family had left Edinburgh for London when he was six, so little of his native accent remained. Except when it was needed.

Bert began to speak, but Mary took over. "My husband's not been himself lately, Doctor. I think he's suffering from depression. And his job is very taxing. He comes home every night really tired and irritable."

Bert wondered why Mary hadn't mentioned what she felt was the real reason for his malaise, but then he supposed that doctors were men of science who probably wouldn't take kindly to talk of things going bump in the night. His wife therefore, very sensibly, had decided not to divulge any of her real misgivings to MacTavish.

It was ironic, however, that, if she had told the good doctor what was really on their minds, she would have found a sympathetic ear. Robert MacTavish was a regular attendee at séances and had read up on the supernatural in some detail. He would have relished the story of Mary's 'haunted house' theory but, as it was, they were just another couple wasting his time. What could he do for Bert besides advising lots of rest and prescribing a fairly useless tonic?

"Aye, I see," he said as Mary finished speaking. Bert, meanwhile, had remained silent. The man looked tired, but not unduly. MacTavish went through the motions of taking his blood pressure, checking his pulse and examining his pupils. The man seemed healthy enough to him.

He scribbled on his prescription pad. "Take a spoonful of this three times a day, and if you don't feel better in a week or so, come and see me again."

Bert took the prescription and looked hesitantly at him and then at Mary, who coughed and rose to leave. "Thank you doctor," she said. "Come on Bert, we might just catch the chemists if we hurry."

MacTavish watched the couple go out the back door of his surgery into the street. He had seen something strange in Bert's eyes and it puzzled him. He was sure the man wanted to confide something to him, but it was obvious his wife didn't want him to. Still, he was much too busy to wonder if Bert Allardyce had something more serious than just tiredness. His cursory examination hadn't shown up anything of significance. He put Bert's file to one side and buzzed in the next patient.

ᴂ

Bert turned to Mary as they left the surgery. "Why didn't you let me tell him about the effect the house was having on me? He might have had some suggestions or advice to give."

"He might and, then again, he might not. Honestly, Bert, do you think he would have had any sympathy with us if we'd told him all that? I only wanted you to see him so that we can eliminate anything physical."

As they reached the front door of number 57, Mary noticed Bert was visibly shaking. "I don't think I can go in there, Mary. Not yet. I feel terrible."

"Oh Bert, this is awful! It's your home, for God's sake. Come on, gently does it." With that, Mary took her husband's trembling hand and led him into the hall. He leaned against the wall, sweat pouring from his forehead.

"What are you feeling now, Bert? Can you say?"

"No – no – I can't! It's too terrible to tell you. It's much worse this evening. I've never felt this bad before." He grabbed her by the throat, as if about to strangle her. Then he pushed her away from him and she landed on the floor. Ignoring the pain in her backside, she scrambled up quickly and ran into the kitchen, slamming the door after her.

She leaned against the door, breathing quickly. She could feel her heart pounding. At least the boys weren't here. That was a blessing. She could hear Bert blundering about in the hall and then his feet on the stairs. He was going to bed. At least she hoped he was. What should she do? Call the police? No, that was ridiculous. Bert wouldn't really harm her. No, of course he wouldn't.

But then she remembered his dream, the dream he said seemed so real. Was it a premonition? Was something awful really going to happen to her? Something as awful as what happened here only a few years back? Suddenly, she felt unable to move. There was nothing to be done but wait.

24

When Dr Robert MacTavish finished his Friday evening surgery he found himself at a loose end. A bachelor from choice, he did very well being looked after by his efficient and doting housekeeper, Lucy Carter, although he sometimes felt the lack of other female company. But mostly he preferred the company of men, purely on a platonic basis, and liked nothing more than a companionable drink and smoke with his old friend, Bernie Paltoquet. He would just see if the good fellow was at home to callers this evening, after all it was only eight-thirty.

The vicar himself answered the door. "Hello, Robbie," he greeted him, smiling. "Come on in and have a 'wee dram' with me, won't you? I could do with a chat."

"I'd be delighted," said the doctor.

The living room looked cosy and inviting after the rain of the day. It had stopped, but a chill was definitely in the air. Robbie rubbed his hands before the blazing fire that the vicarage always seemed to have, rain or shine, summer or winter.

"Have you just finished surgery?" Bernard asked when they were both ensconced in comfy armchairs by the fire with their drinks of choice. Robbie's was the Glenfiddich that Bernard kept hidden at the back of the sideboard away from the prying eyes of his housekeeper, Mrs Harper. She didn't approve of strong liquor although she allowed Bernard, rather grudgingly, an occasional sweet sherry.

"Yes. It was the usual coughs, stomach aches, headaches and imagined illnesses," sighed Robbie. "All except for one man."

"Oh? You look puzzled."

"Well, to tell you the truth I am a bit. The man came with his wife and he started to tell me what was wrong when she jumped in and said he'd been overworking and was tired all the time. But I think he was going to say something else."

"You mean he was going to tell you something that his wife obviously didn't want him to tell you?"

"Yes, that's what it seemed like to me. Of course, it could just have been my imagination, or simply an embarrassing 'man's complaint'. But I don't think that was really at the bottom of it."

"Why?" asked Bernard.

"Oh, nothing specific. But you know me, Bernie, I always try to find a more interesting explanation when a more mundane one is much more likely."

"I don't think you do that. If you felt something was wrong, I'm sure there was some foundation for it. And, I mean this in the kindest possible way, Robbie, you're not exactly the most imaginative person in the world, are you?"

Robbie laughed. It was hard to take offence at anything his friend the vicar said. It was something in the inflection of his tone or maybe just his innocent baby face. "Well, no, I suppose not. Anyway, there's nothing much I can do about it unless he comes to see me on his own."

"No, that's right, you can't. Mind you, I had a strange visit this afternoon myself. It would have interested you, Robbie, I think. She's new to the district and hasn't been to my services before, although she said she and her family would be coming to the Easter service. I hope so."

Robbie raised a bushy eyebrow at him. "And you could do with a few more 'bums on seats' in your congregation, couldn't you?"

Bernard sighed. "Yes. But it's the same everywhere. People seem more interested in worshipping those Beatles than God."

"You've hit the nail on the head, there, Bernie. Anyway, go on. Tell me all about your 'strange' visitor."

"Well, she wasn't strange herself, but she certainly had something strange to tell me. She said she was very worried about her husband's state of mind. They live in that house in Bockhampton Road, you know, the one where that awful double murder took place about fourteen years ago."

"That's it!" Robbie jumped up and hit his forehead in sudden enlightenment. "No wonder I was concerned. That's where the couple live! 57 Bockhampton Road! I remember glancing at their address after I'd showed them in, but it didn't hit me then."

"Of course!" Bernard looked animated now. "Mrs Allardyce told me she and her husband were going to see you this evening."

"No wonder I sensed something was wrong," said Robbie. "So, what did Mrs Allardyce have to say?"

"Well, she just told me how moody her husband was when he got home at night, but that these moods only seemed to affect him at home. Not at work, the pub, or anywhere else."

"So then you told her about what had happened to the people who occupied the house before them?"

"Exactly," said Bernard.

"So it looks as if that bloody place is up to its old tricks again," said Robbie, thoughtfully. "I wish they'd confided in me. I prescribed Allardyce a tonic, can you believe that? Much good it'll do him."

"Oh dear," said Bernard. "I think they're in real danger – at least one of them is, although it could be all of them. Hopefully not the children."

"Children?" Robbie finished off his whisky, smacking his lips.

"Yes. They've got three boys. All five or under. Poor things."

"Good God! Do you think we should go and see them now? As you say, they could be in danger." Robbie was more a man of action than Bernard, and he was already on his feet.

"That's not a bad idea," said Bernard, more cautiously. "Except, they may resent our interference. Besides, Mrs Allardyce will know I've confided in you,

172

and that I'd betrayed her confidence. And it was obvious she didn't want you to know, by what you've just told me."

"Oh, hang all that," said Robbie with impatience. "It could be a matter of life and death, Bernie.

"Yes, you're right, of course." Bernard tapped his pipe out on the mantelpiece in preparation for leaving. "I hope you're wrong, though, because.…"

Robbie pushed him roughly out of the door. "Because what?"

"Because, if you're not, I believe Bert Allardyce is about to murder his wife."

25

"I've been meaning to do this for ages. These privets don't half creep up on you, don't they?" The man was leaning over the incalcitrant hedge, shears in his hand.

Bernard smiled. He recognised one of his regular churchgoers, Brian Franklin. "Hello, Brian, how are you?"

"Very well, thank you, Vicar. You looking for Bert? Or Mary?"

Bernard and Robbie had been relieved to find both Allardyces out when they arrived at 57 Bockhampton Road just after eight o'clock that evening. They had probably gone to the pictures.

"Well, both, actually. We didn't say we were coming, so no harm done. We'll catch up with them later," said Bernard.

"Do you know where they've gone?" Robbie asked Mr Franklin.

"Well, I know Bert's gone to the Bricklayer's. Mary wasn't with him, though. Not sure where *she* is. My wife still has the kids, you know."

"Oh," said Bernard. "Are you looking after them this evening?" This corroborated his theory that the Allardyces were at the pictures.

"Yes. Well, actually my wife's a bit cross," he said, leaning further forward and crushing his privet into submission in the process. "Mary left them with Jean while she and Bert went to the docs – oh, they were coming to see you, Doc." The light of recognition was in Brian's eyes. The evening was overcast, but there was still enough light to see Robbie's face, as well as the privet, apparently.

"Yes. Well, didn't they come back?"

"That's just it. We heard them come in and my Jean was getting the kids ready to return them when Bert came out again."

"So?" Robbie recognised Brian Franklin now. One of the worst hypochondriacs on his panel. "Why didn't she return them?"

"She tried. But when she took them round, the place was in darkness and Mary didn't answer. She must've gone with Bert, although I can't say I saw her go. And it's a bit rich, going to the pub and saddling us with their kids all night. We've got two of our own, which is enough."

Bernard and Robbie thanked the man and, leaving him muttering to himself, they hurried as one man to the Bricklayer's Arms.

"Let's hope that's where they are," said Robbie, distinctly alarmed.

"Oh, I'm sure they are," said Bernard, a little out of breath in his attempt to keep pace with his friend's longer strides. "He just didn't see her go, that's all."

"That man wouldn't miss anything," said Robbie grimly. "Why would he be trimming his hedge at this time of night, if he wasn't being nosy?"

Bernard, too out of breath to speak now, just nodded, as they arrived at the door of the Bricklayer's Arms.

The pub was packed which wasn't unusual at the end of the working week. Robbie grinned at his friend. "I bet you wish all the regulars here attended your church, eh Bernie?"

Bernard sighed. "In a perfect world, dear friend. Come to think of it, I haven't seen you at my Sunday services very much lately."

MacTavish gave an embarrassed cough. "You know what it's like, Bernie. I'm often called out to see patients on Sundays – I can't always get there in time."

"Don't worry, Robbie. I was only teasing. You do a great job, and I'm sure your patients are very grateful. It seems that more and more doctors are employing locums these days. At least you only use them when you go on holiday."

"I don't believe in letting other people do my job for me," said Robbie, elbowing his way through the crowd towards the bar. At first it was impossible to distinguish anyone amongst the dense mob, but as their eyes adjusted, they caught sight of Bert. He was propping up the bar, chatting to one of the pretty barmaids, obviously enjoying himself immensely. There was no sign of his wife, which was just as well, as it was flirting outrageously.

As they reached him, they could hear him telling her about his daring feats of scaffold climbing. Bernard looked at Robbie, and they both smiled knowingly.

What man didn't like to impress a pretty girl with his tales of derring-do? They tapped him on the shoulder, and Bert turned to see both his vicar and his doctor eyeing him with some amusement.

"Hello," he said, surprised at the interruption from so unexpected a quarter and splashing his beer over his hand as he clumsily put his pint down on the bar.

"Hello, Mr Allardyce," said Bernard. "Do you know me? Reverend Paltoquet?"

"Er yes, Vicar," said Bert, clumsily mopping his hand with his hanky. "We – we'll be coming to church next week. We've not been before as we've not been in Wandsworth long."

"It's all right," laughed Bernard, "I've not come to strong-arm you to a service tonight."

"Oh, no, I didn't think – you meant, er, I just thought I'd mention it, that's all. My wife told me she'd been to see you. What's up? Is something wrong? Has Mary sent you to find me? Is she all right? Is it one of the boys?"

"Mary's fine, as far as we know. The boys, too," Robbie informed him. "Are you feeling a bit better now, Bert? Did you manage to catch the chemist's?"

"Er, no, it was shut," said Bert, a guilty look on his face.

"Well you seem happy enough now, I must say," said Robbie with a sly wink at Bernard. "Where *is* your lovely wife, by the way? Is she not joining you?" He tried to make this enquiry sound casual, but there was an anxious edge to his voice that didn't escape Bert.

"I left her clearing up the supper things. She was going to collect the boys and then I think she planned to watch the play on the telly after. Why?" he asked.

"So, she's definitely at home, then?" said Bernard, giving Robbie a quick look.

Bert nodded. "Of course, where else would she be?"

"We went round to your house before coming on here and – "

"I assumed Mary had told you I was here?"

"Well, actually no. We got no answer. It was your neighbour, Brian Franklin, who told us he'd seen you head off here."

"He's a nosy old sod, that one. But he doesn't mean any harm. You say Mary didn't answer?" Bert looked worried now.

"No. And your neighbour seemed annoyed that you hadn't collected the boys."

"Not collected them?" Bert finished his pint in one swallow. "I'm going home right now. Are you coming?" He looked from one to the other of them. "Please?" His worried expression had changed to one of fear.

They didn't need asking twice. Bernard and Robbie followed the doctor out of the pub.

≈

"I'm sure she's fine," Bert was saying as they rushed along.

"Of course, she is," agreed Bernard. Robbie, hands thrust deep into his pockets, said nothing.

It had started to rain again, as they approached 57 Bockhampton Road. It was still in total darkness. There was no sign, either, of Brian Franklin who had either finished pruning for the evening or had been sent indoors by the rain.

They walked slowly up the path, each man deep in his own thoughts. Now they were there, they weren't anxious to have their fears proved right. After hesitating for a moment, Bert turned the key in the lock and pushed open the door. He called out to his wife, his voice echoing eerily in the darkness of the hall. There was a faint smell of brussel sprouts and something unnameable. If fear had a smell, that was it.

The three men remained standing in the hall for a few minutes, not speaking. Finally, Bert turned on the light and in the sudden glare they saw that the door on the right was firmly closed.

He cleared his throat. "That's funny," he said. "Mary never shuts that door, in case one of the boys wakes up and wants something."

Gingerly, he moved towards the room and paused with his hand on the door knob. "I don't want to go in there," he said. "I *know* what we're going to find."

Bernard put his hand on his shoulder. "Come now, Bert. It's just an empty room. Mary must be out. She's probably gone to fetch the boys."

Bert didn't reply but continued to dither outside the living room door.

Robbie broke in. "Let's get it over with. We're three silly sods. What on earth could have happened to her, really? As Bernie said, she's probably at your neighbours."

Bert smiled wanly. "I don't think either of you really believe that." But he hesitated no longer. He turned the handle and opened the door. Although the room was in darkness, there was a glow from the fireplace that wasn't coming from the dying embers in the grate. Bert reached for the switch and a hundred-watt light bulb lit up the scene more clearly.

In front of the fireplace was Mary Allardyce's lifeless body, a blood-stained poker by her side. She was lying in exactly the same position as Bert had seen in his premonition.

26

It wasn't long before Bert was charged with his wife's murder, with Bernard and Robbie unable to bear witness to where he was between six-thirty and eight o'clock, the time when the pathologist estimated the death had occurred. Robbie could, of course, vouch for Mary being alive at six o'clock when he had seen her with Bert at his surgery. Both men could also account for Bert after eight o'clock when they met him in the Bricklayer's Arms. But, no matter how many times they asserted that Bert wasn't a wife murderer, it had made no difference.

Of course, the police couldn't just take their word for it, even though Bernard and Robbie were respectable professional men with a standing in the neighbourhood. When tasked with providing an alternative explanation for the murder, a poker wielded by an unseen assailant was unlikely to cut any ice with the constabulary. They both knew that, but it was hard on poor Bert.

Bernard knew, without a shadow of a doubt, that Bert was innocent. Even though his dreadful mood swings could have accounted for him taking the poker to Mary, the man would have been hardly likely to kill his wife and then turn up at the Bricklayer's as if nothing had happened, smiling cheerfully and chatting up the barmaids. Bert Allardyce was no killer. Besides, the coincidence of yet another murder in 57 Bockhampton Road couldn't be easily brushed aside.

∽

It was the week before Christmas when Bernard arrived at Cambridge train station once more. The last time he had been there was over fourteen years ago, when he had been met by the charming Maltraverses, and he had talked to little Henry Freeman in their pretty garden in Longstanton. Now, here he was again, waiting to be picked up by Alf Maltravers in almost identical circumstances to the first time.

He had told Robbie of his intention to see Henry again to try to find out if time and maturity had helped him recollect any more details about that fateful evening when his parents had been done to death in front of his eyes. If he could remember anything, anything at all, that would help the police with their enquiries into this latest tragedy, then it wouldn't have been a wasted visit. It was just a shame it was in such sad circumstances, as otherwise it would have been delightful to see them all again.

It was Henry Freeman himself who greeted him and escorted him out of the station to his waiting car.

"How do you do, sir?" the young man said. "I'm so pleased to see you again. It gives me a chance to thank you for all your letters. I always looked forward to receiving them. They really helped me." He shook Bernard's hand warmly.

Bernard's eyes were gladdened at the sight of the tall, good-looking boy in front of him. He had recognised Henry immediately from the recent photo he had sent him, but it hadn't done him justice. His dark-brown hair reached fashionably over his collar, like the Beatles, and his top lip had the first sprouting of a moustache à la Paul McCartney. Must be fighting them off with clubs, thought Bernard, as he prepared to sit in the passenger seat.

"Do hop in. Sorry about the mess," said Henry, stowing Bernard's overnight bag in the boot of his rather beaten-up red mini.

Bernard smiled as he removed the debris of several crisp packets and an empty Tizer bottle before sitting down. "How have you been keeping? How are your grandparents?"

"They're both fine and looking forward to seeing you again. They've killed the proverbial fatted calf for your visit, by the way."

"How nice," said Bernard, remembering Winnie Allardyce's delicious stew on his last visit. "I understand that you've got a place at Cambridge University, young man. Congratulations."

"Thanks. I'm taking a year out, though. I want to go to India and Australia before I give up three years of my life to study. My girlfriend and I have it all planned, and we're leaving shortly after Christmas. We're really looking forward to it."

Bernard eyed the young man fondly as he watched him expertly negotiate a round-about and a one-way system.

"What are you going to study at Cambridge, by the way?"

"Modern languages. I want to become bilingual, at the very least. If I can perfect my schoolboy French and then get familiar with Spanish and German as well, I can go and work anywhere in Europe or even South America."

"That's great, Henry. What sort of work did you have in mind?"

"Not sure yet. Possibly economics or politics. I haven't really decided."

"Well, there's plenty of time."

Bernard was pleased Henry had turned out so well, but he noticed a sad, faraway look in those tender brown eyes. He dreaded having to bring up the subject of his parents' murders at some point during his short visit, and almost wished he didn't have to. It was only the thought of a miscarriage of justice, that kept him at the sticking point. But all that could wait awhile, he thought, and sat back to enjoy the drive to the Maltravers's pretty cottage, looking forward to a delicious supper and, given the season, the inevitable mince pies.

❧

Bernard sipped the mulled wine that was being copiously provided by the Maltraverses. The meal had been as delicious as he had expected and the company similarly as congenial.

He had been introduced to Henry's girlfriend, Maddie, later that day, and he had been no less delighted with her. Petite and pretty, she seemed the perfect adjunct to the handsome young man that Henry had become. No more marbles or stamp collecting for him, Bernard imagined.

Bernard was seated in the place of honour nearest the fire, and he let the pleasant atmosphere seep into him. Mrs Harper and the vicarage seemed a long way off at that moment. He and Robbie had planned to spend the festive season in each other's company with Bernard's housekeeper providing the meals. He had been looking forward to it, as Mrs Harper's cooking was easily on a par with Winnie Maltravers's. But the cosy family scene he was now enjoying reminded him wistfully of a family life he had never really known since his boyhood and probably wouldn't ever know now.

"Maddie's not keen on flying," Henry was saying. They had been discussing the young people's itinerary for their world trip. "So, we're travelling mainly by sea, train and coach. We'll see much more that way, as well."

Bernard nodded. "It will be a great adventure. You young people have so much more opportunity these days. When I was your age, you went from school to college, if you were good enough, then to paid employment. There was no such thing as 'gap years' then. I envy you."

Maddie grinned at him. "Go on," she goaded him affectionately. "I bet you had your moments."

Bernard wondered if that were really true. Not so many, he could count on the fingers of one hand. But he just smiled at her for reply. How lovely she was, he thought. And so sweet. She seemed to have taken to him just as much as he had taken to her. For the first time he could truthfully think, 'lucky old Henry'.

As the time approached ten-thirty, Maddie rose to leave. "I'd better be getting back," she said. "I've got a big day tomorrow. The Birmingham contingent's arriving – at least ten of them. Aunts, uncles, cousins. We're doing Christmas here this year. Mum and Dad are going spare trying to get everything organised in time."

Henry jumped up at once. "I'll drive you back," he said.

"Thanks. It's only a ten-minute walk, but it's very dark out there."

The young couple left the room, laughing happily together. "They make a handsome pair, don't they?" observed Alf.

"They do, indeed," agreed Bernard.

Winnie smiled indulgently. "Not only is she pretty, but she's the sweetest girl," she said. "I do hope they stay together. It would be lovely to see Henry settle down with her eventually."

"Steady – they're very young yet!" laughed Bernard. "Is she going to university too?"

"She's got a place at Sussex. Didn't get quite good enough 'A' Levels for Cambridge," Winnie said. "I don't suppose the relationship will survive the separation." She sighed.

"Well, who knows? They'll obviously make new friends at their respective universities. But there's always holidays and weekends."

"True. But you know how it is with the young folk."

Bernard knew only too well. He thought back to the time when he had it all before him. He had been up at Leeds and had met Sophie. She had been the one girl he would have married if things had been different.

"More wine?" Alf asked him. He could see Bernard had a faraway look in his eyes.

"Sorry?"

"I said more wine, Vicar?"

"Oh, yes please. Just a drop."

When his glass was replenished, Alf sat down beside him. Winnie had retired to the kitchen to finish the washing up. "Can I ask, Reverend, to what we owe the pleasure of this visit? Not that we're not happy to see you again."

"I thought it was about time I came to see Henry. I haven't seen him since he was a small boy."

"But why now?"

"Er, well…"

"I think I know why." Alf was serious now. He looked gravely at the vicar as he sipped his wine.

"Mince pies, anyone?" Winnie called from the kitchen.

"Oh, give it a rest, Winnie," Alf shouted back.

"I – I'd rather like one," Bernard said timidly. He knew what Alf was leading up to, and the interruption of yet another mince pie seemed a good idea while he collected his thoughts.

Once Bernard had a plate of hot mince pies in front of him, Alf continued undeterred. "There's been another murder in that house, hasn't there? I've seen the news and read it in the papers."

Bernard took a bite from a pie and nodded. "Well, yes, there's been another unexplained murder. I was with the husband when we found his wife's body. She was bludgeoned to death by the fireplace, just like your daughter and son-in-law were, the only difference being that Bert, the husband, has been charged with the murder. You see, there were no witnesses and he couldn't account for his movements when the murder was committed."

"Yes, I saw all that. What I hope is, you're not going to drag Henry through it all again. He's a happy boy now. He's met a lovely girl, he's going to Cambridge. You're not going to spoil it all for him, are you?"

"I sincerely hope not. But an innocent man is going to be convicted unless I can prove he didn't do it. Or at least cast enough doubt on his guilt for a jury to hopefully acquit him."

"I see that. But we're more concerned about Henry. His state of mind is erratic. He still has black periods when he remembers what happened."

"I do understand, Alf. I do really. But if we don't try and help Bert, we'll never get any closer to discovering the real motive for these crimes and, hopefully, stop any more from happening."

"You'll have to do that without Henry's help," said Alf with determination.

"Won't you just let me ask him if he'll tell the police what happened in his own words? It could help to convince them that Bert had nothing to do with his wife's death."

"Look, if the guy didn't do it, then I'm sorry. But there's no way I'll let Henry get involved. What happened, happened. It's all over and done with as far as Henry's concerned. Besides, he'll be out of the country the first week of January for a whole year. And a good thing too."

"Yes, for him, maybe. But don't you think it's up to Henry whether he helps or not? You can't make the decision for him. He's not five anymore."

"Oh, can't I?" Alf was getting angry now and he started to pace the room. "Look here, Reverend. I know you mean well and we'll always be grateful for what you did for Henry back then. But Henry's my and Win's responsibility now, and we'll decide what's best for him."

At that point, Winnie came into the room, wiping her hands on a tea towel. "What's going on? Why the raised voices?"

"The vicar here has come to ask Henry to go to the police and tell them what happened to his parents. He's trying to help this man accused of murdering his wife. We both think it's just a coincidence it happened in that bloody house, don't we, Win?"

Winnie looked unhappy but turned to Bernard with a friendly smile. "Alf is just worried about Henry," she said. "And you know I don't agree it's just a coincidence." She gave her husband a look that spoke volumes. "I think Henry *should* help, if he can. I don't think this man killed his wife either."

"Thank you, Winnie, for being so understanding," said Bernard. "I'm sure it's the right thing to do."

Just then the front door opened, and Henry's cheerful voice rang through the house. "Hi everyone, I'm back!" He bounced into the room, but soon sensed the awkward atmosphere. "Hey, what's up?"

Alf looked daggers at Bernard, silently forbidding him to tell him.

"Nothing at all, Henry, love," said Winnie, giving her grandson a hug. "I've got some hot mince pies for you."

❧

The next morning dawned bright and clear. Frost glistened on the branches of the apple tree that stood outside Bernard's bedroom window. He surveyed the scene with pleasure. The smell of Winnie's cooking wafted up the stairs, and he realised he was ravenous. It must be the country air, he thought. When he had bathed and dressed, he trotted down to the warm kitchen. Bacon and eggs were piled high on a steaming plate, together with mushrooms, tomatoes and fried bread.

"Good morning, Bernard. Do tuck in," said Winnie.

He rubbed his hands and sat down at the kitchen table. "Tea or coffee?" asked Winnie, placing a glass of freshly squeezed orange juice in front of him.

"Tea, please. Lovely! I'm going to enjoy this."

"You need a good breakfast inside you to start the day, especially on cold mornings like this. Henry's already had his and is in the garden refilling the bird feeders."

"I think I'll join him when I've eaten."

"You do that. Never mind what Alf says. He just can't get over Carol's death and he's scared that Henry will come to some sort of harm if he doesn't watch over him all the time. Understandable, I suppose, but Henry finds it a bit claustrophobic at times."

When Bernard had finished his breakfast, he strolled out into the garden to join his young friend who was inspecting an unusual-looking evergreen, stroking its leaves and cooing softly to it.

"Hello," Henry greeted him. "I hope you slept well. Was the bed comfortable?"

"Very. I slept like a log. What plant is that supposed to be?"

"A form of hemlock, I think," said Henry.

"Really? Poisonous, then?"

"I should think so," Henry laughed. "Anyway, let's go and sit on the bench and talk. Will you be warm enough in just a jacket?"

"I'm fine. The sun is quite warm for December," said Bernard. They sat in silence for several minutes, watching the blue tits and robins pecking at the feeders. Bernard remembered sitting on just this same bench all those years ago with a heartbroken little boy beside him and felt sad for a moment.

"These little chaps need feeding in winter, especially when it snows," said Henry tenderly.

"Do you know a lot about birds?"

"Only what I got from my 'Observer's Book of Birds' as a child," said Henry. "But they fascinate me. And we have all sorts of breeds come here all the year round so there's much to see. I love them."

After a couple more minutes of companionable silence, Bernard broached the subject that was in the air between them. "Henry, do you ever think about that awful time?" he asked gently.

"Of course, I do," said Henry vehemently. "I shall never forget it. How could I?"

"No, who could? Do you remember when I found you there and you told me certain things about what you saw?"

"I remember –"

"Since that time, do you have any reason to believe you could have been mistaken? Do you think your young mind just blotted out the worst of it? That you only saw what you could take in at such a tender age? Or that you simply imagined that 'pretty lady' as you called her?"

"I've often thought about it. But, all I can recall is the sight of my parents' dead bodies by the fireplace and that woman wielding the poker over them."

"Is there anything else you can remember? Please try to think. Anything at all that might help. Did this woman say anything, for example?"

"Well, I can't be sure. But I have a feeling she was sort of chanting something. Like she was in a trance."

"What did she look like?"

"She was the woman who I always saw around the house while I was growing up. Her and the children."

"So, do you now suppose they were actually ghosts or spirits haunting the place? I take it your parents never saw or heard them?"

"No, only me. I asked my mum what she thought of my playmates and she said they were sweet. But I suppose she was only humouring me."

"You were living in a haunted house, Henry," said Bernard, looking at him closely.

"Yes, I know."

"Do you think the attack on your parents was for some specific reason?"

"No. My parents were lovely people." Bernard could see Henry was close to tears now.

"You said just now that the woman was chanting something. Can you remember what that was?"

"I'd tell you, if I could," said Henry, wiping his nose with the back of his hand. He sniffed back further tears manfully. "Wait a minute, though," he said suddenly.

"What?"

"I vaguely remember something about 'being happy' and 'having no right to be'. Something like that."

"That would make sense. Maybe when the woman was alive she had a very unhappy life, or something awful happened to her, or she did something awful to someone else. They say that evil begets evil, don't they?"

"That's right. And something about 'the evil that men do lives after them'...."

"'The good is oft interred with their bones'," Bernard finished.

Henry shivered. "That seems the wrong way round, doesn't it?"

"You're right." Bernard smiled. Henry was so young, yet so wise. He had to grow up quickly, poor thing.

Bernard put his hand on his shoulder. "I suppose you know about the murder that took place in your house a few weeks ago?"

Henry shivered. "Yes, of course. I'm sure the man didn't do it, at least not if it happened in the way it happened to my parents."

"That's just the trouble," said Bernard. "We can't prove it. We – that is, my friend Dr MacTavish and myself – know the man in question and we're sure he didn't do it. That's why I came to see you to see if you could remember anything that might help convince the police they're barking up the wrong tree. Or at least cast a doubt in their minds."

Henry turned to Bernard with a serious expression on his face. "I would tell the police like a shot, if I thought it would help. But I don't see how all this vague stuff I saw as a child will be of any use."

Bernard had to agree with him. "I know, Henry. It was a silly idea of mine in the first place. All it's done is dredge the past up and made you unhappy."

"No, please don't worry about that. I've come to terms with it now. And, if I can do anything to help, I'd be more than happy to."

"Thank you, Henry, that's all I wanted to hear. I'll go to the police and tell them your story, although they'll have it all on record. The one thing I really wanted to make sure about is – er – "

"Yes, Bernard?"

"Will you be prepared to give evidence at Allardyce's trial?"

Henry looked very sad. "But what about my world trip?"

Bernard had forgotten about that. "Oh dear, of course. Never mind …."

"I'll cancel it! We can go after it's all over."

"Oh, Henry," said Bernard, tears starting in his eyes. "Thank you!"

"If I can prevent a miscarriage of justice, it will be worth postponing our trip."

They walked back to the house together, both of them now aware that the sun had disappeared and had left a viciously playful wind in its place.

"Nobody believes in ghosts these days, do they?" said Henry as they entered the house through the kitchen. "But they *do* exist!"

"Henry, I know they do. You're preaching to the converted," said Bernard with a sad smile.

27

As far as the police were concerned, the murder in 57 Bockhampton Road was an open-and-shut case. The husband did it. Bert Allardyce was to go to trial in three months and, in the meantime, was being detained at Her Majesty's pleasure.

One day, in early February, Bernard arrived at Wormwood Scrubs with his visitor's permit. Bert looked defeated and unkempt, a beaten man. Bernard sat down opposite him, the grill between them.

"Hello, Bert. How are you?" What a silly question, thought Bernard. The man's a wreck, and I don't know how to help him.

"As you see, Reverend. It's good of you to come and see me, especially as you hardly know me."

"Not at all – I would have come sooner but I've been trying to convince the police of your innocence. But, as you know, I've failed dismally. For that I'm deeply sorry."

"Thanks for all you've tried to do, anyway. No one else has bothered. But I could have told you you're wasting your time. The police don't go in for ghost stories – understandable, I suppose."

"All is not lost, Bert. We'll prove your innocence yet. Dr MacTavish and I will be called as witnesses and, our trump card, Henry Freeman will also give evidence for your defence. We'll convince the jury that you didn't do it, don't you worry."

"Who's Henry Freeman?"

Bernard proceeded to explain.

"The poor kid," said Bert. "What a dreadful thing to happen to someone so young. I want to be home with *my* boys, Reverend. I've only seen them a couple of times since being incarcerated here. They looked so unhappy. But, what's worse, I think they believe I killed their mother. So, even if I'm found not guilty, mud sticks."

"I know, I know." Bernard felt totally inadequate. Even if he assured him it wasn't the case, Bert wouldn't believe him. Besides, mud *did* stick and, unless the real murderer was found and convicted, it always would. And, of course, the real murderer, as far as Bernard was concerned, had been dead and buried for many years. "How are the boys, by the way? Who's looking after them?"

"They're staying with Mary's brother's family in Barnstaple. So, as you can imagine, I don't get many visits from them."

"Have you seen Mary's brother?"

"No. The boys came with my sister-in-law. A nice woman, but she clearly thought I was Jack the Ripper. They're probably filling the boys' heads with all sorts of wrong ideas about me. They don't mean to, I'd imagine, but nevertheless, what they believe must get through to them, the twins especially. I think Terry's too young to understand what's happened. I hope so, anyway. It's just so hard to take – that your own sons could believe something so awful of you."

Bernard's heart went out to him. It was one thing to be wrongly accused of murder, but quite another to have your own flesh and blood believe you capable of such a crime. But they were too young to know any better. If a grown-up told them black was white, they were at the age when they would believe it.

A bell rang, signalling the end of visiting time. Bernard stood up and gave Bert a not altogether convincing smile. "Chin up, Bert. All is not lost. You must believe that."

"Thanks again for coming."

"I'll come again soon, hopefully with some better news."

Bernard walked out of the room, along with the other visitors, deep in thought. He'd forgotten about the Allardyce children. They, like poor Henry before them, must be suffering deeply.

Bernard learned the dreadful news two days later. Mrs Harper had brought in the evening paper with his tea and buttered crumpets. What a treasure she was to him. So loyal. She cooked and cleaned, and her cooking alone was worth her weight (which was not inconsiderable) in gold. Who needed a wife, when he had a housekeeper like Mrs Harper? She did everything for him a wife would do, apart from sleeping with him and suing for divorce.

After he had finished his fourth crumpet, licked his buttery fingers and drained his teacup, he had picked up the evening paper. It was the best time of the day. The lamps lit, the fire glowing, and he had thought how perfectly content he would have been, if only he'd been able to help Bert Allardyce.

Then he had seen the headline, half-way down the second page of his evening paper:

ACCUSED MAN DIES OF HEART ATTACK WHILE AWAITING TRIAL

There had been no point in reading any further. Bert Allardyce had died of a broken heart – literally. He had phoned Robbie MacTavish at once but had been told by his housekeeper he was still seeing patients in his surgery. He had at least another hour to wait before he could talk it over with his friend.

When Robbie finally arrived, Bernard could tell by his face that he had also received the news of Bert's death.

"We weren't able to save him after all," said Robbie with a deep sigh. "What an utterly sad situation, especially for his boys. First, their mother is murdered, then their father is arrested and charged for the crime, and now they've lost him, too."

"You've summed it up only too well, Robbie. Here, down this," said Bernard handing him a glass of

Glenfiddich. "You need it." Bernard poured himself his usual tipple, a sweet sherry. "So do I."

They sat in front of the fire, not speaking for several minutes. The only noise was the comforting sound of the clock ticking on the mantelpiece and the logs falling in the hearth. Finally, Bernard broke the silence.

"Did Bert have any history of heart problems? Did you have any reason to believe he could be heading for a heart attack?"

"That's just it. I should have thought about that. I looked at his medical records when Bert came to visit me that evening. Just a cursory glance to see if there was anything I needed to look out for. I do that with all my patients."

"And?"

"Well, according to his notes, he'd had a bout of rheumatic fever when he was a child, which, as you probably know, can cause heart problems in later life."

"So you knew he had a weak heart?"

"I suppose I did. But I didn't think there was any danger, as long as he lived modestly and didn't overtax himself."

"But he was a builder – a manual labourer."

"Yes, but I understood that, since moving to the district, he was more of an overseer. He wasn't doing any actual building work as such. If he had been, I would have advised him against it."

"I see. But didn't you think about the strain he must have been under since the murder?"

Robbie nodded sadly, sipping his whisky and cradling the glass fondly. "I should have checked him over. I shall never forgive myself. I should at least have warned the police and saw that he got some medical attention while he was in prison."

Bernard leaned forward and patted his friend on the knee. "Don't blame yourself, Robbie. It might be for the best in the long run. Even if Bert was found not guilty, the stigma would remain, and probably his boys would never be sure of him again. I doubt if he'd have been able to live with that."

"You're probably right. Life is so cruel sometimes. Why can't we do something about that house now, Bernie?"

"Like what? Blow it up? Burn it down? I think the authorities might have something to say about that."

"I was thinking of something more in the exorcism line. What about Dorothy?"

Dorothy Plunkett was a close friend of both men, although she favoured Bernard as her first choice for life partner. Bernard knew this but, deep down, was unsure of his feelings towards her. He loved her like a sister, he had finally convinced himself.

"She's a psychic medium. She doesn't perform exorcisms. We need a bishop for that. Anyway, I've tried to contact her, but she's on some sort of countrywide tour at the moment."

"I still think it would be a good idea. If she could contact whatever's in that house, maybe she could help prevent another tragedy. I presume some other family will move into that house soon enough?"

"I don't think it's all that likely just yet. I mean, would you want to live in a house where a murder had just been committed?"

"Estate agents have a way of skimping over little details like that, Bernie."

"Only too true, my friend. Only too true."

The two friends sat on into the late evening with their drinks and pipes, chewing over the events of the past few days. Eventually they found refuge in a game of chess, but the tragedy that had befallen the Allardyce family was never very far from their thoughts.

PART FOUR

TO: robf@garfieldco.com; emmat@garfieldco.com; nitinp@garfieldco.com
FROM: jbracegirdle83@googlemail.com

Tues, 24/09/2009

Hi guys,

Thanks so much for visiting me the other day and for the card. I don't know when I'll be back at my desk as things are a bit sticky right now. Please pass on my thanks to Mike for his understanding. I know he wants me back at the end of next week, so I'll try and get my act together by then (LOL).

Don't quite know what to do at the moment, what with the police enquiries and me obviously the number one suspect. Thanks, by the way, for not taking sides although I'm sure there's a lot of speculation in the office. I hope I don't have to tell you I didn't do it, but – well, there you are. I've said it.

I want to get back to normality ASAP, of course, but I've got to sort my head out first. What happened is so horrible, I don't even think I really believe it did happen. I keep expecting Beth to text me any minute and tell me to stop being an idiot. If only she would.

Anyway, that's it for now. Your card has pride of place on the mantelpiece which never seems to get dirty. The rest of the place as you saw could do with fumigating.

Missing you lots,

Take care,

Jerry x

28

Harry Grimes stared out of the rain-spattered window that formed part of the Doggett and Finn's shop front and sighed for the umpteenth time. He had been in the estate agency business for nearly twenty years and had never known the property market so depressed. There'd been lean times, admittedly, but this recession was the worst he could ever remember. Why wasn't anybody interested in looking at the 'for sale' ads even? There were usually a few window-shoppers at least, and there were always some who came in, asked stupid questions and took away a few flyers to peruse at leisure. "Time wasters" he used to term them, but these days he would have been grateful for even a few of those.

He looked across at the two young people who made up the full complement of his staff. Barry John-Harrington had been with him the longest, the double-barrelled smart-arse. But he was a good salesman, he had to give him that. Eve Mason was a definite asset too, although for a very different reason. With that pretty face and those slim legs, she could sell pork pies to rabbis, she could. But, although they were both good at their job, even they couldn't pull off more than one sale a month between them, if that.

He glanced back at the window as Eve put his mid-morning coffee down in front of him. There was a young man staring at the ads and, it seemed, by the concentrated look on his face, he was serious about buying. Harry had a nose for a potential customer; he could always winkle them out from the time-wasters. No danger.

He studied the young man standing in the pouring rain, crouched under a broken umbrella, the spokes dangerously threatening people as they squeezed past him on the narrow pavement. He looked very young, now Harry came to think about it. Still, it didn't mean he didn't have the means to buy. He could have rich parents, or a job that paid enough for him to have been able to save for a mortgage. Mind you, thought Harry, you'd have to have been saving from the moment you came out of the womb to have enough to buy these days.

❦

Jerry Bracegirdle saw at once that the price of the flats on sale was way beyond his budget. He was about to go on his way when he noticed the estate agent eyeing him hopefully. Business not as brisk as usual, then? Poor man, he didn't think. Still, he thought, might as well go in and see if there was anything remotely within his budget.

He watched with amusement as Harry squirmed Uriah Heep-like to his feet and shook his hand. He even called him 'sir'.

"Hi," said Jerry, "I'm just looking at the moment. Are the properties advertised in your window typical of what's available? Because I really can't afford anything there."

"I'm afraid the flats in the window are all around the same sort of price, depending on location, number of bedrooms, decorative condition et cetera," Harry told him. "I'm sorry."

But, as Jerry shrugged and turned to leave, Barry John-Harrington spoke up. "What about that house in Bockhampton Road, Harry? Have you shown the gentleman that?"

Grimes smiled. "Of course. Thanks for reminding me." He took out a flyer from the bottom drawer of his filing cabinet. "This property might suit you, sir," he said, offering it to him. "This little terraced house is quite a bargain."

The young man took it from him tentatively. "This wasn't in the window, was it? I don't remember seeing it."

"Er, no. I'll be frank with you," said Harry, looking anything but. "It hasn't been a best-seller this one. As you can see there's an obvious reason for that."

Jerry studied the photo of a run-down terraced house, squashed in between two much smarter-looking dwellings. It certainly didn't seem very promising on the face of it. But he was desperate to leave home. His parents were driving him mad, trying to run his life for him. He had never stopped being their 'little boy', despite being all of twenty-five. Jerry knew he'd have to get a place of his own soon or be had up for patricide stroke matricide. Was there a word for killing both parents? he wondered idly.

"What do you think, sir?" Grimes prompted.

"Oh, sorry, I was miles away."

To say the house was uninviting was to understate the case by miles. Not only was it in a very dilapidated state, it looked strangely forbidding. It had an eerie air of abandonment about it which Jerry picked up just by looking at the photograph. Still, it had a roof and walls and, although it would need renovating from top to bottom to make it habitable, if the price was right, it'd be better than nothing. He'd soon have it knocked into shape. He was an optimist.

"Hmmm. It's very run-down, of course. What's the vendor asking for it?"

Harry riffled through his file. "The odd thing is that there *is* no asking price, as such," he said.

Jerry had the feeling the riffling wasn't necessary. This man knew all along that was the case. "What do you mean?"

"Just that. The vendors are living in Spain and just want shot of it. Any price you care to name will be considered. Within reason, of course."

"Of course." Jerry smiled. "What's the catch?"

"Catch?"

"Yes – catch. The property is obviously in need of a great deal of renovation, but it's certainly worth investing in, I should imagine. So, if I offer a price well below its market value and I'm accepted – well, there must be a catch."

"I think it's just that the owners are in need of ready cash to continue living the lifestyle they're used to in Spain. They've got property out there and it's in need of renovation too, so they need to get their hands on some money quickly."

"Hmmm. How long has it been on the market?"

"A fair while. Most people don't want to be bothered with refurbishment. They just want to move in as is. As long as there's a new fitted kitchen, modern bathroom, wooden floors throughout and magnolia on the walls, they're happy. Most people don't have much imagination."

"Okay," Jerry said. "I'll be interested to view at least. It can't do any harm to have a look at the place."

"Exactly!" Harry said.

"Can we go and see it now?" asked Jerry, aware of how eager the man was. Something wasn't quite right, but it couldn't do any harm to go and see it. Could it?

"Certainly! Barry – can you get me the keys to 57, please."

Barry disappeared into the back of the shop, returning swiftly with a set of keys. Harry pocketed them.

"There. All set. Let's go, young man. It's not far from here. Shall we walk as it's stopped raining, or would you rather we drove there?"

"Walking's fine. Lead on"

❧

After they'd left, Barry turned to Eve and grinned. "There goes a sucker if ever there was one."

Eve gave him a dirty look. Jerry had made a very favourable impression on her and she didn't like the idea of him being hoodwinked. "Shut up, Barry. Why did you mention that house? You know the stories about it as well as I do. I wouldn't want my worst enemy to live there – well, apart from you, of course."

"I love you too," Barry grinned, and blew her a kiss. "Don't you want to sell? That's what we're in business to do, after all."

"I just don't think it's right not to tell him, that's all. Then it's up to him whether he buys it or not. At least he'd know."

"Oh, come off it, Eve. We don't want to put people off. How on earth are we supposed to make a living otherwise?"

"Do you have to?"

"Do I have to, what?"

"Make a living, arsehole."

"Well, this is it. What d'you think?"

"I thought the photo was bad, but the real thing is much worse."

"Yes, well that's why I wasn't going to bother to lie to you."

"Let's go in, anyway." Jerry gritted his teeth. No way could he see himself living in this dump. It would take him a lifetime to make the place habitable. It would also cost a fortune to bring it up to scratch, even if he got away with paying under the market value. The fact that it had started to rain again didn't help either. It made the place look like something out of a horror film. He wouldn't have been surprised to see Norman Bates in drag looking out of an upstairs window.

Harry had trouble turning the key in the rust-jammed lock but eventually, it gave, and they were inside. The first thing that hit them was the smell. Nothing could describe it.

"Pretty strong, isn't it?" Harry looked suitably apologetic. "Sorry about that. Must be rats or mice, I suppose."

"Well, I hope it's not rotting human flesh!"

Harry seemed more nervous than apologetic now. Jerry could see something was wrong. "Look," he said, "I think it's a waste of your and my time to go any further. This place is awful. I can't see myself living here – ever!"

"Yes, I can understand that. Perhaps you're right. However, let's just see if there's anything to make you change your mind."

And then Jerry saw it. The thing that made him change his mind.

"Wow!"

"What?" Grimes turned round and saw Jerry staring at the ornamental fireplace in what passed for the living room.

Everywhere was dust, cobwebs, dark corners and stench, but the fireplace stood out as clean and pristine as the day it was installed. There wasn't a speck of dust on it anywhere. The side panels depicted two Pre-Raphaelite angels blowing trumpets. The colours were so vivid they almost reflected off the opposite walls like prisms.

"This is the most amazing thing I've ever seen," Jerry gasped. "How is it possible that there's no dust on it when everything else is so filthy?"

Harry Grimes coughed. "Beats me," he said, not very convincingly.

Jerry eyed him quizzically. "There's something you're not saying, isn't there?"

"I don't know what you mean. It's as much a puzzle to me as it is to you." Harry's eyes were darting around the room, avoiding meeting those of his would-be client.

"There's something about this house – something that makes the owners want to get rid of it quickly. You said yourself they're prepared to take practically any offer I cared to make. I think the reason's more sinister than they just need ready cash to renovate their Spanish property."

"Look, I'm only the go-between here," said Harry, obviously irritated now that he saw his chance of a sale slipping away. "I'm just here to sell a property. The vendors have told me they need money fast and to sell to the first buyer with a reasonable offer. What more can I say?"

"Lots, probably." Jerry was looking at him as if trying to see into his mind. "But that fireplace intrigues me," he said. "What d'you know about it? Does someone come in and clean it every day?"

"It's a mystery to me," said Harry with a shrug.

"Well, I don't know if I'm completely out of my tree, but something is telling me to take a chance," said Jerry, running his fingers along the mantelpiece.

"Are you telling me you're prepared to make an offer?" Harry looked stunned.

"More fool me, but yes, I suppose I am."

"These ornate Victorian fireplaces are all the rage," said Harry, ramming home the advantage this piece of furniture had given him. "A few years ago, they were being snapped up by yuppies everywhere, paying a fortune for them."

"I bet they never got hold of one quite like this, though," said Jerry.

"Well, if you've seen enough, shall we head back to the office and get down to the nitty-gritty?" said Harry, hardly bothering to hide his eagerness.

"Okay by me," said Jerry, casting a last look at the fireplace as they turned and left the room.

They stepped out into the pouring rain and wished they had driven after all.

29

Jerry began to think he must be mad. He had put in an offer on a total wreck euphemistically called a "terraced house". It was an extremely low and insulting offer made with a vague hope the vendors would turn him down flat and save him from dithering anymore. He had changed his mind at least six or seven times on the walk back to Doggett & Finn's, but in the end the offer had been made. Jerry had sat there while Grimes put through the call to Spain and found he was the owner of 57 Bockhampton Road when the call had ended a mere five minutes later. And that's what bothered him. The house was his for practically nothing, but he doubted very much he had snagged a bargain.

His mind was in a turmoil as he rode the mile and a half back to his parents' home on the number 485 bus. On the one hand, he had a house; he was a property owner. On the other, it was a house that had been empty for years, obviously unsaleable until Jerry Muggins came along. He prided himself at being handy with a hammer and chisel, but he rather thought a demolition squad would more suit his purposes now.

Still, he decided, when he was two stops away from his destination, he'd signed the contract and, barring any unforeseen problems with the solicitors at his end, the property was his and he now had to tell his parents the news. They would protest, of course, putting all sorts of obstacles in his way. But he wasn't asking them to stump up any money, so they could go and take a jump. He was determined to lead his own life from now on. He was fed up with his mother's constant nagging and fussing, and his dad was always on his case, at him to get his hair cut and "smarten himself up". He was the "it's about time you bucked your ideas up" kind of father, and Jerry had had enough of it. He knew they both meant well, but he wasn't twelve anymore. His ghastly little brother would have to take all the flak now and serve him right.

He smiled to himself as his thoughts turned to Beth. He had met her at a friend's party last Christmas, and they had hit it off straightaway. They had sneaked up to an unoccupied bedroom and, before they knew what was happening, they were under the bedclothes. She was a fast worker, that one, he thought smugly. But she, like him, still lived at home with her parents, so it wasn't easy to be alone together. With the house now in his possession, they could enjoy each other's company without worrying about one or the other's parents coming in on them mid-clinch. That, alone, was worth all the aggro. He just wished his property was a bit more prepossessing. Heaven only knew what she would think of it, the state it was in at the moment. Still, all he needed to do was buy some paint and clean it up a bit. It wouldn't look too bad, then.

≥

Harry Grimes smiled grimly as he stamped "SOLD" in big red letters on the file he never thought he would see the back of, let alone any commission from. The sale had gone through like a dream. No hitches, no chain, no unforeseen little problems that generally held up proceedings. Exchange and completion could go ahead simultaneously. It was a dream sale.

As he put the file away, he looked across at Barry who gave him the thumbs up. "So, it's sold at last, eh? Don't forget you owe me some commission. After all, it was me who suggested it."

Harry glared at him. "Okay, Barry. I'll see you're all right. I don't feel right about this sale, though. He was a nice guy."

Eve looked up in surprise. "I didn't know you had a conscience, Harry," she said. "I'll see you in a new light after this. I hope we don't all live to regret selling that house, though."

"Why should we?" asked Barry, taking a swig at one of his endless Starbucks coffees. "We sold it in good faith. The buyer's happy. The vendors are happy...."

"In good faith, you say?" demanded Eve crossly. "How can you say that? That poor man's got a shock in store for him, I'm certain."

"Come on, just because a few murders have taken place there, you think it's haunted!" Barry countered. "This is the 21st century, doll. What century are you living in?"

"The same century as you, unfortunately. And don't call me 'doll'!"

Harry smiled to himself. Those two were always bickering. He found it amusing to watch them batting insults to and fro. If Eve wasn't married, he'd bet they'd have got it together at some point. It was just as well she had a ring on her finger as she didn't deserve to be landed with a shit like Barry. Come to think of it, he didn't know a girl who did.

He closed the filing cabinet and locked it. 57 Bockhampton Road was off his hands at last, but somehow he didn't think he'd heard the last of it.

"Is this *it*?" Beth Morrison stared around her, a look of pure disbelief on her face.

"Yep." Jerry cleared his throat, prepared to defend his purchase tooth and nail. "Okay, it's a bit of a dump I grant you. But think of the possibilities, Beth. I'll spend every weekend and evening renovating it. It'll be a palace when I've done."

"You think so? Well, I hate it. Even allowing for all the dirt and the foul smell, there's something not quite right about this place. I don't know exactly what, I can't put my finger on it, but...."

She stopped in mid-sentence as she entered the living room and saw the fireplace. She put her hand to her mouth as if to stop herself from screaming.

Jerry watched her reaction in amazement. "What's wrong?" he asked. For answer, she turned and pushed past him down the hall to the front door. It was as if all the hounds of hell were after her.

"Just let's get out of here, Jerry, please. There's something evil in there."

"Evil? Don't be so melodramatic, Beth. The place is run down, I know. But what makes you say it's evil?"

"It just *is*." Beth let in a gulp of fresh air as she stepped out of the front door. "It positively reeks of something horrible. It's haunted, Jerry. What you have just bought is a bloody haunted house."

"Oh, don't be so ridiculous! It's just needs some TLC. Which I intend to give it."

"Good for you, Jerry. It's a pile of shit. No amount of TLC will improve it."

"For goodness sake, Beth, just wait and see. I'll have it ready for you in a few days. You won't know the place." Jerry's optimism knew no bounds.

"I'll believe it when I see it. Now, are you going to get rid of it or are we finished?"

"Look, Beth, this is crazy. Are you saying you're dumping me just because you don't like the house?"

"It's much more than that, Jerry. Much more."

She walked down the front path and slammed the gate after her. Jerry watched his tall, slim, pretty girlfriend (correction, ex-girlfriend) go, her long blonde hair flying in the wind as she quickly put the distance between herself and him – and his house.

"Beth!" he called after her, rather forlornly. He knew she wouldn't turn back. Was this house just an excuse to break up with him? True, their relationship hadn't been going anywhere lately, but that was mainly because they had nowhere to go to be together. Sitting in the back row of the pictures or necking in the park was a bit like being stuck in a Barbara Cartland novel, he'd imagine, never actually having read one of that good lady's books. In this day and age, they needed space. Now they had it, in spades, it seemed she wasn't satisfied with that either. Couldn't she see the house's potential? He had to admit, though, it was hard for him to see it either, at that moment.

Jerry sat down on the only chair he had so far managed to install in his new home. Buying bits of furniture from second hand shops was proving a slow and difficult business. Money was so tight that he could just about afford to buy paint and wallpaper. Actual furniture would have to wait.

His parents, after the initial shock of seeing their oldest son leave home had worn off, had offered him an old, rickety gate leg table and an old cast-iron bedstead. They were the ugliest bits of furniture he had ever seen, but he supposed they were better than nothing. His mum and dad had fumbled around in the attic for these pieces and brought them down to him with pride. He hadn't had the heart to refuse them. Besides, the alternative would have been upturned crates and a sleeping bag on the filthy floor.

Now he was installed without Beth for company, he was fast regretting ever setting eyes on the place. He wanted to walk into Doggett & Finn's and strangle Harry Grimes and that other bloke who'd suggested it in the first place. He sat on and stared at the strange fireplace, the only thing he felt was worthwhile about the whole venture.

The price of the house had been a snip but, even so, it was too much to pay for just a fireplace, ornately Victorian as it obviously was. And why *was* it so clean? It just didn't make any sense. And why had Beth got so agitated when she saw it? She hadn't liked the house, it was true, but it was only when she clapped eyes on the fireplace that she had reacted so violently.

He tried calling her mobile for the umpteenth time. Surely, she hadn't meant that their relationship was at an end, all because of this stupid fireplace? If it meant dismantling the thing to bring her back, he would do so. It was a fine example of its type, but not worth losing Beth for.

Her phone went straight to voice mail as usual. "Hi Beth. It's me – Jerry. Look, love, whatever's worrying you about the house, we can sort it out. If it's the fireplace, I'll get rid of it. Just say the word. Just get in touch. I love you."

He clicked off and rose to his feet. All enthusiasm for doing the house up had deserted him, and it was late, and he was tired. He climbed the stairs and lay down on the bed. The mattress his parents had given him was hard, but clean and firm. He drifted off into a fitful sleep.

He saw Beth in his dream. She was sitting by the fireplace, the poker in her hand, stirring the embers. She was smiling at him and beckoning him to join her. He came towards her and, as he did so, he saw her expression change to one of hatred and anger. He stood there while she took the red hot poker from the fire and jabbed it in his eye.

He woke up, silently screaming, bathed in sweat.

30

Jerry's mobile shrieked. Muttering curses, he sat up in bed and rubbed his eyes, wondering what the time was. It was pitch-dark. He peered at the caller's ID and suddenly his mood lifted. It was Beth. For over three weeks he hadn't heard a word from her and now she chose this unearthly hour of the night, or morning rather, to come back into his life. What an annoying, irritating, irrational, lovely girl she was.

He pressed the answer button. "Oh Beth, thank God you called I've been so...."

"Shut up, Jerry and listen." She cut him off.

"Uh?"

"Look, I've been doing some digging. That house you've bought is all wrong. I've just got off the plane from Spain. I've been to see the previous owners, and I need to see you at once. You've got to get out of there. You can't live there. Put it back on the market *now*. Get rid of it at any price." With that, the phone went dead.

He tried to call her back, but it went straight to voice mail. "Uh?" was all he could manage. The time on his mobile said 2.05 am. He was whacked. Sleep overtook him before he could think anything else.

As soon as he woke the next morning, he called Beth. It went straight to voice mail.

"Oh, for goodness sake," he muttered. "What's the matter with her? Waking me up in the middle of the night to tell me to get out of the house and then leaving me to wonder why."

He tried her phone several more times while he ate his meagre breakfast of toast and instant coffee, about all his primitive kitchen could stretch to. The first thing he needed was a microwave, he made a mental note to himself. Why wasn't she answering?

Didn't she say she'd just got off a plane from somewhere? He racked his brains. Didn't she say she was on her way to see him? So where was she and why wasn't she answering her stupid, bloody phone?

He tried again when he reached his office, but she just didn't pick up. Then he called her office. He was told she hadn't come in yet. It was almost ten o'clock, where could she be? What was going on? Jerry tried to absorb himself in the plans for a new indoor swimming pool that his firm was working on, but he couldn't concentrate. His young colleague, Rob Faulkner, watched him with amusement.

"Hey, you look done in, mate. Had a heavy night?"

Jerry looked up from his work. "No, I wouldn't mind if I had. I got woken up at 2 am by my mad girlfriend telling me to leave the place right away. I've tried calling her back ever since, but she doesn't answer. She's not at work either. She seems to have disappeared off the face of the earth."

"There's no accounting for women. Mad as snakes, most of them." Rob was a man who spoke with some authority on the subject of the fair sex, being already twice married and divorced at the tender age of twenty-six.

"Beth's always been so sensible, though. She's never acted in this way before. I don't know what to make of it."

"Oh, she'll be in touch when she's ready, don't you worry. But why d'you think she wants you to get out of your house? Does she think it's haunted or something?"

Rob had uttered the word Jerry had been skirting around ever since Beth had said it. 'Haunted'. He didn't really believe in ghosts, second sight, premonitions and all that other paranormal psychobabble rubbish. The house certainly had a weird atmosphere, though. "She's just got a bee in her bonnet, that's all," said Jerry.

He tried, on and off, throughout the day to get hold of her, both at work and on her mobile, but drew a blank every time. Her office said they hadn't heard from her, and all he got when he rang her mobile was her cheerful voice saying: *"Hi, you've reached Beth Morrison. Leave a message and I'll get back to you if I like you. Bye."*

All day he had cursed her every time he heard that voice message. But, by the time he left work, he was beginning to feel more worried than annoyed. As he entered the house, he felt a strange, unpleasant foreboding descend on him, as if someone was walking over his grave. He wanted to turn and run, just the way Beth had done.

However, he resisted the urge and went into the kitchen to put the kettle on. What with all the Beth drama, he'd forgotten to go to Robert Dyas in his lunch hour to pick up a cheap microwave. It would just have to be more toast, he supposed. It was a good job that Garfield's Architects had a staff canteen, he thought, otherwise he'd starve. While the kettle boiled, he tried Beth once more. This time he didn't even get her voice message. The phone was dead. She'd let the battery run down, silly cow.

Drinking his coffee and munching his toast, he was becoming more and more alarmed at the lack of any further communication from her. He couldn't understand it. He would just have to go round to her house. Maybe she'd lost her phone – that was the most likely explanation. But then why hadn't she been at work? He made up his mind to pay her a visit right away.

He was about to leave the house, when he remembered he still had the book she'd lent him. Better return it, he thought. Now where had he left it? Then he remembered – it was in the front room. He'd put it on the mantelpiece so that he would remember to give it back to her next time he saw her.

As he entered the room, he saw the fireplace, still gleaming and shiny as a new pin. But underneath was a body. A very dead, bloodstained body. It was Beth.

He rubbed his eyes and looked again. No, there was no mistake, this was not a hallucination. Beth was lying there, completely stone cold dead. She must have been there for some time, as rigor mortis had set in. When he touched her hand, it felt completely stiff and cold. Her skull was all matted blood and smashed bone. She was a horrific sight. He saw the phone clutched in her left hand. There would be hundreds of missed calls from himself on it. No wonder she hadn't answered.

His eyes filled with tears. His Beth was dead. But what was she doing here? How had she got in without his knowledge? And what was he going to do now? Call the police, of course. But, wait a minute. He'd bound to be their main suspect; never mind the fact he'd called them in the first place.

As he dithered, he heard a clatter and saw a cloud of soot fall from the chimney into the grate. The clatter had been caused by the fireside poker. It had blood all over it. The murder weapon! He reached down to touch it but remembered just in time. If his fingerprints were found on it, the real criminal's would be smudged. He left it where it was, as he punched '999' into his mobile phone and waited.

The police lost no time in carting off Jerry to the local police station. Detective Superintendent Bob Drake and Detective Inspector Indira Patel watched their interviewee with detached, professional interest. The young man sitting before them seemed nervous, but that was natural enough. He had discovered his girlfriend's dead body in his own house. At least that was what he'd told them. The only bit he'd missed out had been when and why had he killed her. It was always a struggle getting a confession, even from a suspect so obviously guilty as they were convinced Mr Jeremy Bracegirdle was.

"As I keep saying, I didn't know she was there. I'd been trying to contact her by phone all day," Jerry insisted. Beads of sweat were standing on his brow.

"So, are you saying that you called her mobile while in the kitchen at breakfast, and didn't hear it ringing in the living room where her body was? The phone was found on her, you know."

"Well, obviously I didn't hear it. If I had, I would have found her body sooner. I was in the kitchen with the door shut – the door's quite thick, you know. Even if I'd heard a faint ringing, which I didn't, I wouldn't have necessarily thought she was on the premises, would I?"

"Unless you were being particularly clever," said Drake, drumming his fingers on the table. "You could have known she was there all the time and made the calls to establish you didn't know what had happened to her or where she was."

His second-in-command, a sloe-eyed brunette, took over. She smiled ingratiatingly at Jerry. "Look, sir. We're only trying to get at the true facts. You say that Miss Morrison called you at two o'clock in the morning, telling you that you were in danger if you stayed in the house any longer and that you should clear out right away. Is that correct?"

"Yes, I've told you."

"Right. So, you go back to sleep and then try to call her the next day to find out what she meant?"

"That's right. I couldn't think what else to do. I was at work all day. It was only when I got home that I found her body."

"That must have been a shock, Mr Bracegirdle," said DI Patel.

"To say the least!"

"So, you want us to believe that Miss Morrison broke into your house sometime during the early morning hours and promptly got herself murdered downstairs while you slept blissfully on upstairs?" Bob Drake eyed him with distaste.

"Well, that's what happened. I've no more idea of how she got there than you have."

"Did she have a key to your house?" Drake asked.

"No."

"Then how do you explain how she got in, if you didn't let her in yourself?"

"I don't know. I only wish I did," sighed Jerry.

Reverend Bernard Paltoquet relaxed in his easy chair by the fire. His eyes opened and closed, as he tried to fight off the sleepiness he felt more and more these days. Now an old man in his mid-eighties, his faithful housekeeper, Mrs Harper, had long since left his employ as well as this life. His few wants were now catered for by Mrs Ruddock, a friendly, apple-cheeked woman, moulded along the same lines as dear old Mrs Harper.

He was jolted into wakefulness by that good lady bringing him his supper tray and evening paper. He had long since retired, but still lived in the same parish, close to the old vicarage where the current incumbent now dwelt. The Reverend Bickerstaffe was a likeable young man and would often visit his predecessor in the evenings for advice and a chat.

"Thank you, Mrs Ruddock. Those muffins look delicious." Indeed, they did, piping hot and oozing with butter.

"So they should. I made them myself," she told him with a sniff. She was proud of her culinary skills, even though she knew she had a lot to live up to. Mrs Harper's prowess in that department was legendary. "Are you warm enough? Shall I turn the gas fire up?" she asked him, moving swiftly on.

"No, thank you," he said, sitting up and tucking his napkin under his chin. "I'm very comfortable."

After Mrs Ruddock had returned to her kitchen domain, he picked up the paper and stared at the headline.

LONDON MAN IN MURDER PROBE

There was always something of the kind going on these days, he sighed. Murders, rapes, knife attacks, terrorist bombs. Life today wasn't what it was. He wouldn't be sad to leave it. Although in fairly good health for a man of his age, he had moments of depression and thoughts of his impending demise were never far away. He put the paper on the table beside him while he stirred his tea. Then his eye caught a word in the text of the article, and he dropped his cup with a clatter and splash. *Bockhampton*!

LONDON MAN IN MURDER PROBE
A young man is being questioned by police following the bizarre murder of his girlfriend in his own house sometime in the early hours of this morning. The man, as yet unnamed, of Bockhampton Road, SW, is said to be shocked by her death, and can throw no light on how the body of his 25-year-old girlfriend, Beth Morrison, got into his own living room while he was allegedly sleeping upstairs.

It made grim reading for Bernard. The curse had come upon that house once again. Another brutal murder, and they wouldn't stop until 57 Bockhampton Road had been obliterated from the face of the earth.

31

Omar Kemal approached the police station with some trepidation. The desk sergeant looked at him with suspicion, something he was used to. He couldn't help looking like a terrorist.

"Good morning, sir. How can we help you?"

Omar cleared his throat. "Errm, I'd like to see whoever's in charge of the Beth Morrison murder case, please," he said.

"Do you have some information relevant to the case, sir?" The man was scrupulously polite, but Omar could see the mistrust in his eyes.

"Yes. I need to see whoever's in charge at once," Omar asserted. He wasn't daunted by the desk sergeant's officious words or manner. Too much water had gone under the bridge for that.

"Very well. Can I take your name, sir?"

"Kemal – Omar Kemal."

"Right. Wait there, Mr Kemal. I will see if the Inspector's free."

Omar looked around him, taking in the various graphic posters that adorned the walls. It seemed there were many murders and other assorted crimes still unsolved, so he didn't feel particularly reassured by the police's apparently poor clear-up rate.

"Mr Kemal?"

Omar swung round to see DS Bob Drake bearing down on him.

"You wanted to see me?" His manner was gruff, and there was no pretence of politeness in his tone.

"Yes, please, sir. I've come about the Beth Morrison murder."

"Well, what about it?" Bob Drake stood in front of him. "Did you do it?" He made no move to show him into a private room.

"Of course not!" Omar exclaimed. "I – I think I'd rather tell you why I've come in private." He looked around as a woman with a fractious child came into the station, followed by two ominous-looking young men who might, or might not, have been with them.

"Just spit it out. I haven't got all day."

Omar Kemal felt like walking out but stood his ground. "All right, then. I saw the murder."

"*You saw the murder?* What exactly do you mean by that?"

"Well, if you'd let me explain...."

"Okay, come on. This way." DS Drake led him into an interview room and closed the door. The room was small and claustrophobic, and Omar almost regretted asking for somewhere private. It could have been a prison cell; it was certainly built along the same lines, with one postage stamp-sized window situated high up in the grey stone wall. He reached inside his collar and wiped the sweat from his neck. It was stiflingly hot, and the smell of stale sweat was making him feel nauseous.

"Can you please open the window, sir?" he asked timidly.

Drake tutted as he yanked open the window and sat down at the bare wooden table, beckoning Omar to sit opposite. "Right, let's have it," he said, a sarcastic edge to his voice. "Unless you'd like me to adjust the air conditioning – which we don't have – or would you like me to fetch you some iced lemonade?"

Omar felt like hitting him now. DS or no DS, he needed to show him some respect. Who did he think he was? "Er, no thank you," was all he said, however.

"Okay, let's get on with it."

"I – I know I should have called you straightaway, but I was worried you wouldn't believe me."

"Try me."

"It's just that the circumstances of the murder are – very – well, not easily explained."

"Look, Mr Kemal, I've not got time for 'Alice in Wonderland' stories. If you've something to tell me, do so. Otherwise – "

"I'm a taxi driver and I picked up Miss Morrison from Gatwick on the night of the murder." Omar decided to gabble out his story quickly before Drake could pass any more sarcastic remarks. "I drove her to 57 Bockhampton Road. I remember the number and everything. I've got a good memory, especially when I drive people on nice long journeys."

Drake was taking notice at last. "That would be the night before last?"

"That's right. It was about two-fifteen in the morning when we arrived at the house. She had been telling me about her visit to Spain, and I asked her if she had had a good holiday. She told me that she hadn't been on holiday but had gone to see some people who had sold their house to her boyfriend. They're living in Spain now apparently."

"Do I need to hear what you chatted about?" Bob Drake drummed his fingers on the table impatiently. "What I need to hear is how you witnessed the crime."

"Yes, well, I'm coming to that. As we got chatting I noticed she seemed very agitated and she kept checking the signal on her mobile. Apparently, she was having trouble with it. I asked her if she wanted to use mine, but then she was able to call out on hers..."

"Again, Mr Kemal, the relevance?"

"Please, let me tell the story in my own way. It has a bearing on the crime, I assure you."

"Hmm!" was Drake's only response.

"Anyway, as I was saying, I overheard her talk to someone, telling that person he or she must get out of the house immediately. She seemed very worried, as if something in the house was very dangerous. I drew up outside number 57 Bockhampton Road...."

"What time did you say that was?"

"About two-fifteen, I think. Anyway, she made to get out of the cab, but something made her stop. She looked very scared. I asked her if she wanted me to go in with her, but she said no, she would be fine. However, I didn't drive off. I decided to wait to make sure she got safely inside the house. She rang the bell a couple of times, but it obviously wasn't working. Then she pushed at the front door and I saw it open. It was either unlocked or someone inside had opened it for her. She disappeared inside so I decided she must be okay. But something made me stay."

"Why did you do that?" Drake leaned towards him, his grey eyes boring into Omar's brown ones.

"Well, it was what she had said in the cab. About the house. She told me that she didn't like the atmosphere in the house and that her boyfriend had bought it and she wasn't very happy about it. I thought that was who she was on the phone to. Anyway, I thought she might be in some kind of danger."

"As it turned out, you were dead right, mate." Drake looked at him grimly. "So, what did you do then?"

"Well, I waited for about ten minutes and, as she hadn't appeared, I thought I'd just make sure she was all right. I thought she'd be with her boyfriend, and I didn't want to intrude myself, but I just wanted to be sure. Well, I got out of the cab and walked up the path. The door opened as I got up to it – almost like those automatic doors they have in supermarkets. It was weird. I nearly turned and ran, but I thought about the girl and decided to go in. It was very cold inside there, but I could see an almost luminous glow from under the door on the immediate right. I went towards the light and pushed the door wide open. It was the fireplace, glowing in the dark. I'd never seen anything like it."

Omar stopped and gulped. "Could I have a drink of water, please?"

Omar Kemal wiped the sweat from his forehead, as Drake went in search of the required refreshment. He wasn't being sarcastic anymore, the little cab driver thought grimly. Just wait until he hears the worst bit, then there'd be trouble. He just didn't know how the policeman would take it. But it was the truth, that's all he could say. It was up to him how he dealt with it.

Drake returned with a bottle of water and a steaming mug of coffee. Sitting back down, he took a swig of his coffee.

"Okay. Let's hear the rest of it."

Omar gulped down his water and wiped his forehead again. "What I'm about to tell you won't make any sense. You won't believe me, I know."

"Let me be the judge of that, Mr Kemal."

"Okay. What I saw was the girl by the fireplace. She was staring at it, obviously wondering what was making it glow like that. Then this poker just lifted itself up from the grate and smashed down on her head. The poker still swung over her head and then smashed down on her again. I was too scared to go up to her in case I got hit too."

"You're right, Mr Kemal. I *don't* believe you."

"I knew you wouldn't. That's why I didn't come sooner. But I saw in the paper that her boyfriend was being questioned about the murder, so I wanted to let you know he had nothing to do with it. He wasn't anywhere near."

"Mr Kemal, do you really expect me to believe that a low-flying poker was responsible for killing Beth Morrison while her boyfriend was asleep upstairs?"

"Yes. That is what happened." Omar knew he'd wasted his time in coming, but he didn't really care now. He'd salved his conscience by telling him what he'd seen.

"What I can't understand is why didn't you call an ambulance at the time? You might have been able to save her life."

"Because I could see she was dead. She was beyond help."

"So, you just left her there and went home and forgot all about it?"

"I know it was wrong, but I was so scared. What I saw was beyond human understanding. All I know is that it wasn't the boyfriend. If you've charged him, he didn't do it."

"Okay, so lover boy didn't do it. The poker did. Is that the theory?"

"It's the truth."

Omar left the station some fifteen minutes later, after having signed a witness statement. The look on the detective's face was enough to tell him he'd made a complete fool of himself. However, they hadn't locked him up for wasting police time, so that was a positive, at least.

32

It had been many years since Bernard had visited 57 Bockhampton Road. He had hoped, the last time he came, that he would never have cause to visit it again, but here he was standing outside the troubled house once more, trying to pump some life into the rust-encrusted doorbell.

It was eight o'clock on a crisp, early autumn evening, the twilight casting eerie shadows around the unlit house. He assumed the absence of light meant that no one was home but decided to try the knocker to make sure. The noise echoed through the mournful house, followed by an almost unnatural silence.

"Oh well," he thought, "He's probably at the pub drowning his sorrows." As he retraced his steps down the path, however, he heard the creak of an opening door. He turned to see an unkempt, bleary-eyed young man with a few days' growth of stubble on his face, wearing an egg-stained dressing-gown.

"Hello?" said Jerry Bracegirdle. "Who are you? What do you want?"

"I'm sorry to disturb you, I – "

Jerry interrupted him. "I don't know who you are, so if you've come to pry, then I'm sorry to disappoint you. I don't want any visitors at the moment."

Bernard smiled tentatively at him. "I can understand that. I used to be the local vicar and I've just read about your girlfriend's murder."

"I told you, I'm not at home to callers...."

"Please, just listen for a moment." Bernard could understand how he felt and wondered if newspaper reporters had found out where he lived and had been bothering him. More than likely, he thought. "I'm not a reporter or anything like that," he assured him. "I've come to try and help you. You see, I know quite a lot about what's been going on in this house over the years and I – "

The young man looked contrite. "Oh, I'm sorry. I apologise for my rudeness."

"That's all right," smiled Bernard now. Jerry reminded him of Henry Freeman, and he liked him already. "I've just come to see if there's anything I can do. I know quite a bit about the history of your house, so I would like to help, if I can."

Jerry showed Bernard into the kitchen, by-passing the closed door on the right. Bernard knew that room only too well. It was where poor Beth Morrison's murder had taken place. And all the other murders, come to that.

"Do sit down," said Jerry pulling out the only chair from under the kitchen table. "Can I get you anything? I've got some tea, I think. Or a beer, if you'd prefer?"

"Tea would be most welcome, thank you."

As Jerry busied himself preparing the tea, Bernard looked around the sparsely furnished kitchen. The sink drainer was piled up with unwashed plates and cups, and the ancient cooker had a thick layer of grease on its hob that looked like even a blow-torch wouldn't be able to shift.

As if reading his thoughts, Jerry laughed. "Yes, the place *is* a bit of a mess, I know. But I haven't been here long, and, well, what with what's happened, I don't intend to stay here. I've put it back on the market in the meantime, but I don't really expect to sell it."

When the rather weak tea was placed before him, Bernard cleared his throat and asked him the obvious question: "Did you kill Beth Morrison?"

It was blunt, but the question had to be asked and got out of the way. Bernard was sure he hadn't done it, but he had to hear it from Jerry's own lips.

"No, I didn't."

"Forgive me for asking," said Bernard, "but I just wanted to make sure."

"Well, now you know." Jerry looked cross for a moment. "The police have interrogated me thoroughly, as you know from the papers."

He refilled Bernard's cup from the ancient teapot he had found discarded in a cupboard. It had a faulty spout and dispensed the tea haphazardly, with most of it missing the cup and ending up in the saucer. Bernard calmly tipped the saucer into the cup. "Thank you," he smiled.

"I don't think it's been reported about the taxi driver, though," Jerry continued, passing Bernard a piece of kitchen towel to mop up the tea dribbles that had missed both the cup and the saucer. "That's why you found me at home. I'd probably be still at the nick if he hadn't shown up."

"Taxi driver?"

Jerry told Bernard about Omar Kemal. "He came to see me after he'd been to the police and told me what he'd seen."

"I don't suppose the police believed him," said Bernard.

Jerry shrugged. "You can't really blame them, can you?"

"No." Bernard knew only too well, from his own experience, how the police felt about what they called 'fairy stories'.

"Anyway, I can only feel grateful that Mr Kemal came forward."

"But have you thought that he could have called the emergency services on the spot and saved your girlfriend's life?"

"Well, yes, I did think of that. But I suppose he thought she was already dead and beyond help."

"Did it cross your mind that he might have killed her himself?"

"No, it didn't. He would hardly have gone to the police, if he had, would he?"

Bernard let that pass. "Anyway, what I really came to tell you was that I know you didn't kill her, and I'm also sure the taxi driver didn't, either. I think the real killer is this house, or rather the evil spirits that are trapped inside this house."

"You mean you think it's haunted?"

"I do," said Bernard. "What I came to give you was this." He handed Jerry the battered cardboard file he had brought with him. "I've made a study of the history of this house from the later Victorian times up to the late sixties. There have been several unexplained murders here, all in front of the living room fireplace."

Jerry opened the file and began flicking through the pages.

"What I suggest is you read what's in there, and you'll see that the murder of your poor Beth follows a similar pattern to the other murders documented in there. I came to see you tonight to tell you I'm determined to put an end to all this killing."

Jerry looked up from the file. "How are you going to do that?"

"There's a psychic medium I know. I'm sure she'll get to the bottom of it. I wanted to call her in when the last murder happened, but I'd lost touch with her then. She was going around the country, giving mass séances and there weren't any such things as mobile phones then."

"So, you're back in touch with her, now?"

"Yes. She sent me a Christmas card out of the blue with her new address on it." He had been delighted to receive the card from Dorothy Plunkett, shortly after the death of his good friend, Robbie MacTavish. Her renewed presence in his life had given him the comfort he needed at just the right time.

"I'll be honest, Reverend," said Jerry, "I don't really believe in the supernatural…"

"Even after all that's happened?" Bernard eyed him quizzically. Some people took a lot of convincing.

"Well, I suppose – well, I'm beginning to change my mind." Jerry's smile was infectious.

"So I should think," Bernard giggled. "Anyway, keep the file as long as you want. If you're not convinced there's something evil in this house after reading it, I'll eat my hat."

33

Omar drew up outside 57 Bockhampton Road and eyed its unprepossessing exterior with a shiver. It looked even more forbidding in the light of day, having only seen it in the dark on the two previous occasions he'd had cause to visit it. The first time had been to deliver that poor girl to her death, and the second time had been that evening when he had told Jerry about his witness statement.

How could anyone contemplate living in a place like this? he wondered, as he walked up to the front door. It should have been condemned years ago.

"Hello, Omar," Jerry greeted him. "Good of you to come."

"Look," said Omar, "I'd rather not get involved. I told the police all I could. I'm sorry for your loss, but I don't see how I can really help you."

"You might be able to. Please, Omar." There was a pleading look in Jerry's tired eyes. "I'd very much appreciate it. Won't you come in and talk to me and my friend, Reverend Paltoquet? We just want to try and get to the bottom of the mystery. You're the only one who saw what happened."

Omar was in two minds. He was beginning to regret giving Jerry his card, but he thought he was a genuinely nice man and felt sorry for his situation. And it was only natural, he supposed, that Jerry would want to talk to him some more, being probably the only one who believed in his innocence.

"It was a wicked thing," said Omar, following Jerry into the house. "A very wicked thing."

They went straight through to the kitchen, where Bernard was sitting with a cup of tea and a plate of biscuits in front of him.

"This is Reverend Paltoquet, Mr Kemal."

"How do you do?" Omar shook hands with the old gentleman, taking an instant liking to him.

"Hello, Mr Kemal. May I call you Omar?"

"Of course."

"Tea?" Jerry asked.

"No, thank you. I don't drink stimulants," replied Omar, looking around for another chair.

"I'm sorry I don't have any more chairs," said Jerry, looking embarrassed. "I'll fetch a packing case."

When they were all settled, Bernard asked Omar why he hadn't called the police or an ambulance at least. Omar repeated what he had said to Jerry and DS Drake: that Beth was already dead, and it wouldn't have done her any good.

"But it still doesn't explain why you left and didn't report the crime to anyone," Bernard pointed out.

Omar helped himself to a biscuit. "I know. I can't really explain. I don't like the police at the best of times. They don't treat people like me with much respect, you know. As it is, I'm surprised they didn't arrest *me* for the murder."

Bernard nodded sympathetically. "It must be difficult, Omar. But perhaps if you had called them straightaway, a life may have been saved."

"I'm sure she was dead," Omar repeated.

He watched Bernard pass a look to Jerry. Didn't they believe him? Had he been brought here under false pretences? When Jerry had called him, he'd simply asked him to come because he thought he could help. But maybe he suspected him of killing his girlfriend, after all?

"All right, Omar, we believe you," said Jerry.

"Thank you," said Omar, relieved.

"So, what we need to do now is find the previous owners. Did Beth say anything to you about them?" Jerry sounded upbeat now.

"The young lady had come back from Spain when I picked her up at Gatwick," Omar informed him. "I remember she mentioned that she had been to see the people who had sold you the house."

Jerry nodded. "That makes sense. The estate agent told me the vendors were living in Spain. Only problem is, we don't know where. It beats me how Beth found them."

Bernard drained his teacup and rose creakily to his feet. "Let's go and visit that estate agent of yours, Jerry. That's where Beth must have got the information from."

"Yes, I'll be pleased to see *him* again. I'll give him a piece of my mind. Selling me the place when he knew all the time why it was so cheap."

250

Omar had been only too happy to drive them to Doggett & Finn's. As they pulled up, Harry Grimes was looking idly out of the window. He dropped his pen when he saw that among the people getting out of the taxi was the young man to whom he had sold 57 Bockhampton Road.

Barry John-Harrington, finishing a call, looked across at Harry. "Isn't that the chap we sold that spooky house to?" he asked. "Isn't he supposed to have done in his girlfriend? Can't understand why the police haven't charged him yet."

"It's him, all right. And he's brought some old geezer with him," said Harry. He watched as Jerry, Bernard and Omar entered the shop, making straight for his desk.

He smiled gingerly at them. "Hello, gentlemen. How can I help you?"

"Hello, Mr Grimes. Remember me?" asked Jerry.

"Yes, of course. How – how are you?"

"As well as can be expected, as the saying goes," said Jerry, leaning forward and making Harry lean back in his chair as he did so. "Can I introduce you to Reverend Paltoquet? And this," continued Jerry, "is Mr Omar Kemal." Omar stepped forward and shook Harry's hand.

Harry wondered if Jerry had brought these two men along to help duff him up. On the whole, he thought it unlikely, as the little Asian chap didn't look as if he could knock the skin of a rice pudding and, as for the old vicar, unless he was Arnold Schwarzenegger in disguise, he was hardly any threat, either.

"Can we talk privately, do you think?" Jerry asked him.

"What you have to say can be said in front of my colleagues, here...."

"Very well," said Jerry. "I'm here about the house you sold me, and these two gentlemen are helping me to solve the mystery of my girlfriend's murder."

"I – I don't quite know how you think I can help with that," said Harry. "I sold you the property in all good faith. Please leave my shop."

"Not until I have some answers. So, do you have a private office where we can talk?" Jerry asked again.

"Okay, okay, anything you say," Harry capitulated. "Barry, I leave you in charge. Call me if there're any problems. I won't be long."

Once inside the office with the door shut, Jerry started to pace the room. "I don't want to cause any trouble, Mr Grimes, and I know it's your job to sell property, but I think it would have been helpful to know exactly why the previous owners were willing to let me have their house so cheaply."

"But I told you – it was because they wanted money quickly for renovations to their Spanish property. Also, it was the condition of the place...."

"And, thirdly, because it was haunted," Jerry finished for him.

"Now, please, that's something that I know nothing about. Anyway, it wasn't my place to deal in mere speculation."

"Agreed. But I thought, at the time, you were holding something back. The owners had told you about the house's history, hadn't they?"

Harry looked at the three men's faces and shrugged. "Well, they may have mentioned something, but they requested me to keep it to myself."

"Well, they would, wouldn't they?" smirked Jerry. His manner relaxed a little, and he sat down. "Look, Mr Grimes, as I said, I'm not here to cause trouble, but I would like to get to the bottom of what's been going on in my house."

"But, as I said, I don't see what you expect me to do," said Harry. He was beginning to feel a little less threatened now.

"Well, you can give me the address of the previous owners, for a start. You must have given it to my girlfriend?"

"Your girlfriend? The one who was murdered?" Harry asked, puzzled.

"Yes. She must have got the information from here. How else would she have known where to find them?"

"I – I didn't know she had. Anyway, she didn't get it from me. Wait a minute, let me call Barry."

He called through to the shop. "Barry, can you come here a minute?"

253

Barry, on one of his interminable cold calls, put his thumb up, acknowledging Harry's request, but showing no sign of terminating his call.

"Like now, please," said Harry impatiently. Barry put his thumb up again and this time made an effort to wind up his call.

When he finally entered the office, four faces turned expectantly towards him. "Barry," said his boss. "Did you give a young woman the address of the vendors of 57 Bockhampton Road?"

"In Spain, do you mean?"

"Yes."

"She said she was the buyer's girlfriend, and she wanted the address on his behalf. I thought it was okay to give it to her."

"You should have asked their permission first," Harry pointed out.

"Well, I only gave her the address, not the phone number. As it was in Spain I thought it would be all right."

"Never mind. That's all," said Harry, dismissing him.

"No, wait," said Jerry. "How did she seem to you?"

"In what way?"

"I mean, was she upset, worried, annoyed?"

"A bit of all those, I'd say. Said she needed some answers from the vendors of the property. I thought she meant, like, the condition of it. I thought she had a right to...."

Harry interrupted him angrily. "She had no right! We do not give out our clients' addresses to all and sundry. You know that full well, Barry."

Barry didn't look the slightest bit embarrassed or abashed. "Sure, I know that. But she was very insistent, and I decided to help her."

Harry glared at his underling, whose days were now well and truly numbered. "Just get out. I'll talk to you later."

Barry did as he was told, looking anything but contrite.

"Does that mean you're not going to tell us the address of these people?" asked Jerry.

"Certainly, it does," said Harry. Put that in your pipe and smoke it, he thought with satisfaction. Teach him to come in here, strong-arming him and making threats. Count himself lucky he hadn't called the police.

Bernard spoke up for the first time. "Mr Grimes, while appreciating your position, this is a very delicate matter and circumstances are such that we need to contact these people urgently. We're trying to prevent a miscarriage of justice, that's all. We must speak to the vendors, if at all possible. I'm sure they won't mind and will understand why you divulged their details to us."

"Look, all I can do is call them and ask," replied Harry.

Jerry smiled at him for the first time. "Yes. Please do that, Harry."

"If you wouldn't mind waiting outside, gentleman, I will call them now."

～

There was no sign of Barry as they made their way back into the shop, but Eve was at her desk searching through a file index. Jerry gave her one of his most charming smiles. She returned it and asked him if he and his companions would like some coffee.

They sat around companionably, drinking coffee with Eve until Harry came out of the office. He shrugged his shoulders and spread out his well-manicured hands. "No dice, I'm afraid," he said, "They don't want to talk to you. They were very angry that your girlfriend turned up as she did and are considering suing us for giving out confidential information without permission as it is."

Jerry looked at his companions and sighed. "That's a shame. We don't want to make any trouble for them. We just want some answers, that's all."

Then he noticed Eve's expression. She was raising her eyebrows and nodding her head slightly in the direction of the file index on the desk between them. There was one card up-ended, and all three men gathered at once what Eve was trying to do. But how could it be managed? Jerry didn't want to get this nice girl into any trouble with her obnoxious boss. Then Eve called across to Harry.

"Did you know that the property in Silver Street is still on display, Harry? I thought it had been sold weeks ago. Shouldn't you remove it before we get any more enquiries?"

"I thought I'd told Barry to take it out. I'll go and attend to it right away."

That got rid of Harry for a few seconds and Barry was still away from his desk. With a deft flick Eve passed the card to Jerry who put it straight into his pocket it without looking at it. "Thanks!" he mouthed at her, making a mental note, not only to post the card back to her as soon as he could, but also to ask her out for a meal when this whole mess had been cleared up.

Once outside the shop, Jerry pulled the card out of his pocket and all three men saw that Eve had given them the address of a Mr and Mrs Miles-Harris in Almeria, Spain. There was also a phone number and e-mail address.

Bernard pointed out that the only thing to do was get on a plane and go out to them. They were hardly likely to answer e-mails and would probably hang up once they knew it was the poor sap who'd bought their blighted house. Also, they had to find a way of contacting the Miles-Harrises without getting that pretty young woman into trouble.

Omar, who had been silent during much of the meeting with Harry Grimes, pointed out that he was really an outsider in this affair and couldn't see how he could be of service to Jerry any further. But he'd be more than happy to drive him to the airport.

"Thanks, Omar. That'd be great," said Jerry. "But I'd really like you to come with me if you can spare the time. I hate travelling alone and I'd like someone to back me up and bounce ideas off, if possible. Please say you'll come."

Before Omar could answer, Bernard butted in. "Hello, what about me? Don't you want me along? After all, I know much more about the house than either of you. I've read up extensively on the subject."

Jerry turned to the old man and put his hand gently on his shoulder. "Oh, Bernard, I'd love you to come! But won't the flight be too much for you?"

"Are you saying I'm too old?" Bernard was indignant.

"No, no," laughed Jerry. "If you think you're up to it – all right – I mean, I'd be delighted to have you with me. I just didn't want you to think I was expecting you to come, that's all."

"Young man, I'd have you know that I've travelled much further afield than Spain in my time. Why only last year I was on the Nile admiring the Pyramids!"

"Well, if you're sure.... it could be quite an ordeal with these people. They may chase us off their property with Rottweilers!"

"Pooh! Rottweilers, schmottweilers. I've faced tougher foe."

The two friends shook hands and agreed to fly out to Spain as soon they could book the flights, with Omar acting as their personal chauffeur to Gatwick.

34

The first thing Jerry did, on returning from Doggett & Finn's, was to go online and book himself and Bernard on a cheap flight to Almeria the following evening, leaving from Gatwick at 5 pm. The next thing he did was inform the police of his intention to leave the country and furnish them with the Miles-Harris's address. It was touch and go but, in the end. he was given permission as long as he wasn't away for more than a couple of days. Jerry thought that would give him and Bernard ample time to consult the Miles-Harrises and be kicked out afterwards. He was under no illusion that the interview would be easy, or even if it would be granted at all.

"Passport in order?" Jerry asked Bernard on the phone that evening.

"Of course. I shall pack a small suitcase and be ready as soon as you like. What time is the flight?"

"Five o'clock tomorrow afternoon. We need to check in two hours before. So we'll get Omar to collect us at two o'clock tomorrow afternoon, to give us enough time to drive there."

"Good. I'll be ready."

Jerry began to wonder just how they were going to approach the Miles-Harrises. They would hardly be pleased to see him and Bernard so soon after Beth's visit, but he was determined to ask them what they knew about the goings-on in 57 Bockhampton Road. They had warned Beth about it, so it was only fair that they should tell him all they knew, too. Whether it would help with the police was another matter, especially if all they could tell him was the house was haunted. He needed more than that if he was to get off the hook.

He slept fitfully that night, dreaming of Beth. She looked beautiful in his dream and then, suddenly, she was covered in blood. She was calling out to him: "Take care, Jerry darling. Get away now. You're in great danger. They told me in Spain. You cannot live there, you can only die..." Jerry awoke with a start, his heart pounding. "Oh, Beth, darling, I miss you!" he called out to the darkness. Then he noticed the atmosphere in the room. It was icy cold, and an intangible sense of menace was oozing all around him, as if through the very walls.

He leapt out of bed and ran out of the room, but the menace had followed him onto the landing. It seemed to be rising upwards, emanating from the living room, where that vile fireplace still stood. Why hadn't he destroyed it?

He crept slowly down the stairs and hesitated outside the living room door. Should he go in? Face the evil head on? He wished Bernard was with him. Then he thought he heard someone talking. It was just a low mutter and he couldn't make out the words. But he could tell it was a woman's voice, even though it was low and guttural. It reminded him of the voice of the possessed child in that horror film he had seen recently in a National Film Theatre revival season. The film had disturbed him more than he would have thought possible, particularly when the little girl's eyes fluttered open, giving a foretaste of the evil to come.

"Get a grip, Jerry, you soft sod," he said to himself. He turned the door handle and entered the room. A woman was standing by the fireplace, a poker in her hand. The fire was blazing in the grate and she was gently stirring the coals. She wore a long gown and her hair was piled high on her head. He thought immediately of a prettier version of 'Jane Eyre'. As he thought this, she turned and smiled at him, showing blackened teeth. The grin was uncannily evil. Before he knew what was happening, she ran at him, wielding the poker like a cheerleader. She gave a cackling laugh and smashed the poker down on his head. As she did so, he could hear her evil words: "Didn't you know I don't allow anyone to live here who has a happy relationship? Your girlfriend had to die, but you'll soon find another girl to take her place, won't you? Then she will suffer the consequences, just like your first girlfriend. You will never be happy here."

Jerry screamed and forced open his eyes. It was as if they had been glued down. Sunlight streamed in through his bedroom window. What had seemed so real a second ago had only been a nightmare. "Thank God!" he said.

After a skimpy breakfast, he packed a few clothes, toothbrush and towel into a small suitcase, just enough for an overnight stay. He had several hours to kill so he made sure, for the umpteenth time, that his passport was in his holdall, along with the flight tickets. Only ten o'clock. He decided to go for a stroll in the park.

It was a pleasant feeling, after the horrors of the night, to be seated and relaxed on a park bench, watching the pigeons eyeing him hopefully. He was free to come and go, even though the police were far from finished with him. They hadn't questioned him again, but he had no doubt they would do so sooner or later. There was no one else on their radar.

He had dreaded a visit from Beth's parents but, so far, they hadn't even called him. What must they be thinking? he wondered. They probably thought he'd killed her. What else were they to think?

And then he thought about work. His boss had called him yesterday, asking when he planned to return, which was a good sign in itself. It didn't seem like he was intent on sacking him, unless he wanted to do it face to face. He had been gratified when he'd received the card from Rob, Emma and all the others in his office. Their offer of condolences for his loss moved him more than he could say. At least they were giving him the benefit of the doubt. Innocent until proven guilty, wasn't that how it went? He decided to return to the office at the beginning of the following week, whatever happened in Spain. Life had to go on.

Then he remembered. He had still to return the Miles-Harris's index card to that pretty Eve at the estate agents. It was still in his jacket pocket. He jumped up from the park bench at once and ran out of the park, leaving the pigeons to pick on someone else. As he reached Doggett & Finn's, he slowed his pace. He had to make sure he got the card back to Eve without Grimes or that other guy seeing him do it. The last thing he wanted was get her into trouble. He was relieved to find Harry's desk empty. The younger man was there, but deeply engrossed in a phone call, his feet on the desk as if he owned the place.

Eve was also at her desk, leafing through some flyers. "Hello," she said to him as he approached. "How are you?"

"Fine, thanks." He noticed the ring on her finger and suddenly felt a fool. Had he really been thinking of her as a Beth replacement? How shallow can you get?

He slipped the card unobtrusively under her mouse mat. "Thanks!" he mouthed at her.

She winked at him. "Are you all right in that house?" she asked. "I see you've put it back on the market."

"Well, wouldn't you?" grinned Jerry. "Sorry that you're saddled with it again. I don't expect many viewings."

"We'll do what we can," she said seriously.

"I don't intend to sell it to anyone until I'm sure the house is safe."

Eve glanced at her watch. "Look, it's coming up to my lunch break. Harry's due back from his in a minute. Do you fancy a drink?"

❦

Promptly at two o'clock, Omar Kemal drew up outside number 57. He found Bernard waiting on the doorstep with his little suitcase beside him.

"Hello, Mr Paltoquet," said Omar. "Have you just arrived?"

"No. Actually I've been here for five minutes at least. Jerry doesn't appear to be here."

Omar scratched his head in puzzlement. "He definitely said two o'clock to give us enough time to reach Gatwick by three..."

Just then they heard their names being called and turned to see a flushed and breathless Jerry racing up the street towards them.

"Sorry! Got delayed. I'll just get my bag. I'm all packed."

❦

As the plane began to taxi down the runway, Jerry looked out of the window at the receding tarmac. It was just after five o'clock and everything was going according to plan. Bernard was seated comfortably beside him, a chocolate bar and coffee in front of him.

"Have you thought about how to tackle the Miles-Harrises?" Bernard asked.

Jerry, who was staring out of the window, didn't reply.

"Jerry?"

"Oh, sorry, I was miles away."

"Is everything all right? You seem distracted."

"I'm okay, Bernard, don't worry."

"Is it anything to do with why you were late this afternoon?"

Jerry smiled. Bernard was a wise old bird, he could read him like a book. "Yes, sort of."

"Care to tell me what's up?" Bernard munched into his chocolate bar and slurped his coffee as the plane began to gather speed.

"Oh, it's nothing, really."

"It must be *something*," said Bernard, screwing up his chocolate wrapper and putting it in his empty paper cup.

"I just feel a bit bad, that's all."

"Why?"

He's a persistent old bugger, thought Jerry, not unkindly. "It's just that I had lunch with that girl from the estate agents. That's why I was late."

"So, why should you feel bad about that?"

"Because (a) Beth's not been dead five minutes and (b) Eve's married."

"Eve?"

"Eve Mason. The girl in the estate agents."

"Oh, I see. So, are you telling me you're interested in her?"

Jerry thought the use of the word 'interested' was understating it now. All through their Starbuck's lunch, he had watched her and grown more and more to like her as he did so. It wasn't that she was pretty, although she was. Not as pretty as Beth, but she was cute in a button-nosed sort of way, and he realised she had, what most girls seemed to lack in his experience, a terrific sense of humour. They had got on like a proverbial house on fire.

"I think I'm falling for her."

"I see." Bernard smiled. "Well, it's nothing to feel bad about. We can't help our feelings." Jerry noticed a wistful look cross his face suddenly.

"I know. But I feel I'm getting over Beth too quickly. It can't be right, not after what happened to her. Besides, Eve's married, don't forget."

"Even so. Falling in love is a God-given gift. It's not everyone who's so fortunate."

"Oh, Bernard. You never married, did you? Did you ever get close?"

The wistful look was back. "I had a girl when I was a student at University. Sophie."

"What happened? Do you want to tell me?"

"Maybe."

Jerry smiled and patted his sleeve. This old man had a sad secret, he could tell. His own romantic entanglements were nothing beside what Bernard had probably suffered. After all, why had he spent his life alone if, once upon a time, he'd had a woman to love?

35

"Oops, was I asleep?" Bernard jerked awake suddenly, as if from a bad dream.

"Yes but carry on. It's good if you can get some rest now," Jerry told him. "We've a hard time coming up. The Miles-Harrises might very well refuse to speak to us. They may even call the police, saying we're trespassing, if we make too much of a nuisance of ourselves."

"Let's hope they'll be more reasonable than that," Bernard smiled. "Anyway, I don't feel sleepy anymore. Is there any food coming our way?"

"They've brought the trolley along a couple of times while you were dozing. Here, I've saved you a sandwich and some crisps."

"Thanks, Jerry. Just the ticket." He dug into the crisps.

"Bernard?"

"Hmm?" came the crisp-filled reply.

"I'm curious. What happened to the girl you met at Uni? Sophie, you said?"

Bernard's eyes misted over as he got to grips with the packaging around his sandwich. Jerry took it from him and released the rather dried-up cheese and tomato sandwich from its plastic prison.

"Would you tell me about her?"

Bernard continued to work his way through his sandwich without answering.

"I mean if it's too painful, then I quite understand."

As Bernard swallowed the last mouthful of his sandwich, the air hostess was at his side with a selection of drinks. He chose a miniature bottle of red wine of undetermined origin, and Jerry followed suit.

When the drinks were poured into their respective plastic cups, Bernard wiped his mouth and spoke. "She was just a girl I got friendly with when I was up at Leeds. I was studying theology and she was reading English classics. We met in a cafe and got talking."

"Go on."

Bernard smiled at his young friend. This was the first time he'd spoken about his love affair with Sophie. Not even his dear old friend, Robbie MacTavish, knew all the facts.

"I was a shy student and found it hard to mix. I think my studious nature and reticence put off most of my fellow students. I shared a room with a chap called Ron when I first went up, but he was a great socialiser and loved going to parties and living it up. It was all very tame by today's standards, mark you. No drugs or sex, or not that I was aware of. How he found time to study or attend lectures was a mystery to me, but I liked him, even so.

"Then, one day, I was sitting in my favourite cafe, a nose in a book as usual, when this young woman came up to my table and asked if she could sit with me as there wasn't another table free. I think I fell in love with her on sight. She was so beautiful even with spectacles on. She was obviously a student, what with the glasses and a pile of books under her arm. So we started chatting, and then she said she'd often seen me in the café, always on my own, reading something or other. When she learned I was reading theology, she said she thought I'd make a good vicar. I was slightly put out by this, as I didn't want to give her the impression I was a prude or stick-in-the-mud. But, instead of putting her off, she seemed to like me all the more for it.

"Anyway, I felt suddenly emboldened to ask her out, although I suppose I'd expected her to say no. But, to my surprise, she said she'd love to and told me about a film she wanted to see that very evening, some French thing, I can't remember what now. Something worthy in black-and-white with sub-titles. You know the sort of thing."

Jerry smiled. "Boring, I think you mean."

"I suppose I do. But I made out I'd enjoyed it because she so obviously did. It's silly what you say and do just to impress a girl, isn't it?"

Jerry nodded knowingly.

"After that first night, we became almost inseparable, except when we went to lectures and returned to our respective lodgings. It wasn't long before we decided to move out of halls into a communal flat, shared with two other student couples. It was a bit squashed and informal, but at least we had a room to ourselves.

"We were so happy together then. It didn't seem to matter that we were at war with Germany. By then, Ron had enlisted in the Royal Navy, and I supposed it wouldn't be long before I was called up. I dreaded it, because I was a pacifist, but I was prepared to drive ambulances and bind up wounds. It was the least I could do, but when I got my papers, I was rejected because of my flat feet. It was a relief, I have to admit, although I felt a bit guilty about not doing my bit.

"But Sophie told me not to be silly and, as long as she still loved me, I continued to be happy. I planned to ask her to marry me as soon as I graduated and had taken up a curacy. I suspected she wouldn't be the normal run of vicars' wives, being so lively and happy-go-lucky. I don't think I've ever met a more disorganised person than Sophie, before or since, but none of that mattered. She was the only woman for me.

"Then, one day, she wasn't there anymore. I came back to the flat from a lecture and ran straight up to our room as usual. She often got back before me and I couldn't wait to take her in my arms. Sorry, Jerry, if this sounds a bit Mills & Boon...."

"Don't be silly, Bernard. I'm interested. What happened then?"

"All I found, when I got to our room, was a scribbled note on my pillow. It said, and I can still remember the exact words, 'Darling, forgive me. I've let you down. I love you, but I can't stay. Don't try to find me – it will only bring you pain. But remember this – I will always love you. Be happy. Your Sophie.'

"I broke down then and wept like a baby. I just couldn't understand what had happened. Why had she gone away, like that? Everything had been fine up until then, although I'd begun to suspect something was wrong a few days before. She'd become a bit moody, and not her usual cheerful self. Nothing so dramatic as having a row, or anything. It was a real mystery to me. I couldn't think where she would have gone, unless to her parents, who lived in Chesterfield somewhere. I didn't even allow myself to think that she might have found someone else.

"I know what you're going to ask, Jerry. Why didn't I try to find her? Looking back, I don't really know now."

As Bernard finished his story, the plane touched down on Spanish soil. Jerry was choked. What a sad tale. How could such a seemingly perfect relationship end so abruptly?

"Did you never find out what happened?" he asked, as the plane taxied to a halt.

"No. And I never saw her again from that day to this."

"How sad," said Jerry, unbuckling his safety belt. "You really should have gone after her, you know."

"What's the point of regrets, Jerry? It only makes you bitter and life's too short."

"But love is all there is in the end. We only get one stab at life, so shouldn't we do all we can to be happy while we're here?"

"I'm a man of God. I think God tests us, and I don't think we're put on this earth to be happy all the time. After all, Jesus wasn't. He had His trials, so why shouldn't we? Anyway, I've no complaints. My life's been good, and I'm well looked after."

Jerry didn't altogether agree with the old man's philosophy and secretly thought Bernard had been pretty feeble to give up so easily. He put his arm around the old man as they made their way through customs.

36

In the taxi on the way to their hotel, Jerry brought up the subject again. "But, honestly, Bernard, wouldn't you like to know what happened to your Sophie – even now?"

"Perhaps. More so now than in the past. I had the business of living to get through then. My work as a vicar and father confessor kept me fully occupied. But now that I've retired I've found myself thinking more and more about Sophie. I lost a dear friend recently, so I feel a gap in my life now."

"Once this is over, maybe I can help you find her? After all, we've got the world wide web now. You never know…."

Bernard smiled. "Do you think there's a chance?"

"Sure – why not?" Jerry smiled encouragingly. "I want to know what happened to her almost as much as you do!"

Bernard laughed as they pulled up outside the accommodation that Jerry had had the foresight to book before leaving London. Both men felt at home at once inside the small, family-run hotel, as they made their way to the reception desk.

❧

After a good night's sleep, they felt ready for breakfast and for the prospect of meeting the Miles-Harrises. They gazed out of the window at the early autumn sunshine as they finished their meal. It was going to be a lovely day, but they weren't particularly looking forward to it.

Once in the taxi on their way, Jerry turned to Bernard and reminded him that, under no circumstances, were they to implicate Eve when asked how they had got their address. "Just say we sneaked a look in the file while her back was turned," said Jerry.

Bernard nodded. "Of course. Don't worry, I won't give the game away."

The Miles-Harrises' house was very impressive from the outside. The white façade looked pristine in the autumn sunshine, and they could see a swimming pool as they approached it from the street where the taxi had dropped them.

"Talk about the lap of luxury. They moved from Bockhampton Road to here? What a change!" observed Jerry.

"Very nice," agreed Bernard. "Is this what's called a hacienda, d'you think?"

"I think so," said Jerry, thoughtfully. He looked forward to moving himself, although maybe not so far as Spain, just to the next street would do.

They both stood, admiring the house for several minutes. It was situated in a quiet cul-de-sac, and there was hardly a sound to be heard. No cars, nothing. Then their ears attuned to the cicadas and various bird songs.

It was magical, like something out of a Walt Disney cartoon.

Finally, they steeled themselves to walk up to the front door and ring the bell. It wasn't long before a tall, grey-haired, rather elegant woman of indeterminate age stood before them, a friendly smile on her open, pleasant face.

"Yes? Can I help you?" she asked politely.

Jerry returned her smile. "Hello. I'm Jerry Bracegirdle, and this is Bernard Paltoquet. We've...."

He stopped. She was staring at Bernard and Bernard was staring at her.

"Bernard? Is it really you?"

"Sophie?"

Yes, it was she. Bernard's long-lost sweetheart stood before him, the Spanish sun highlighting her English rose complexion which still seemed as fresh as the day he had met her.

"H- how did you find me?" she asked. The shock on her face was the only thing that marred her beauty for Bernard at that moment. "Have you been looking for me for long?"

"I – I – forgive me, Sophie, but I haven't been looking for you at all," Bernard replied, not altogether tactfully.

"Then how – why?"

"It was a completely different matter that's brought me here," Bernard told her. "Can we come in?"

"Of course, please do, both of you." Sophie stepped aside to let the two men enter the house.

"Let me get you some tea. I always remembered you liked your tea, Bernard. Or do you prefer coffee these days?"

"Tea would be lovely," Bernard said. "But my young friend here may want coffee."

"Tea's fine, thanks," said Jerry.

While Sophie went off to the kitchen to prepare it, the two men looked at each other in amazement.

"What a coincidence!" said Jerry. "You must be over the moon."

"I can't quite believe it yet," said Bernard. "It's like a miracle. To find her after all these years."

Jerry looked across at the sideboard and noticed the photograph of a smiling, grey-haired man. And then he saw the black crepe draped around the frame.

"Bernie," he whispered. "Look! The picture of that man over there. It's got black crepe around it. What does that mean?"

"It means he must have recently died. Don't be so nosy – oh, I see what you mean..."

"Do you think it's Mr Miles-Harris? Do you think he's dead?"

"If that's who it is. I should say that's what it means, yes."

Then they looked along the sideboard and saw an array of cards, mostly tastefully decorated with flowers. Sympathy cards, of course.

"Oh my God," said Bernard, when the full import of the display sunk in. "Do you suppose her husband has just died?"

"Looks like it," said Jerry. "Sshh! She's coming."

Sophie came back into the room with a tea tray. She placed it on the coffee table between the two men and sat down opposite them.

As she poured the tea, Bernard coughed politely. "Er, we couldn't help noticing that you have recently been bereaved. We're so sorry to come at such a time. Of course, we didn't know, otherwise we wouldn't have dreamed of bothering you."

"Oh please, don't give it another thought. Of course, you didn't know. How could you? My dear husband died of a heart attack just over a week ago. He didn't suffer for long, which was a blessing."

"How long had you been married, Sophie?" Bernard asked as he sipped his tea.

"Just over fifty years," she replied. "We'd only just celebrated our golden wedding anniversary."

Neither man knew how to respond to this piece of information. "That's nice" seemed inappropriate in the circumstances.

"He hadn't been well for several weeks," she continued, "but he was doing all right until that girl turned up. That sent him over the edge and caused his fatal heart attack."

"'That girl'?" asked Jerry.

"Oh nothing. I didn't mean to say anything. After all, it's no concern of yours."

Jerry cleared his throat. "I think that's where you're wrong, Mrs Miles-Harris. The girl you mean was Beth Morrison, wasn't it?"

Sophie looked taken aback. "Yes, I think so. I know her name was Beth, anyway. I can't remember her surname. But – how did you know?"

"Does my name mean nothing to you?" Jerry asked her.

"No, I don't think so. Are you her husband?"

"No. I *was* her boyfriend. My name's Bracegirdle."

"Yes, I know. You told me. I think I would remember a name like that."

"I was the poor idiot who bought 57 Bockhampton Road off you," Jerry told her. Bernard shot him a warning glance.

Sophie looked at the young man in surprise. "I – I didn't know. My husband handled that side of things."

Bernard decided to intervene at this stage. "Look, Sophie, as I said to you just now, I haven't been actively looking for you at all. You and I finding each other again is a pure coincidence. I came here today with Jerry as his friend and confidante. His girlfriend was murdered in the house you sold him."

Sophie suddenly looked scared. "Murdered? But how? By whom?"

"I think you know the answer to that one, Sophie," said Bernard. "Shall we stop playing games? We came here to find out what happened to you and your husband in that house and why you sold it so cheaply to my friend here."

The old lady looked deflated. Her eyes began to fill with tears. "That house has been nothing but trouble to me and my family almost from day one. I wish we'd never seen the place. It should be blasted off the face of the earth."

"Our feelings exactly, Sophie," said Bernard gently. "We're not here to make trouble for you, especially at this sad time." He cast a glance at photograph of Mr Miles-Harris on the sideboard. "But Jerry is under suspicion by the police, and you know, don't you, that it wasn't him?"

"I don't know anything of the kind," she said, defensively, looking from one to other of them. "How should I?"

The two men waited patiently while she seemed to be gathering not only her thoughts, but her scattered wits. Finally, she spoke. "I – I didn't know anything was really wrong, honestly I didn't. I just thought it was all in my daughter's head."

"Your daughter? She had some bad experiences in that house?"

"She did. But we didn't really believe her."

"But if you didn't believe her, why did you want to get rid of the house? Surely you wouldn't have sold it for so little if you thought it was just your daughter's imagination?" Bernard was puzzled.

"Because what it did to her frightened us. We couldn't keep on the house after it had caused so much trouble for her."

"Where is your daughter now?" asked Bernard. "Did she move with you to Spain?"

"She's still in England," said Sophie. She paused before continuing. "In a mental asylum, actually."

"Are you saying the house sent her mad?" asked Bernard.

"Look, I think I need to explain a few things. My daughter, Catherine, was a beautiful child, but the trauma of her birth caused a problem with the workings of her brain, and she was what you would call 'sub-normal', I suppose. She had 'learning difficulties' as I think they politely call it these days and, as she grew older, she became more and more isolated from the other children and clung more and more to me. I was a single parent at the time, which didn't help matters – "

Bernard jumped in. "So, Mr Miles-Harris wasn't Catherine's father?"

"No. He took her on when he married me. He was a saint."

"A good man indeed," agreed Bernard. "You must have loved him very much."

"Oh yes, I loved him. We enjoyed our life together – at least we did until we moved into Bockhampton Road."

"But, Mrs Miles-Harris, in what way was your daughter disturbed by the house? Did she see ghosts? Hear voices? What?" Jerry asked eagerly.

"Nothing so precise as that. She kept telling me she felt miserable, especially when she was sitting in front of that fireplace. She also felt cold most of the time. There were days when she would run out of the house and refuse to return for hours. We had to coax her back in with the promise of her favourite video and a box of chocolates."

"All that sounds upsetting, but I don't quite see how it would have sent her so deranged as to warrant her being put in a mental home," observed Bernard.

"No, well, it's hard to explain. But she was getting more and more introverted. Her condition hadn't really improved since she was a child. In fact, as she grew older, she got worse. She was on medication, which helped, but really, she wasn't relating to the outside world at all. Which was such a shame as she was a very pretty young woman. But men frightened her, and any attempt by a young man to befriend her was repulsed almost at once. And, by the time she reached middle age, she had become bitter. She used to pick rows with me and Charlie, my husband, and there were many times when we just didn't know how to deal with her. Then, when we moved to Bockhampton Road, she started to go completely off the rails. One time, she tried to throw herself off the roof. She said she was being hounded to her death by the house."

"I'm so sorry," said Bernard, "I can see why you needed to move right away. But why did you put her in an institution?"

"We didn't do it lightly, I can assure you. And she's a voluntary patient. She wasn't sectioned, or anything. But the doctors convinced us that travelling to Spain would be traumatic for Cathy, and that a stay in a hospital that specialised in her sort of problems would be better for her. Once she was stabilised, we could then think about getting her over here."

"So how long has she been in the hospital?" asked Bernard.

"Two years. We went to see her several times, but each time she seemed worse, not better. I think she was being kept on medication most of the time. Although, they said she was receiving regular counselling as well as occasional electric shock treatment."

"Do they still do that?" asked Jerry, aghast. "I thought that went out with the Victorians."

"No, they still perform what's called electroconvulsive therapy – ECT for short. It's supposed to help severe depressive cases and bipolar disorders – or so we were told. My husband was not happy that Cathy was getting this ECT treatment and said so to the psychiatrist in charge of our daughter's case. Charlie told him we could see no improvement in Cathy and that, in fact, she was worse. But we were talked round and told we needed to give the treatment more time to work. Neither of us was really convinced, but we didn't know any different and had to assume that the professionals knew best."

"How sad for you – especially now that your husband is dead," observed Jerry. "But what about

Cathy's real father? Does he know? Does he keep in touch?"

Sophie lowered her gaze. "Can we talk privately for a few minutes, Bernard?"

Jerry stood up at once. "I'd love to look round your garden and the swimming pool. May I?" he asked tactfully.

⁑

When they were alone, Sophie topped up Bernard's teacup and seated herself in the chair vacated by Jerry. She gazed gently into Bernard's eyes. "I need to tell you something, and I'm not sure how you're going to take it."

Bernard sipped his tea. "Go on, I'm listening."

"There's no way to break this to you gently. So I'll just come out and say it. Cathy's your daughter."

"Mine?" Bernard nearly spilt his tea as he replaced the cup in the saucer. "Mine you say? But how?"

"How do you think?"

"Do you mean she was conceived while we were at university?"

"Of course. I thought you would have understood why I left in such a hurry. I thought you would have read between the lines of the note I left you."

Bernard had never, in his wildest dreams, thought that was the reason she had left him. He sat there, trying to come to terms with the fact that, for all these years, he had been a father without ever knowing it. He also had to come to terms with his feelings for the woman now seated beside him. She was the woman he had worshipped and loved throughout the long years of his celibacy. Now he realised he had loved a mere figment of his imagination. The woman in the room with him now was a stranger.

37

"Is it okay if I come back in now? Have you finished your private conversation?" Jerry asked, looking from one to the other.

"Of course," said Sophie, getting up and coming over to him. "Come in. I think Bernard would like to talk to you." She walked past him out of the room. Jerry noticed, out of the corner of his eye, she had been crying. He walked over to Bernard and sat down beside him. He, too, looked close to tears.

"Is everything all right?" he asked.

Bernard reached for his handkerchief and blew his nose. "I've just had rather a shock, Jerry. I don't know where to begin."

"Begin at the beginning, as they say," said Jerry with an encouraging smile. "That's the best plan."

Bernard gave him a thin smile. "Well, you know the beginning already."

"Yes, I do. Is there an ending now?"

"Well, hardly that. Anyway, you know I told you she left me suddenly after two years together?"

"Yes, of course I do. Do you know the reason now?"

"Yes."

"Well, what is it?" Jerry prompted, obviously impatient as Bernard remained silent for several moments.

"Can't you guess?" Bernard asked finally.

"I'm not a mind reader."

"Sorry, Jerry. I'm just finding it hard to put into words. The reason Sophie left me was because she was pregnant with my child." The last sentence was said in staccato, each word pronounced with stark solemnity.

Bernard continued to wipe his eyes and blow his nose.

"My God!"

"It's a bit of a facer, isn't it?"

"It certainly is. But why on earth would she have left you if she was going to have your baby? She loved you, didn't she? And there was no doubt you were in love with her. What a waste!"

"I just can't begin to comprehend her motive for abandoning me and bringing up the child on her own."

"Well, I suppose back in the mid-nineteen-forties, it was a social disgrace to have a baby out of wedlock...."

"But she must have known I would have married her like a shot. She knew I wanted to...."

Jerry put his arm around the old man's shoulders. "So you lived most of your life not even knowing you were a father. I don't think I'd ever forgive that woman if it were me."

"Well, you're not me, are you?" There was an accusatory look on Bernard's face. "However, I don't blame you for feeling like that. I don't think I can forgive her, either. Certainly not yet, anyway."

"So, what are you going to do now? Meet your daughter? I mean, Mrs Miles-Harris can't stop you, can she? You've a right."

"I don't think Sophie would stop me but she's obviously in no fit state to meet a strange man claiming to be her long-lost father."

"But you *must* meet her," insisted Jerry, "and, you never know, it may make all the difference to her to finally know who her father is. Think about it, it's not only you in this."

"I know, Jerry. But I'm so nervous. And, by my reckoning, she'd be in her mid-sixties now. To think I never knew her when she was young and growing up...."

"With all due respect to you, Bernard, I think Sophie didn't treat you well at all."

Bernard sighed. "She must have had her reasons."

"Why don't you ask her? Don't leave it like this – you can't!"

"No, I suppose...."

Just then, Sophie came back into the room. Jerry got up and headed for the kitchen. "I think you two have some unfinished business. I'll make a fresh pot of tea. Do you have anything cold to drink, Mrs Miles-Harris?"

Sophie, now quite dry-eyed, gave him a sad smile. "Call me Sophie, please. There's coke and orange juice, I think. And water, of course. Help yourself."

"Tea for two coming up," he said, leaving the room and closing the door quietly. He glanced over at Bernard as he did so, mouthing something at him.

Bernard, who hadn't understood exactly what Jerry was communicating to him, had got the general drift. He gave Sophie a wary look as she came and sat down beside him again.

"I think I owe you an explanation," she said.

"It's hard to remember everything exactly after all these years," she began, "but most of that awful time is etched on my memory. Everything was fine, except I started to be sick in the mornings. I thought nothing of it, at first, thinking I'd just caught a bug or had some sort of food poisoning. The last thing I thought was that I was going to have a baby. Can you believe it? But I was so innocent, I didn't even connect it with being pregnant, even though I hadn't had a period for three months. Sorry, Bernard, if this is embarrassing for you."

"Not at all," he assured her. "I should think I know the facts of life by now. Carry on."

"Anyway, it was Lallagy – you remember her? – one of our flatmates? She was always singing and being generally noisy."

"Oh, yes. I remember accusing her of being too cheerful in the mornings."

"That's her," smiled Sophie. "She was the one who told me. Said it was as plain as a pikestaff. And even when the doctor confirmed it, I still didn't quite believe it. Everything was about to fall apart. You – me – my future – *our* future. When it finally sunk in, I knew there was no question of 'getting rid of it', as Lallagy suggested. The very idea was abhorrent. All I could think, then, was I'd have to leave university at once and go home to my parents. There wasn't any other choice or, at least, that's how I saw it at the time. I couldn't tell you. No, Bernard, hear me out. I knew, if I told you, you'd want to marry me, and two lives would be have been ruined instead of one."

"Don't you think I had a right to make that decision for myself?"

"Maybe, now. Looking back. But you can't turn back the clock. At the time, all I knew was I loved you enough to set you free. You'd never have been able to become a vicar, would you? And it was your dearest wish. Just think what people would have said if they knew you'd got a fellow student pregnant out of wedlock."

"That's ridiculous! We'd have been married long before the baby was born. No one would have been any the wiser."

"But you hadn't got your degree! You would have had to leave university – at least that's what I thought at the time. No, the only thing for me to do was go home. I knew my parents would go up the wall, but there was no help for it. So I just wrote you a note and left it on your pillow. You'd already left for a ten o'clock lecture, so I packed my suitcase and walked out of your life."

It was a melodramatic statement, and Sophie paused, waiting for Bernard to assimilate what she had said so far. Then she continued.

"There was a dreadful scene with my parents when I got home. Worse, even, than I'd expected. But, in the end, they supported me through my pregnancy. They were the kind of people who cared what other people thought and, back then, it was a social stigma to have a baby 'on the other side of the blanket', so I was very grateful to them that they didn't turn me out. And, when Cathy was born, it was all forgotten. They were such proud grandparents.

"All was well, for a while. It wasn't apparent that Cathy was subnormal and, by the time we found out, there was no question of putting her into a special home. So I brought her up with the help of my parents, and I eventually consigned you to history. I *had* to. You were better off without me, I was convinced. Anyway, as you'd made no attempt to find me, I began to think you hadn't really cared about me so much, after all. It's all right, Bernard, I know now I was wrong about that, but at the time that's what I thought. I knew you didn't know where my parents lived, but it wasn't beyond the bounds of possibility for you to find me if you'd wanted to enough.

"Water under the bridge now, of course. Things could have been different, I suppose, if you'd turned up on my parents' doorstep."

Bernard looked her in the eyes. His usually soft brown eyes had taken on a steely hardness. "I nearly came to see you, Sophie. I found your parents' address easily enough. I remembered you'd told me they lived in Chesterfield, and it only took a quick look in the telephone directory to get the exact address."

"But you didn't come?"

"No, and for that I shall be eternally sorry."

"Never mind, Bernard. As I said, water under the bridge. When Charlie came along, it was like a miracle. I'd reached the end of my tether with being a single mum. Cathy, as you can imagine, wasn't the easiest of children, and my parents could only do so much. When he proposed, I just thanked God for him. He was prepared to take on the care of Cathy, who was then about ten-years-old. He had a good job with a Chartered Accountancy firm in the city of London and, for many years, we were all very happy.

"Until we moved to 57 Bockhampton Road, and I curse the day."

There was little more to tell after that. Jerry, who had been discreetly making tea all this time, put his head round the door. He saw the two old dears sitting together silently. He coughed.

"Oh, do come in, young man," said Sophie briskly. "Where's that tea?"

Bernard wanted Sophie to return with them to London by the next available flight, but Sophie pointed out that it would be quite impossible to up and leave just like that. There were arrangements to be made, people to notify and friends to say farewell to.

Her husband's funeral had taken place only the day before and she still had to collect his ashes from the crematorium. She was planning to scatter them on Hampstead Heath, the place where he had lived as a boy and been happiest.

"Well, as soon as you can, then," said Bernard. "Once you've scattered the ashes, maybe you can take me to meet my daughter?"

"Oh, Bernard, you're running away with yourself. I don't think you can just turn up out of the blue without some sort of prior preparation. Don't forget she's not well and still in the institution."

"And *that's* going to change," he said with determination.

"What d'you mean?"

"No more electric shocks for her, not if I have anything to do with it."

"We must let the experts know what's best, Bernard."

"I think Bernard's right," chipped in Jerry. "You just put her in there out of your way so you could move to Spain."

"Jerry!"

"Sorry, Bernard, but I have to speak my mind about this. I'm sorry, Mrs Miles-Harris, I know you haven't had an easy time, but Bernard has suffered too. And not telling him about the baby was just plain wrong."

Sophie looked at him severely, then her face softened. "You're talking from a twenty-first century perspective, young man. This was the nineteen-forties."

There was an awkward silence. "'The past is another country – they do things differently there'," quoted Bernard into it.

Suddenly, the phone sprang into life. Both Bernard and Sophie seemed unable to move, so Jerry went to answer it.

"Is Mr or Mrs Miles-Harris there, please?" said an official-sounding voice.

"There's a man asking for you or your husband," he said, passing the receiver to Sophie.

"Hello? This is Mrs Miles-Harris speaking. What can I do for you?"

"This is Dr Mallory of Ticehurst Priory here. I'm afraid I've got some bad news, Mrs Miles-Harris."

The two men watched her in growing alarm. Her face had turned ashen and she looked about to faint. However, she remained upright, as she listened to her caller.

"I see," she said finally. "Well thank you, Doctor, for informing me. I shall catch the next flight to the UK tonight and be with you as soon as I can. In the meantime, have you told the police?"

Jerry and Bernard were standing beside her now.

"I understand," she said, "but there is one place you should concentrate your search, Doctor. Tell the police to go to 57 Bockhampton Road, Wandsworth. That was her last family home. Try there – now!"

She slammed the receiver down and turned to her companions. "That was the Priory where Cathy is being treated," she told them. "They tell me she's run away.

She wasn't sectioned so she was free to come and go. Apparently, she's been gone for several hours and the police have been searching for her without any luck."

"So you suggested that she might have gone back to her old home?" Bernard asked.

"It seems the most logical place. She's probably missing me and Charlie. How could we leave her alone there for so long? What a wicked and cruel thing to do!"

"Don't be so hard on yourself, Sophie," Jerry said, obviously undergoing a slight change of heart. "The important thing now is to find her."

"But she could be anywhere – I only hope she's at Bockhampton Road."

"And I only hope she's not," said Bernard sternly. "She could be in grave danger if she's gone there. Have you thought about that?"

Sophie began to cry in rage and frustration. "Just book the tickets, can't you? We must be on that plane tonight."

Jerry pressed a number on his mobile and did as he was bid.

Three hours later they were on a plane bound for Gatwick, estimated time of arrival: ten fifteen at night. The three companions sat in silence. Sophie cradled her husband's ashes in her lap. Jerry, armed with the necessary paperwork, had somehow managed to get them from the crematorium before they left. She had wept with gratitude as he had handed her the urn.

"I don't deserve friends like you," she had wept. "I only hope my darling's safe."

They had rung the Priory before leaving to catch their flight, but they were told Cathy hadn't gone to Bockhampton Road or, if she had, wasn't there now. In one way they were relieved but, in another, they didn't know where else she could be. The sooner they were on English soil the better.

38

In only a few hours, although to them it seemed like an eternity, they were outside the Ticehurst Priory where Cathy Harris-Miles had spent the last few years. It was a pleasant, white building, looking more like a seaside hotel than a mental institution. Situated just outside the pleasant village of Ticehurst on the Sussex-Kent border, most people, apart from the villagers themselves, assumed it was some sort of guest house. There was no hint of Victorian institutional gloom about it, and the only clue to its true purpose was in the wrought iron gates that were invisible from the road, hidden by ornate evergreens. Sophie pressed the bell set in the wall by the side of them.

The trio were soon buzzed in and immediately met by a worried-looking Dr Mallory, his remaining strands of hair awry, and his small, grey eyes ringed by dark circles.

"We thought we'd cracked it when you told us she'd probably gone back to her old home," he said, shaking Sophie by the hand. He looked enquiringly at the old gentleman and the much younger man by her side.

"Forgive me," she said, "This is a young friend of mine, Jeremy Bracegirdle, and this is – this is – Cathy's father." Bernard shook the doctor's hand vigorously.

"But this isn't Mr Miles-Harris." Dr Mallory looked stunned.

"No, Bernard Paltoquet, *Reverend* Bernard Paltoquet." Sophie announced him as if he was James Bond.

The 'Reverend' bit didn't seem to have impressed the psychiatrist at all.

"Sorry, Doctor," Sophie continued, "this gentleman is my daughter's *natural* father. My husband was her adoptive father."

"Oh, I see. Is your husband not with you today?"

"No, I'm afraid he died last week," she told him.

"I'm sorry," he said. "He was a good man. I'm really sorry about your daughter's disappearance. We didn't keep her under lock and key, and she never ever made an attempt to leave before. We're at a loss to know where she could be."

Bernard spoke up. "So, are you telling us she isn't at Bockhampton Road?"

The doctor eyed him with a hint of suspicion. "The police told us that the place was completely deserted. There was no sign of life."

"But did they go inside?" Bernard persisted.

"No. The owner wasn't at home."

"No, because I'm here," Jerry interjected.

"Oh, right." The poor doctor looked even more bewildered now. "Anyway, the police were satisfied there was no one there."

"How can you be sure if they didn't go inside?" Bernard stamped his foot with impatience. "Why are we wasting time? We need to get to Bockhampton Road right away!"

Dr Mallory sighed. "I can assure you...."

Before the doctor could finish assuring them, Bernard turned to Sophie. "Has Cathy got a key to the house?"

Sophie thought for a moment. "I wouldn't have thought so. We handed all the keys to the estate agents. Although I suppose she could still have one."

"Then I think we'd better just make sure for ourselves that Cathy isn't there," he said. "Because it's my belief she *is* there and in great danger."

And with that he pulled Sophie back down the corridor and out of the building, Jerry following in his wake. Dr Mallory called after them, "You're only wasting your time. We need to discuss this...."

But nobody was listening to him. Jerry pressed Omar Kemal's number on his mobile.

"Hello?" came a sleep-sodden voice. "Who's that?"

"Sorry, did I wake you, Omar? It's Jerry."

"It's after midnight," Omar complained. "I knocked off early as I'd been driving for over sixteen hours, and now you wake me...."

"Shut up and listen," interrupted Jerry. "I can't explain now. But we need to get to Bockhampton Road soonest and we need *you* to get us there. You said you'd be glad to help and I wouldn't ask, only it's really important. A woman's life's at risk...."

"Okay okay!" protested Omar, sounding wide awake now. "I'll be with you right away. Where are you?"

"That's just it, we're in Sussex, in a small village called Ticehurst. There's a place here called the Priory – it's a mental home of sorts. Do you think you can find it?"

"No problem. Let's see – the time's now twelve-thirty-five. I should be with you in about an hour?"

"Great! But don't kill yourself. We want you here in one piece."

"No problem. There won't be much traffic at this time of night."

"Okay," said Jerry, clicking off the call. "We've got about an hour to wait. It's a good job it's not too cold as there's nowhere we can go till then."

"Never mind," said Bernard. "It's all in a good cause. Let's just pray we're not too late."

When Omar arrived some fifty-five minutes later, he found them sitting on a bench outside the village pub. Although the night was reasonably mild, they were now pretty cold after nearly an hour of inaction. Jerry wasn't too bad, but the old bones of Bernard and Sophie were beginning to protest. Luckily, Omar had thought to prepare a flask of hot coffee for them.

"Hold tight," grinned Omar, after they were all seated inside his cab, gratefully hugging their coffee mugs. "I'm going for the world land speed record – again!"

As they counted down the miles, Jerry explained everything to their kind chauffeur, including who Sophie was and why they had to get to that dreadful Wandsworth terrace as quickly as possible. Omar stepped on the accelerator after waiting uselessly at the traffic lights. He was tempted to ignore the red lights when there were no other cars to be seen but didn't dare chance it. Surveillance cameras were everywhere, and they couldn't afford to be stopped by the police now.

∾

57 Bockhampton Road looked just as Jerry had left it the day before yesterday. No lights on and, to all intents and purposes, completely deserted. There was no sign of a forced entry, and all the windows were firmly closed. The 'For Sale' sign, re-erected so soon after being taken down, creaked slightly in the gentle night breeze.

All four of them made their way up the path and waited while Jerry wrestled with the lock. "It's still very stiff," he complained. "I was going to do something about it, but I don't see the point now."

When they were inside, he switched on the hall light. They looked around them. All looked normal and nothing seemed to have been disturbed. Sophie called out softly: "Cathy? Are you there? It's your mummy, come to take you home with me."

They waited for an answer, but none came. Sophie couldn't hide her disappointment, so convinced had she been that Bernard was right and they would find her daughter there.

"Not to worry," said Bernard. "Maybe she's asleep upstairs."

"Oh yes," said Sophie, brightening. "She could have gone to her old room. She felt safe there." They all made their way up the unlit stairs. Jerry hadn't got around to putting a bulb into the landing light fitting, but there was enough light from the hall to illuminate their way. They followed the owner of the house slowly up the stairs, all of them sensing a change in the atmosphere as they did so. The natural chill of a house uninhabited for a time was replaced by an unnatural and unhealthy dampness that seemed to envelop them.

Reaching the landing, feeling chilled to their very marrow, they set about searching the upstairs rooms. The two smaller bedrooms were empty and there was no sleeping form in Jerry's bed, the only one in the house. If Cathy had come there, she would certainly have found her way eventually to it, they felt sure. The police were right after all. Cathy hadn't come back here. So where was she?

As they all trooped back down the stairs, Bernard cleared his throat and spoke softly to Jerry, so that Sophie wouldn't hear. "We still haven't tried the living room. Will you go with Sophie and Omar back to the cab while I take a look?"

"Don't go in there on your own, Bernard," Jerry whispered. "It could be dangerous. Remember what happened to Beth."

Not to mention the others, thought Bernard. "I've had my life," he said out loud. "If it ends here, so be it. But I must find out if I'm right."

Jerry patted him on the shoulder. "Wait here," he told him and, raising his voice, addressed Sophie and Omar. "You two had better get back to the cab. Can you drop Sophie at a B&B, do you think, Omar?"

Omar said he knew of a really good one, but it would probably be shut up for the night by now. He could put Sophie up in his spare room, though.

Sophie looked at Bernard. "Aren't I staying with you?" she asked him.

"No. I'm going to stay here with Jerry. I think he shouldn't be left alone. And I'd rather know you were safe away from here. Omar will look after you."

"You will be safe with me," said Omar, looking at the elegant old lady with an appraising eye. "My landlady will make sure of that."

Sophie, much too tired to argue, allowed herself to be settled into the front passenger seat.

Bernard turned to Jerry as the cab disappeared into the early morning shadows. "You should have gone with them. I don't want anything to happen to you."

"Did you think I'd let you go in that room on your own?" Jerry demanded. "It's my house, remember? I must be the one to go in there first."

Without further discussion, they made their way back to the living room door. Jerry stepped forward and turned the doorknob.

What greeted their eyes didn't surprise them in the least. It didn't really even shock them. It was what they had both expected but had hoped to be proved wrong. Without the aid of the electric light they could see the body of Cathy Miles-Harris in the glow of the fireplace. Her skull was smashed in and her hair was matted with blood.

Jerry grabbed Bernard as he toppled against him. He closed the door quickly and supported the old man into the kitchen, where he sat him down and fetched him a glass of water.

"That's my daughter in there, Jerry." Bernard's hands shook as he drank the water. "I didn't even have the chance to speak to her, let alone save her life."

39

Over a year had passed since the discovery of Cathy's body in 57 Bockhampton Road. It had been a sad year for Bernard and Sophie, coming to terms with their grief over the loss of their daughter. Added to their misery had been the painstaking probing by the police. Naturally, no motive or suspect was ever found for her murder and, after several fruitless months, the investigation was scaled down and the grieving parents were left in peace.

It had soon become evident to the police or, as Jerry put it, permeated their thick skulls, that the murders of Cathy Miles-Harris and Beth Morrison in the exact same place by the exact same means couldn't be put down to just mere coincidence. The murder weapon, too, had puzzled them. Although the blood-stained poker found by Beth's body had been taken away by the police for forensic tests and eventually labelled and added to all the other gruesome things found at murder scenes, the precise same weapon, covered in blood stains, was found by poor Cathy's body. It couldn't be rationally explained away.

DS Bob Drake had almost suffered a nervous breakdown over the whole business. He couldn't pin Beth's murder on Jerry Bracegirdle, and there was no one to pin Cathy's murder on, either. Jerry was, for a short time, a suspect, but nothing stuck and nothing made sense. Drake finally let Jerry off the hook in order to finish having his nervous breakdown in peace.

Since then, life had looked up for Jerry. Back at work, with his colleagues treating him as if nothing had happened, and Eve Mason playing a rather important part in his life, he was a contented young man. Eve's impending divorce was the cherry on the cake for him. She had been unhappy for a while before she had even met him, so he had showed up in her life, or at least in her shop, at just the right time for both of them.

The only fly in the ointment for Jerry now was 57 Bockhampton Road. If only he had been able to sell the bloody place. However, Eve hadn't objected to visiting him there and even staying over occasionally. That had made him very happy, as he had feared a reaction similar to Beth's when she first set foot in the place. "It's a bit quaint," was all Eve had said on seeing it for the first time.

Quaint it wasn't, certainly not to Jerry, after everything that had happened in it. Still, he had to admit, it had been behaving itself lately, its blood lust seemingly quenched for the time being, at least.

Bernard hadn't seen Sophie off when she finally decided to return to Spain. She had asked him to come with her, live out his remaining years with her in sunnier climes. It would be the perfect solution for them both, she had urged, then cried, then cajoled. They should be together, consoling each other in the loss of their child. But, as Bernard had pointed out, Cathy had never been his child. How could he mourn her loss in the same way his mother could, who had known her all her life? It had been meant to hurt and hurt her it did. Vindictiveness had never been in Bernard's nature but now, in his dotage, he found he was more than capable of it.

Jerry had tried to intervene, suggesting that Sophie was right. Although he didn't really like her, he could see the sense in the two old people joining forces in their old age. They would be company for each other, loving companions. But it hadn't moved Bernard one iota. He had never hardened his heart against anyone who had needed him. His Christian duty had always come first. To love and forgive, that's what his life had all been about. But he had found no forgiveness in his heart for Sophie, and he certainly had no love for her, either. Not anymore.

After Sophie's departure, Bernard settled back into a routine of sorts, with dear old Mrs Ruddock serving him faithfully with tea, sympathy and her own individual brand of companionship. It was all he needed now, he had told Jerry and Jerry accepted Bernard was happy with that. But he still thought he had been wrong to turn his back on Sophie. Life was too short.

ℒ

Jerry found he cared more for his old friend than even his parents, these days. He often visited him to make sure he was all right, in good health and had all he needed. He became a favourite of Mrs Ruddock, too. Bernard was always delighted to see him, even if a little anxious about his safety in that house. But, as the days, weeks and months wore on, he began to relax. Perhaps 57 Bockhampton Road was at peace at last.

But, just as Bernard, a few streets away, was thinking this, Jerry and Eve were sitting in that very living room in front of the fire. It was a cold December evening, and they were hugging each other for warmth, as much as anything else. There was no proper fire in the grate, just an electric two-bar job which wasn't very efficient. Love kept them warm, of course, but suddenly it wasn't enough. There was an icy blast that seemed to emanate from the boarded up chimney breast. The fire was still throwing out the same amount of heat, but they couldn't feel it now. The house was up to its old tricks again.

Eve got up from his lap, her teeth chattering in her head. They had been on the verge of going to bed, so Jerry thought she had decided it was time. They needed to get between the sheets to keep warm and to, well, do what came naturally. He reached down to turn off the fire.

"You need to get out, Jerry," said Eve, almost echoing Beth's very words. "I'm going home."

He didn't even try to stop her. What was the point? Besides, the last thing he wanted was Eve ending up like Beth.

∼

Jerry was at Bernard's door after work the following evening. "It's started again," he said without preamble.

Mrs Ruddock had shown him straight through to Bernard in his cosy study. She was used to the pleasant young man's visits, but he looked worried tonight. More than worried. As Jerry addressed Bernard with these dramatic words, he realised he wasn't alone.

"Oh, sorry," he said, seeing a plump, but still pretty, old lady by the fire opposite Bernard.

"Let me introduce you," smiled Bernard. Dorothy Plunkett held out her hand to Jerry and he shook it gently.

"So, this is the lady you were telling me about," said Jerry, turning to Bernard. "I'm so sorry to interrupt, but I'm worried."

"I know," said Bernard. "I always expected the spirit, or spirits, in that house would reappear sooner or later. I've just been telling Dorothy all about it."

"Are you still doing séances and that sort of thing?" Jerry asked her, taking the seat indicated by Bernard.

"Not so much these days, dear," she said. Her voice was like melting chocolate, a voice to comfort, a voice to soothe the sorrows of the bereaved. "I'm a bit too long in the tooth."

"But you've still got the gift, Dorothy, haven't you?" Bernard interjected.

"I have. If I'm needed. And, from what you've been telling me, Bernard, it seems I am."

"Do you really think you can help?" asked Jerry. "Can you contact these spirits in my house and find out what they want or why they're there. And then can you stop them doing it?"

"One thing at a time, Jerry dear," laughed Dorothy, "although the answers to your questions are yes – probably."

"So, what will you do? When can you start?"

"Is tomorrow soon enough, young man?"

"I should think so," laughed Jerry. "If you can rid my place of whatever is haunting it, then I'll take it off the market and do it up. Eve and I plan – or, at least, we *had* planned – to live there together. But I'm sure she'll come back when the evil has gone." His eagerness was all too palpable.

"Don't get your hopes up too high, dear," she warned him. "I'm not infallible. But I promise I shall do my very best. In fact, I shall regard it as my biggest challenge. Probably my swan song as well." She said this wistfully. "So, I don't intend to fail."

40

Christmas had come and gone, leaving in its wake a cold, snow-covered January. Bernard, although he always enjoyed the festive season, being such a special time in the church calendar, had enjoyed this last one more than any others he could remember for a long time. Henry and Maddie Freeman had come to stay with him, bringing their only daughter and her husband, and their only daughter, with them. It was a houseful, but it was a house of happiness.

Against all the odds, Henry Freeman had survived the trauma of his childhood to marry his delightful Maddie, and their daughter and granddaughter were equally delightful. Bernard had been slightly wary of the son-in-law at first. His sole topics of conversation seemed to be *Star Wars* and Formula One, but his heart was in the right place, and Bernard eventually warmed to him. Mrs Ruddock, despite having her hands full, had enjoyed every minute of their visit, too, pampering the little granddaughter within an inch of her life.

Bernard had invited Jerry to stay for as long as he wanted, following the latest manifestations in his house, so there was one more to add to the party. Then, on Boxing Day, Dorothy and Eve also turned up. Even Mrs Ruddock, at this point, feared her mince pies wouldn't go round. However, she needn't have worried, there were still a stack of mince pies in the larder on the fifth of January, the date set for Dorothy to try and contact the evil spirits in Jerry's house.

So, after a quick breakfast of mince pies, she, Jerry and Bernard arrived at 57 Bockhampton Road. Snow obliterated the 'For Sale' sign, perched upon which was a tiny robin.

"That's a sign of good luck," observed Dorothy, wrapped in her unfashionable fur coat, for which she had been vilified for many years.

"Let's hope so," said Bernard.

Jerry said nothing, seemingly daunted at being back outside his home again, after the cosy time he had spent with Bernard for the last couple of weeks. This was make or break time for him, and Dorothy Plunkett was his only hope.

They stood outside the gate, surveying the ordinary little terrace house that, apart from its dilapidation, looked just like all the rest in the row. No one passing by could ever suspect what had gone on within its walls. And was still going on. Dorothy Plunkett was an unlikely heroine, as she stood there in her old fur coat and ankle boots but, however unlikely, she was the only one who could prevent another murder.

"Let's begin," she said quietly. "Now, you must both wait here. Key, please, Jerry."

He gave her the key without a murmur. If he was concerned to see an old lady enter the house of death, he didn't say so. This was Dorothy Plunkett's territory, and she was in charge. She had trouble turning the key but held her hand up as Jerry stepped forward to help her. It was clear she needed no one else today. Soon, she was inside, and the front door was closed. Bernard and Jerry remained at the gate and waited anxiously for her next instruction. The front door opened after a few long minutes.

"I've seen the fireplace," she said, "and I'm convinced that that is where the real trouble lies. The whole house is very troubled – there are many restless spirits here. But the fireplace is possessed by a veritable demon."

This really wasn't any news to the two men, of course. What they needed to know was how Dorothy proposed to deal with it all.

"I'm pleased to report that every one of these spirits, including the one responsible for the murders, is anxious to communicate. They've been waiting a long time."

"So, what happens now?" asked Bernard.

"First, I need you both to go away and leave me alone with these spirits. It will take me some time to contact them all."

"When shall we come back? Will you be safe?" asked Jerry anxiously.

"There you go again, Jerry, dear. Questions, questions. But, in answer to your first one, come back in about four hours. Say, at three o'clock."

Before Jerry could ask any more questions, Bernard took his arm and began walking with him down the street. "Dorothy knows what's she's doing," he told him. "You'd better come home with me for a while.

Let's see if Mrs Ruddock has any more mince pies, shall we?"

❧

Bernard and Jerry sat beside the fire, hardly speaking. There was little to say. Mrs Ruddock came and went at regular intervals, with supplies of tea, coffee, left over Christmas cake and a lunch of scrambled eggs and baked beans. They constantly looked at their watches and at the mantel clock, waiting for the hour of three. It was almost dark outside as they made their way back to Bockhampton Road through the snow flurries.

Finally, they were outside 57 Bockhampton Road once more. All seemed quiet, peaceful even. The lamp post situated on the opposite side of the road cast an eerie glow over its facade, but neither man felt afraid. Except, there was no sign of Dorothy Plunkett. Jerry was all for going into the house, but then remembered he'd given the key to her.

"I'll knock on the door," he said with determination. "She may be lying dead in there, for all we know."

This time, Bernard agreed that doing nothing was no longer an option. They both started up the garden path together but, as they did so, the front door opened and there was Dorothy, looking shaken, but otherwise unscathed.

"Dorothy, thank goodness!" said Bernard with relief. He took her hand and helped her down the front doorstep. "Are you all right?"

"Yes, I think so. Up to a point." She turned to Jerry. "Do you possess an axe, young man?"

"Er, I think so. I saw one in the garden shed, but it's very rusty. Why?"

"Get it, sharpen it and – "

"And?"

"Break up that bloody fireplace."

PART FIVE

Ivy Lodge
Harcourt Road, Ealing

2nd February 2010

Dear Bernard,

I enclose, as promised, all the information that I was able to discover when I undertook to rid 57 Bockhampton Road of its evil influence.

Each of the spirits trapped in the house had their stories to tell, and I pass all this on to you in the enclosed pages. You will see I've taken down everything they told me as near as possible verbatim, so their speech patterns and cockney dialect in some cases may prove difficult to understand. I hope, however, that you can glean, from all that I have managed to document, what you need to know about that dreadful house.

The fireplace served as a home for the evilest spirit of them all, and that is why I had Jerry destroy it. However, while I have been able to release the tormented souls and enable them to pass over, I was unsuccessful in one instance. The evilest spirit of all has eluded me and, without its home in the fireplace, still poses a danger wherever it goes.

But, Bernard dear, I have done all I can. The forces of pure evil remain unconquered and, for that, I am sincerely sorry.

Yours always,
Dorothy

41

It was not until several days later that Bernard learned the true meaning of what had taken place in 57 Bockhampton Road sporadically over the past decades. He had pieced together information from various sources, but they hadn't added up to the true and startling facts that Dorothy had managed to discover while communing with the spirits within that troubled house.

She had been physically and mentally exhausted when she had emerged, with just the one instruction to Jerry. He had promised to do her bidding as soon as possible, but she had been adamant.

"Do it now!" she had insisted.

Bernard had then ordered a taxi to take her home, courtesy of Jerry's mobile, and it was Omar Kemal who had turned up, more by design than luck. Bernard was delighted to see him, and so was Jerry. Dorothy had soon learned the part Omar had played in the drama, and she shook him by the hand. "A terrible business," she had said, "but it is at an end now." Then she had paused, looking at all three men as she had said it. "Almost," she had then added ominously.

"Well, Dorothy, dear, how are you feeling now?" asked Bernard, welcoming her the next evening and settling her opposite him by the cosy fireplace. Mrs Ruddock had made a great fuss of the old woman too, and there was tea and an upside-down cake on the occasional table beside her to prove it.

"Still tired, but coping," smiled Dorothy, tucking in to Mrs Ruddock's homemade cake. "Hmm, delicious. What is it with you, Bernard? You always seem to get housekeepers that not only pamper the socks off you, but cook such lovely food, too."

"Must be my riveting personality," he grinned. "Now, tell me, Dorothy, are the trials of that house at an end at last?"

She looked serious now, returning her half-eaten cake to the plate for a moment. "More or less," she hedged. "More or less."

"What does that mean?"

"I shall explain in due course, dear."

"Very well. But do you now know exactly what happened to cause all those awful tragedies?"

"Yes, I do. I'm sure you know most of it, though."

"Well, I have made it my business to find out as much as I can about the place, but there's still so much I don't yet fully understand."

Dorothy sat back in her chair and sighed. "It is hard, I grant you. The whole thing was brought about by a great wickedness. That is nothing new to you, I take it?"

"I know about the triple murders back in – when was it?"

"1896," Dorothy clarified. "That was the start of it. I was able to contact all the spirits still trapped in that house and gradually get their stories from them. Poor

Beth was the first one I spoke to, she having been there little over a few months or so."

"Did she tell you exactly how she was killed and who killed her?"

"Oh, yes, she knew *how* she had died, but she didn't know *who* had killed her. And that was true of Mary Allardyce and the Freemans. They had all been killed by the fireside poker, but not one of them had seen who had wielded it."

"It must have been someone very strong," commented Bernard.

"Not necessarily. The element of surprise comes into play and a few sharp whacks with a heavy iron object like that poker would soon despatch the poor victim to Kingdom Come."

"Point taken."

"Anyway, thanks to my shorthand training, I was able to take down all that they had to say verbatim, and I will let you have printed versions once I can summon up the energy to do it."

"Thank you, dear," said Bernard, patting her knee. "More tea?"

"Yes, please."

When the tea was poured, Bernard watched her as she drank it. She looked tired and old, but there was still that spark of fire in her brown eyes that had always captivated him. They could have made a go of it, he thought with a tinge of bitterness. All that devotion he had wasted on Sophie made him angry every time he thought about it. Why had he always kept Dorothy at

320

arm's length? After all, he had never expected to see Sophie again. He forced his thoughts back to the present.

"Can you tell me who killed Hayter and those poor Lomax children?" It was the crux of the story, and he needed to know.

"I will tell you, Bernard, but it will take all my strength to go over it again, and I really don't feel up to it tonight. Can I send you the information? It will be better if you read it all for yourself. You will understand the motivation for what went on better than I could ever explain to you over a cup of tea."

Bernard was disappointed but had no option but to agree. "I will await the post with eager anticipation," he smiled.

"I know you need answers, but all those awful tragedies occurred over the space of more than a century. A few more weeks, won't hurt, will it?"

In the event, it was only a matter of five days before the awaited information plopped on Bernard's doormat. He read with sadness, mixed with horror, the fates of Beth Morrison, Mary Allardyce, John and Carol Freeman, and Cathy, his own daughter. The testimony of little Jemima and Georgina Lomax nearly broke his heart. He even felt sympathy for Edith Lomax, their unfeeling mother, when he read her account.

George Arthur Hayter had been a monster, there was no gainsaying that, but his motive for murdering three women was clear. Bernard couldn't condone his actions, but there was at least a spark of humanity in the man that had led him, ironically, to act so inhumanely.

He read and reread the accounts of Hayter and the maidservant, Martha Finch, with growing dismay and horror.

GEORGE ARTHUR HAYTER

I wasn't always a strangler of women. I killed my first victim almost by accident. I had only intended to shut her up and teach her a lesson. No woman should neglect her own child. I had her by the throat and I was just trying to drum this into her, but she struggled so much, my grip grew tighter. It was then I realised I had gone too far. She was a limp rag in my arms. I would like to be able to say that this shocked and saddened me deeply and set me back on the path of righteousness. But, once the killing had started, I am ashamed to say I could not stop. It became my crusade: to rid the world of women who did not care for their children; women like Edith Lomax.

By the time I met Edith, I had killed three women. She was to be my fourth. I was drawn to her, not by her beauty, which I own was considerable, but by her arrogance and vanity. I would see her parading up and down the street, looking at herself in shop windows, and obviously intent on drawing the admiration of the male sex. She thought nothing of leaving her two small daughters with the maidservant. I regret not managing to complete my work. It was ironic, and I suppose poetic justice, that Edith got to me first.

My penance for my crimes has been to be incarcerated here in this house. I took my punishment like a man, and all had been well until Edith herself joined me. But that was some time later. However, I have been able to avoid her company, as the pleasure I would get from killing her is somewhat tempered by the fact she is dead already. I also keep well out of Martha's way, despite the fact that I love her. I still love her, even though she has been a disappointment to me.

Martha Finch was, at first, a means to an end. I sought her out on purpose because it seemed the easiest way to get to Edith. And so it turned out. I found out from Martha how her mistress neglected her children and left them in her care most of the time. Edith Lomax was just like my mother and my wife. They were all cut from the same vile cloth.

But Martha was different, or so I thought then. She seemed to have none of the vices I had come to expect from women in a class above her. She had no airs and graces and I could see her by my side in the years to come, when I had made her my wife. She was a rough diamond, it was true, and would require some polishing. But her beauty and natural intelligence more than made up for what she lacked in breeding.

I was a widower and free to marry, my first wife having died some years before. (No, I did not kill her.) I had married Hermione when she was an innocent young woman of eighteen; pretty, vivacious and very much in love with me. We had met at a mutual friend's soirée and were both equally smitten with each other. It wasn't long before I had walked her up the aisle, everyone agreeing it was a match made in heaven. But it very soon became clear to me that it was a match made in the other place.

My mother had died shortly after the wedding, and my father was happy to welcome my pretty wife into the bosom of the family. My older brother, Maximilian, had shown no intention of settling down, so it was up to me to carry on the family line, which I did dutifully and, I say this in all modesty, well.

Maximilian, meanwhile, was busy running up huge gambling debts and becoming addicted to opium. I was, by contrast, every inch the country squire, ready to follow in the footsteps of my now ailing father. Even though I was a credit to the family, it was Max who got the lion's share of the attention and love. My mother had had time only for her first born, and my father had always been too busy to notice how I was being neglected. I doubt he would have lifted a finger if he had known, in any case.

My mother never forgave me for not being born a girl, and I was a grisly child, which added to my crimes. Max, on the other hand, possessed a sunny disposition that won over everyone with whom he came into contact. I wasn't able to compete for his popularity, even though I was just as handsome, perhaps more so. So, I reached my manhood unloved and ignored by those closest to me, at best merely tolerated, sowing the seeds of hatred in me that rooted and grew deeper with each passing year.

Life looked up when I married Hermione. She gave me the attention and love I had never received from any of my family and I was happy for probably the first, and last, time in my life. I was delighted when our son James was born, even though my wife concentrated all her attention on him. You see, I was assured by everyone it was only natural, and I was glad to see her so happy. All was well until our second son, Reginald, was born a year later. But, instead of loving him just as much as her first-born, she had no time for him, content to leave him to the ministrations of Nanny Perkins. History was repeating itself, and I saw in him the little unloved boy I had once been.

My heart hardened towards Hermione after that, and I began casting around for a way to avenge Reginald's neglect, as well as my own. But, in those early years of our marriage, murder couldn't have been further from my mind. There were other ways of skinning a cat. I would ruin her happiness with James. I would ignore her just as she ignored me and Reggie.

At first, she didn't notice, but eventually she understood what was happening between us. She tried to make amends, but it was too late. I continued to neglect her, just as my mother had neglected me. I could see she was miserable, but she had James, hadn't she? She didn't need me. Then more tragedy occurred. An outbreak of typhoid fever carried off not only my wife, but both my sons as well. I didn't care about Hermione: she deserved it. But the children. My heart bled for them.

After I had got over the worst, I found my grudge against women like my mother and Hermione continued unabated and, this time, my thoughts turned to murder. Yes, I killed those women. I courted them and won them. They were silly and vain with little time to devote to their children, but plenty to spare for me, their handsome suitor. I flattered their egos and they were putty in my hands. I do not regret, for a single moment, what I did. I used a false name each time, careful not to give away anything about myself. They would never know how or why they had met such a fate at my hands.

I was satisfied for a while between each killing, vowing that my vendetta was now at an end. But then I met Edith Lomax. She angered me even more than the others and I realised my work, my crusade, was far from done.

It was Edith that struck me that day when I was in the parlour with Martha. I never knew anything else, except I vaguely remember coming to and someone, not Edith, was screaming. I think it was probably Martha. She is such a disappointment to me.

MARTHA FINCH

It was all 'cos of them stupid brats. I suppose it weren't their fault, really, but I 'ave to blame someone, don't I?

My life weren't going nowhere. I'd been in service since I was fourteen and, in all that time, I'd never 'ad the chance for a lie-in to seven o'clock, even! Up at the crack of dawn, clearing out grates, preparing breakfast, making beds. A girl like me deserved something better. Maybe if I 'adn't thought that, then things wouldn't 'ave 'appened the way they did.

I'd been dismissed from a snooty family in Stoke and been told I'd never get another job if they 'ad anything to do with it. All I'd done was try on some of the mistress's dresses and she'd caught me at it. It weren't a hanging offence – or I didn't think so, anyway. But, no matter, I was sacked anyway and told never to darken their door again. They thought I'd be upset and beg to stay, but I showed them. I was glad to go, but not before I told them what their randy son 'ad been up to. 'E was always trying it on with me. 'E'd creep up be'ind me when I was clearing out the grates and try to interfere with me. 'E never got nowhere, though. 'E 'ad no idea 'ow to work 'is way through my petticoats to get at my knickers. I used to 'it 'im with the dustpan – that usually dampened 'is ardour. 'E was 'armless enough, really, 'e just got on my nerves.

Anyway, now I was dismissed and my employers 'ad it in for me, I decided I'd better move right away, and London seemed to be the obvious place. Luckily, I still 'ad some money left from the pittance I'd been paid so was able to travel by carriage more or less all the way.

When I got to London, I went straight to an employment bureau who fixed me up 'ere with the Lomaxes. Okay, I know. You're probably wondering 'ow I got the job without any references. Well, easy, I forged them. Before I left the Lessways', I took some of their 'eaded notepaper. I didn't like being dishonest – well, not then, anyway – but a girl 'ad to survive, didn't she? The reference I forged weren't bad, I do say so myself, and it did the trick.

I was with the Lomaxes for two years before what 'appened. It was the day I was proposed to by Giles Fortescue. I was so 'appy. Then Mrs Lomax came 'ome and ruined it. Giles was ever so 'andsome. Coo, not 'arf, 'e was. 'E was rich, too. 'E was gonna make me into a proper lady, and girls would be waiting on *me* in future. But I would've been kind to them, knowing what I used to 'ave to put up with when I was a maid. I could afford to be generous and kind, now that I was gonna marry into a wealthy family.

Edith Lomax was jealous of me, though she wouldn't 'ave admitted it. I was just as beautiful as she was, and I knew she couldn't stand that. Circumstances 'ad made me subservient to 'er, but it could just as easily 'ave been the other way round. And, as for the kids. She never wanted to look after them. Always foisting them off onto me, she was. I 'ad no time to myself. I liked the girls well enough, but when did a single woman get the opportunity to go courting if she's always got tiny tots in tow? Look at it from my point of view, like.

But Giles singled me out. 'E saw me one day in the butcher's queue and started taking me for walks in the park and giving me tea at the bakery. We were very much in love, you know. And 'e wanted to marry me. Okay, so 'e did keep picking my brains about Edith. I didn't twig then why 'e wanted to know all them things. I should've realised 'e was up to no good but when you're in love, you don't think, do you?

So you could 'ave knocked me down with a feather when Edith told me that 'e 'ad been courting 'er, as well. And she said 'e was called something different – Abraham somebody or other. It was a stupid name, that's all I remember.

So, back to that day when the murders took place. As I said, Giles 'ad just proposed to me and was bending down to kiss me when Edith came in and whacked 'im over the 'ead with the poker, with not so much as a by-your-leave. 'E just fell to the floor and didn't move. There was blood coming from 'is 'ead and we both could see 'e was dead. Edith then told me why she'd done it. Said that 'e was wanted by the police for strangling young women. Dr Lomax 'ad read something out to us from the paper only that morning about a man the police were looking for in connection with the murders. I thought she was mad. My Giles weren't no killer. She'd got the wrong man, I told 'er. But she was positive.

I was so upset at what she'd done to my Giles, but she didn't care. All she cared about was 'erself. Said she 'ad to run away as she would be hung, sure as eggs. She ran upstairs and five minutes later I 'eard 'er come down the stairs and go out the front door. I then 'eard the kids calling and running after 'er. I let them go, I weren't in no fit state to stop them, even if I'd wanted to. And I didn't want to.

As I sat there with Giles's body, I 'eard the children come back. They came to the parlour door and looked in and screamed when they saw it. Edith came in just be'ind them. But, when she saw that 'er brats 'ad seen what she'd done, she turned and ran out of the 'ouse again. This time she didn't come back. The brats still stood there screaming, though.

I told them to be quiet or else they'd get their mama into trouble. They seemed to take notice of what I said then, 'cos they quietened down a bit. It was then that Giles regained consciousness. 'E weren't dead, after all. 'E smiled at me and 'e looked 'orrible. 'Is teeth 'ad been knocked out of 'is 'ead and 'e looked like 'e was gurning at me. 'E laughed, and then said that Edith always 'ad 'ad a bit of a temper. That's when I was convinced. 'E *did* know 'er – she 'adn't been lying. 'E knew 'er name and all that, 'cos I'd told 'im when 'e asked. But the way 'e said she'd always 'ad a temper on 'er, then it was clear 'e knew 'er like 'e knew me. The swine!

I challenged 'im, then. I asked 'im if 'e'd strangled them women, and 'e didn't deny it. Proud of 'isself, 'e was. Edith was to be next on his list, 'e said. 'E said 'e was serious about marrying me, though. 'Course I didn't believe 'im and I was so furious I just grabbed the poker and 'it him with it again and again. This time 'e weren't gonna come round, not if I 'ad anything to do with it. I'd finish the job Edith 'ad started. But that's when Edith's kiddies started off screaming again. This time there was no bleedin' stopping them.

I grabbed them and told them I'd give them what for if they didn't put a sock in it. But it did no good. They just kept on struggling and screaming the place down. I still 'ad the poker in my 'and, 'Eaven 'elp me, and I just lashed out at them. Before I knew what I'd done, the two little ones were laying dead at my feet. I swear I didn't know what I was doing – except I 'ad to keep them quiet. I couldn't let them tell what they'd just seen, could I? I 'ad to silence them for good. It was 'orrid, all that blood, and they were so small.

Yeah, I can see you're shocked, Mrs whatever-your-name-is. Plunkett? Dorothy? Okay, Dorothy. But what else could I do? I swear it weren't in my 'ead to kill them. Killing kiddies weren't in my nature. Still ain't. But they'd 'ave been sure to tell the doctor that it was me that'd killed Giles, not Edith. She'd gone off anyway, and she'd never know that she 'adn't killed 'im. She'd keep right away now, I was sure. Everything would be all right if I just kept me 'ead.

Anyway, I got my come-uppance later on, didn't I? When I found I was going to 'ave a baby, I thought 'Erbert would look after me, but 'e denied 'e was the father. 'E could 'ave been, though, if I 'adn't been so far gone. 'E weren't no angel. So 'e said I'd 'ave to leave 'cos I'd bring disrepute on 'im. That was all 'e was concerned about. You soon find out who your friends are in this world, don't yer?

So, what was I to do now? You may well ask. I was beginning to show, so getting another situation was out of the question. Even if I managed to get one, I would 'ave soon been out on my ear when the lump got bigger. Corsets would 'ave 'elped for a while, I suppose. But, even if I managed to keep my secret up 'til the birth, what would 'ave 'appened then? The work'ouse – that's all I 'ad to look forward to. My mum and dad would disown me if I went back 'ome, I knew that. My mum 'ad enough kids of 'er own to contend with without me adding to 'er brood. She'd got rid of me once, she'd 'ardly welcome me back with open arms, bringing 'er another mouth to feed. Two, if you count the baby.

I was desperate. My life was over. There was only one way out. So I wrote a note to 'Erbert – that'd show 'im – and then I put my 'ead in the gas oven. What a way to go! Yeah, I know I deserved it, but I wasn't always bad. It was just circumstances...

Taking my own life like that was the last straw, though. Far from ending my troubles, it was just the start of them. I thought once the gas'd done its job, I'd be free forever. But, what with the killings – the kids, mainly – that was unforgiveable. Giles, or whatever 'is name was, was one thing. But innocent children. There weren't no way back from that.

So I woke up, not in 'Eaven, though I suppose I was lucky not to end up in the other place, but 'ere in this bleedin' fireplace. In limbo. For ages, I was 'ere on my own. Except for all the others, of course, but I don't count them. They 'ad it in for me, naturally. Can't say I blame them, but if them kids pinched me once, they pinched me a thousand times. I was miserable, I can tell you.

Then things looked up a bit when Edith Lomax come back. Gawd knows why she did that. I don't know 'ow long after I was supposed to 'ave died that would 'ave been. You lose all sense of time being in limbo, like. Anyway, there she was, large as life and twice as nasty, as the saying goes. Looked good, though, I 'ave to say that for 'er. Older, but still pretty. You know what? I saw red. I just took up the poker and gave 'er a dose of what I give Giles and 'er brats. It felt good.

I don't know 'ow long before the couple moved in with their little boy. Nice little thing 'e was. Edith's brats often played with 'im, but she didn't like it. Don't know why. So, the poor little boy got upset. Didn't really bother me, though. I didn't want anyone to be 'appy 'ere. Especially not the men. I 'ate all men after what they done to me. The little boy was no different. 'E'd grow up to be a man one day. Anyway, I wanted to get 'is father to murder 'is mother so that 'e'd get 'ung and she'd be dead, anyway. I kept trying to put the idea in 'is 'ead, but 'e was resistant. So I finally killed 'er myself, then I 'ad to do 'im in, too. I could've let justice take its course, I suppose, but I was all fired up and let 'im 'ave the poker treatment too. It gave me a thrill, I can tell you. Doin' them in and knowin' I couldn't get done for it. Better'n sex. Much better.

Then I 'ad to wait a bit for the next mugs to come through the door. They were a gift when they did. A youngish couple and their three boys. Tiny little things, they were. I almost felt sorry for them. But, again, they'd grow up to be men, so I tried not to think of what I intended to do to ruin their 'appy 'ome. I just got on with it. Again, the man proved difficult, although I managed to make 'im cross with 'is wife a lot. But not enough to kill 'er. Then I got fed up with playing a cat and mouse game, and killed 'er myself while 'e was at the pub. This time I let the police take over. I knew no one'd believe 'e didn't do it and 'e'd suffer in prison while waiting for the 'angman. 'Course, I didn't know then that 'anging 'ad just been abolished, more's the pity. Still, 'e copped it in prison, anyway, and 'is boys would grow up thinking their dad was a murderer. So I was more than satisfied with that.

Then there was that older couple with the potty daughter. They moved in next. I 'ad a bit of fun with 'er. Nutty as a fruitcake, she was. I could easily tune into 'er brain, or what passed for it. Kept taunting 'er, I did. She weren't 'arf easy to wind up. She thought it were voices in 'er 'ead. Which I suppose it was. Only one voice, though. Mine. Then I told 'er to jump off the roof. She nearly did but was saved in the nick of time. That's what made the family move out. That stopped my fun, I quite missed 'er. I never bothered with 'er mum and dad, though. I would've got round to them in time. If they'd stayed. I tell you one thing, though. That barmy woman should've stayed away. She didn't know when she was well off, that one. Well, it weren't surprising, when you think she didn't even know the time of day most of the time. But I can't tell you 'ow glad I was to see 'er back. Life was getting a bit samey, if you know what I mean,

Anyway, it was just before she came back that the young man got tricked into buying the gaff by that slimy estate agent. I remember watching from my vantage point 'ere in the fireplace as the daft bugger came over and examined it. It was what made 'im buy it, 'cos, up till then, I was sure 'e 'ated the place. Who'd 'ave thought a fireplace could make you buy a whole 'ouse? Seems daft to me. I mean, a fireplace 'ardly constitutes a whole 'ouse, does it? You'd 'ave to like some other aspects of a place, surely? But no, it was just this fireplace. I suppose it could've been the way I kept it clean all the time. Made it look kind of nice and inviting, like. This feather duster 'as seen some service, I can tell you.

I thought 'e wasn't going to be much fun, though. 'E didn't seem to 'ave a family for me to mess about with. All the pleasure I got was watching 'im undress.

'Ad a nice body, I give 'im that. Then 'is girlfriend turned up. So I 'ad my bit of fun once more. Ain't so good now there's no 'anging, of course. I was looking forward to doing 'is new bit of stuff in as well, but I suppose I'm stymied now, ain't I?

Oh, yeah. I forgot. Potty Cathy 'ad come back. The new owner'ad gone off somewhere. 'E'd only been gone overnight when she turned up. Let 'erself in with a key, she did. And, well, what was I gonna do? Sit 'er down and give 'er a cup of tea? You know by now, Dorothy, that's not my style.

EPILOGUE

London, March 2010

Bernard snuggled down into his warm bed. He was tired, dog tired. Dorothy had left nothing out in her verbatim accounts of the trapped spirits in 57 Bockhampton Road. Perhaps he wished she had. The violence and pure evil that she had uncovered surpassed even his own vivid imaginings. But it had to be the truth; he had never doubted Dorothy's psychic powers in the past, and he saw no reason to doubt them now.

He yawned and nestled deeper into his pillow. At least he could sleep more easily now everything had been explained at last. He would combine Dorothy's information into what he had already compiled and try to make some sense of it all. Then people would know that Bert Allardyce had been innocent which, he hoped, would be a comfort to his family. The other murders would be accounted for, too. The police, who had long since given up trying to find the perpetrators, would surely be convinced that they were right to suspend their enquiries. It was still a lot to swallow, but Bernard was sure, once he had written his definitive history of the house in Bockhampton Road, people would, at the very least, be prepared to accept the possibility that such things happen.

But, for tonight, he was much too tired to think any more about it. It would only be a few moments before blessed oblivion overcame him and he nestled deeper into his pillow. Then the vision of the evil Martha Finch wreaking her revenge on all those innocent victims came to him. His own daughter had bccn bludgeoned to death, apparently, just for a lark. The sad thing was, he couldn't feel her loss the way any normal father would. He had never even *seen* her, let alone met or talked to her. Once again, he tried to understand why Sophie had never told him, but he couldn't. He just couldn't.

But there were so many things he had always failed to understand. How people could do such awful things to each other, like Martha Finch. She hadn't been dealt the best hand of cards in life, and he could understand that suicide had been her only option in the end. But he couldn't comprehend her blood lust ever afterwards. He shivered in his warm bed as he turned over.

Jerry and Eve were sleeping in the next room. He could hear the bed springs and knew what they were up to. Had he missed out on that side of things? he wondered. He realised that young love in such close proximity made him feel desperately lonely all of a sudden. It wasn't sex he missed, though. It was companionship.

Jerry had asked him if it was all right for Eve to stay occasionally while he was under his roof, and Bernard had said by all means. But had he really meant it? Now that Jerry's house had been cleansed of its evil, the young man would be returning there soon, only staying until the decorators and plasterers had finished making the place habitable. Bernard hoped it wouldn't be too long. As much as he liked him, it wasn't his company he craved now. He thought of dear Robbie MacTavish. Their evenings together had been special. No woman could have filled the place that Robbie had had in his life.

Still wide awake, the bed springs had stopped now. His thoughts turned once more to Martha. Where was she now? he wondered. Dorothy had been worried about her. Although the fireplace had been demolished, it had only served to dislodge her spirit, not destroy it. She was out there – somewhere. He shivered again.

Downstairs in the parlour, there was a glow from the fireplace. But the coal effect gas fire had been turned off an hour ago.

CPSIA information can be obtained
at www.ICGtesting.com
Printed in the USA
LVOW08s0524140418
573474LV00001BA/32/P